A JEW IN GAZA

HUMANITARIAN HEARTBREAK, HUBRIS AND HORRORS

Allan J. "Alonzo" Wind

ISBN: 979-8-9907983-2-8

Imprint: Independently published

STAY IN TOUCH

As a thank you for purchasing this book, I may provide exclusive free content in my private email newsletter distribution list. Click here to join the email newsletter distribution list for free:

https://enableennoble.net/subscribe/

Or email me at:

Andean Adventures Partner

DEDICATION

This book is dedicated to my former staff in IMC Palestine, who always showed me the utmost hospitality and welcome in a troubled and besieged land, my friends and colleagues in the humanitarian assistance community working tirelessly in Gaza, West Bank and East Jerusalem, and the innocent victims in the occupied Palestinian territories. I also recognize the brave and selfless efforts of the Standing Together community in DC, Israel, and worldwide. I dedicate this book to the memories and souls of the humanitarian workers who lost their lives while trying to help in this misery of unrelenting violence. So many humanitarians, health workers, and journalists have lost their lives in the service to humanity.

I also dedicate this book to the innocent victims and hostages abducted from Israel, Israelis, and foreigners among them: those that have been murdered, those that have been killed in military operations, those who have been released or rescued, and those who may remain alive today.

May their memories be a blessing. May all remain safe and protected; may the better angels and peacekeepers of the region prevail against the enemies of humanity and peace.

The opinions and reporting here are entirely my own and do not necessarily represent the opinions of the U.S. government, International Medical Corps, the membership of the Association for International Development Agencies, or other official organizations.

SELECTED ACRONYMS

AAH	AHLI ARAB HOSPITAL
AIDA	ASSOCIATION OF INTERNATIONAL DEVELOPMENT AGENCIES
ANERA	AMERICAN NEAR EAST REFUGEE AID
ATC	ANTI-TERRORISM CERTIFICATE
BHA	BUREAU OF HUMANITARIAN ASSISTANCE (USAID)
CTL	COUNTER-TERRORISM LEGISLATION
CLA	GOI COORDINATION OF LIAISON ASSISTANCE [IN GAZA]
COGAT	GOI COORDINATOR OF GOVERNMENT ACTIVITIES IN THE [OCCUPIED] TERRITORIES
DFA	DE FACTO AUTHORITY [IN GAZA-HAMAS]
EMT	EMERGENCY MEDICAL TEAMS
EXCOM	EXECUTIVE COMMITTEE
FOST	FRIENDS OF "STANDING TOGETHER"
GBV	GENDER-BASED VIOLENCE
GOI	GOVERNMENT OF ISRAEL
HCT/HF	HUMANITARIAN COUNTRY TEAM/HUMANITARIAN FUND
ICC	INTERNATIONAL CRIMINAL COURT
ICJ	INTERNATIONAL COURT OF JUSTICE
IDF	ISRAEL DEFENSE FORCES
IMC	INTERNATIONAL MEDICAL CORPS

INGO	INTERNATIONAL NONGOVERNMENTAL ORGANIZATION
IOCC	INTERNATIONAL ORTHODOX CHRISTIAN CHARITIES
KYTC	KHAN YUNUS TRAINING CENTER
MCI	MERCY CORPS INTERNATIONAL
MEPPA	[NITA LOWEY] MIDDLE EAST PEACE PARTNERSHIP ACT
MHPSS	MENTAL HEALTH PSYCHOSOCIAL SERVICES
MOH	MINISTRY OF HEALTH
MSNA	MULTI-SECTOR NEEDS ASSESSMENT
OCHA	[UN] OFFICE OF COORDINATION OF HUMANITARIAN ASSISTANCE
OFAC	[U.S. TREASURY] OFFICE OF FOREIGN ASSETS CONTROL
OPT	OCCUPIED PALESTINIAN TERRITORIES
PA/PNA	PALESTINIAN AUTHORITY/PALESTINIAN NATIONAL ASSEMBLY
PCR	POLYMERASE CHAIN REACTION [DEVICE]
PCRF	PALESTINIAN CHILDREN'S RELIEF FUND
PIJ	PALESTINIAN ISLAMIC JIHAD
PRCS	PALESTINIAN RED CRESCENT SOCIETY
ST	STANDING TOGETHER
UNDP	UNITED NATIONS DEVELOPMENT PROGRAM

UNRWA	UNITED NATIONS RELIEF AND WORKS AGENCY FOR PALESTINIAN REFUGEES
USAID	U.S. AGENCY FOR INTERNATIONAL DEVELOPMENT
USG	UNITED STATES GOVERNMENT
WASH	WATER, SANITATION AND HYGIENE [INTERVENTIONS]

TABLE OF CONTENTS

INTRODUCTION

Throughout my life, I worked for nearly 20 years with international non-governmental organizations (INGOs) in development and humanitarian assistance. This was followed by over 20 years as a U.S. Foreign Service and Senior Foreign Service Officer before retiring five years ago. I told the story of the early part of my career and how I came to feel chosen for this work as a life vocation in my book ANDEAN ADVENTURES. I hope you've read it, and if you haven't, please consider looking at it on Amazon or your favorite bookseller. It's available in different formats, including audiobooks and English and Spanish.

Since those earliest formative experiences, I've worked in many environments where we sometimes must deal with adversaries and enemies, even potential or past terrorists. As a former development practitioner and executive with diplomatic assignments, I know that true diplomacy is supposed to help you talk with your adversaries and manage your enemies, not with your friends. Diplomacy isn't needed to speak to your friends. Sustaining positive relationships in the best of times should not be a massive reach.

However, accurate diplomatic skills are required when you reach out to persuade, cajole, demand, or otherwise pressure people who are not your friends to act in ways they might not otherwise do. Yet, we often find ourselves in situations where we give up by default and make no effort to talk to our enemies. What's the harm in not doing that? We'll get to that a little later.

I've written this book to share the story of my work in Gaza and Israel. I recently served as Mission Director for International Medical Corps in the occupied Palestinian territories for two years, based roughly 50/50 divided between Gaza City and East Jerusalem through almost all of 2022 and 2023, present during multiple escalations and conflicts, and a witness to the constant damage and harm to the people of Gaza, the children and youth of

Gaza and communities and civil society, most of whom had little or nothing to do with Hamas, or as the USG preferred to call them, the De facto Authority (DFA).

Living in Gaza, indeed, the experience during two years of going back and forth between Gaza and Israel was profoundly touching, one which I feel enriched me as a person and as a professional, but which also profoundly wounded me. I'm still coming to terms with the experience. In this book, I will talk about the Gaza of today and the implications of humanitarian assistance and its delivery to noncombatants and civilians. Still, I also want to talk about the Gaza and the Gazans I came to know before the most recent spasm of death and violence. I will draw on a series of classes I gave earlier last year online to a mixed group of adult education subscribers, including Jewish and Palestinian people, some Muslim, and some Christians.

I knew little about Gaza at first, beyond the basics of course of the Israeli occupation after they seized it from Egypt in the 1967 Six Day War and the retreat by the late Ariel Sharon from Gaza in the early 2000s, dismantling the Israeli Jewish settlements and supposedly leaving it to fend for itself. I have visited Israel several times since the late 1980s and the West Bank. But Gaza was Terra Incognita for me.

Accepting the job and deploying with International Medical Corps in Gaza and the occupied Palestinian territories (commonly abbreviated as the 'oPt') did give me initial pause when I saw the reaction of several friends. Some who also worked internationally said I would be crazy to take the risk to go to Gaza. They thought I would be in mortal danger if I were to go, as an American with a Jewish background. They insisted I 'sanitize' my social media before going, presumably to hide somehow the fact that I was Jewish. I heard similar advice from the IMC Security Advisor before I traveled. He warned me not to take my usual phone or laptop into Gaza because of the risk of surveillance and possible hacking. It was amusing in the run-up before I traveled to the

Mideast. I had what seemed to be a difficult conversation with my future supervisor at IMC, who seemed disturbed by something but unable to come right out and tell me. I realized after a few minutes that somehow, he and others at IMC must have just realized I was Jewish and perhaps imagined that I had not realized the risk of going into what was expected to be an extremist, fundamentalist-ridden Muslim environment.

I confess that I initially looked through my Facebook and Instagram accounts and wondered if I should do so. I deleted one post and stopped because I thought this would be ridiculous. More than anything, if I were to start sanitizing things, this could be seen as suspicious behavior, as if I was trying to hide something. So, I stopped and decided the best policy would be openness and transparency. I felt I had nothing to hide or reason to do so.

WHAT WAS MY RECEPTION LIKE IN GAZA?

To get to Gaza, I traveled first to Ben Gurion Airport outside Tel Aviv, Israel, spent a few days in Jerusalem to manage some logistics and ensure I had all the proper permissions from both the Israeli military and DFA sides, and then ran the gauntlet into Gaza from Erez Terminal, a substantial airport-like terminal for land pedestrian entry into Gaza about 90 minutes from Jerusalem. I'll talk more about that later.

But for now, I can say this: as I lived and worked in Gaza, I was never molested by the DFA. I had to be interviewed by their security personnel when I first arrived, who had done some homework about me looking into my social media and internet footprint and fingerprints. They were respectful and transparent: "Mr. Wind, we are honored that you, as an American Jew and someone connected with the Baha'i community in Haifa, Israel, would agree to live among us and help the needy. Marhaba! You are most welcome, and we will always protect you." There was no other American Jew like me or my position there.

I wasn't naïve to think this treatment was out of the charity in their hearts. I assumed that with IMC present for 15 years providing essential health services, the DFA had no reason to interfere with our activities. Of course, that's a risk and a calculation that could always change.

For two years, I met with hundreds of Gazans all over Gaza, from Beit Lahia in the north to Rafah in the south. I met with dozens of small Gazan charities and civil society organizations dedicated to social safety needs, the needs of the marginalized, the needs of the handicapped and disabled, and the empowerment of women. I found many points of view, but the vast majority of the people, the civilians I met, said they did not hate Israel; they did not hate Jewish people; they just wanted to live their lives in peace and have the chance to give opportunities to progress to their children. I am not naïve; I have worked in public health and international development diplomacy in many countries, including Iraq and Afghanistan, under kinetic circumstances. I've been shot at and in harm's way more than once. Yet I found civility, courtesy, and humanity in Gaza – as did my wife when she joined me a couple of days on a visit to Gaza in late 2022 – that completely belies the narrative of so many today.

The brutal attack on Israeli border communities on October 7th last year by Hamas and other militants was undeniably savage, even by the standards of the region. The ordeal of the hostages is unconscionable.

However, and this must be understood, this brutal war did not begin on October 7th. The attack grew out of a blockade and siege of Gaza for over 16 years. This is ignored by a mythology spread by news media and pundits alike. Many well-meaning and misinformed people commonly misunderstand the Blockade of Gaza. For example, I hear repeatedly on television pundits refer to the fact that Gaza was handed back or given independence by Israel 17 years ago, and Israel's reward was years of terror and attacks from Gaza. It's true that Israel removed settlers and soldiers from Gaza in 2005 but then blockaded land, sea, and air access to Gaza with very narrow and tightly controlled exceptions, converting Gaza into what has been called for many years the world's largest open-air prison. Israel's justification was the history of solitary lone-wolf terrorist attacks on buses and public places before 2005. But for the Gazans, it meant virtually no escape; only the well-to-do could pay off Egyptian guards. The 2005 Israeli removal was unilateral; it was uncoordinated with the Palestinian Authority or Hamas, and no efforts were made for a normal handover.

WHAT WERE YOU DOING IN GAZA?

I led a USAID-funded $10 million health and humanitarian assistance effort for International Medical Corps across all five governorates of Gaza to support primary health care, Mental Health Psychosocial Services, disaster risk reduction, child protection, and address gender-based violence. The staff included about seven expats and 70 Gazans. Gaza was an area of seemingly incessant repeated and recidivist conflict with Israel, with almost annual escalations and air strikes and previous ground invasions as well from Israel. USAID did not try to undertake a long-term development program. Still, the USAID Bureau of Humanitarian Assistance had funds available to provide humanitarian assistance to the neediest and most marginalized communities in Gaza. Fewer international NGOs were working in Gaza than in the West Bank, given the heavy lifting for access and logistics.

I and my staff were frequently constrained by a counterproductive USG policy naming Hamas a Foreign Terrorist Organization. American diplomacy and Humanitarian assistance since 2007 maintain an official No Contact Policy of the USG that does not allow USG officials or even private humanitarians to talk to the DFA. This involved poorly thought-out government regulations and policies from the U.S. Treasury Office of Foreign Asset Control, which imposed a legal liability and risk on NGOs that felt they had to engage. How can you negotiate peace and reconciliation, or even just the amelioration of suffering, that way?

As a result of this and other counter-productive U.S. laws like the False Claims Act, I know of several INGOs that were sued and accused of giving material aid to Hamas. For example, I heard plenty of anecdotes when right-wing activists from groups like NGO Monitor in the U.S. found photos on the Internet that showed DFA low-level health ministry staff at a table for an NGO health conference. Water bottles were seen on the table and described as illegal "material aid." They threatened nuisance lawsuits against certain international NGOs, nonprofit charities seeking to provide humanitarian assistance worldwide, and Gaza and the West Bank in particular. In several cases, charitable organizations had to shell out millions of dollars in legal fees to fight off nuisance claims. In other cases, they paid millions to settle cases to avoid legal risks.

Most people don't know that the rules and barriers are ever so much tighter and restrictive, specifically with Hamas and Palestinian groups, compared to every single other adversary we have in the world. Senseless – even worse than ISIS, Al Qaeda, or the Taliban, who were and are far more dangerous.

I'll address the Taylor Force Law similarly later. It had the counterproductive effect of disrupting PA finances and blocking any serious capacity the PA could have to outmaneuver Hamas.

As IMC Mission Director in Gaza, I also sat on the UN Humanitarian Fund Advisory Board, and I was elected to the Executive Committee, the Board of Directors for the Association of International Development Agencies (AIDA), a network with over 90 INGO members from the U.S., Europe, and Asia. Even before the war, we faced frequent challenges from Israeli government authorities, questioning and sometimes blocking the flow of resources and the flow of people from Israel proper into West Bank/Gaza. It wasn't universal – many Israeli military authorities welcomed me and others and said they appreciated our humanitarian work with the Palestinians in Gaza and the West Bank. But other Israeli officials and government ministries influenced by the changes from the Netanyahu extremist government sought to try to punitively tax and punish Israeli civil society organizations that were partners; they sought to suppress legitimate Palestinian charities, NGOs, and human rights organizations and block visas and access for humanitarian workers from the UN and NGOs.

WHERE WERE YOU ON OCTOBER 7 (10/7)?

Were it not for a meeting called for by USAID in Jerusalem on October 5th, I would have been in Gaza during the attack. As it turned out, I was in Sheikh Jarrah, East Jerusalem, a Palestinian neighborhood that has had its horrors and oppression by Israeli religious extremists for years and the demolition of their homes for years. But with the attack, I then was forced to spend 16-hour days seven days a week trying to protect and rescue from harm's way over 35 expat staff from IMC and other INGOs trapped by the war until we could finally get them out somehow through Rafah – with little to no help and some obstruction by certain governments.

My hope, and perhaps hubris, was that my extensive experience with many different international organizations and my diplomacy skills would help me negotiate treacherous waters on all sides and find a way to protect our expat and local staff more effectively. I hoped I could bring some common sense to the table. While the evident trauma and rage from the Israeli side was understandably massive, and we know this attack and conflict had reached far beyond the common annual escalations and tit-for-tat attacks, I still had hoped we would be able to continue our support and program.

I also persuaded and looked for ways to identify and protect from Israeli bombing and airstrikes the humanitarian assistance work locations of our over 70 Gazan staff. We reported either directly or through the UN the GPS coordinates of our sites to request deconfliction. Many of my relationships with Israeli Defense Forces (IDF) liaisons were positive and productive, and they respected and trusted me. But over time, I often felt misled; they brought our people into harm's way when they said they would not.

There is no easy way to convey the all-consuming desire for revenge that came over most Israelis after the savage crimes of October 7th. Perhaps the time after 9/11 was comparable for Americans, but I don't quite think so, not on that level.

Perhaps the scale of October 7th was also so much more significant – the murder of over 1000 Israelis at one time was death for Jews not seen since the Holocaust, and the equivalent in a country of almost ten million people of perhaps 30 9/11 attacks, as if America had lost in one day nearly 90,000 people.

10/7 changed virtually all my many Israeli friends, so many of whom were at least somewhat sympathetic to the Palestinian cause and the need to respect Palestinian civil and human rights. This changed fundamentally for so many over the days and weeks after the 10/7 attack.

As December 2023 rolled in, the program I knew and led was dissolved mainly in favor of a USG idea to promote emergency field hospitals in southern Gaza. This was funded all while the many millions of dollars that American and European taxpayers had paid to improve health and humanitarian assistance services were destroyed in systematic policies to destroy every hospital and facility in Gaza.

Far worse would happen within a week and in the ensuing weeks and months.

DO INTERNATIONAL HUMANITARIAN LAW VIOLATIONS APPLY?

I was present in Gaza during several escalations and Israeli rocket retaliatory attacks. Some airstrikes and missiles came within 500 meters of our expat residence. I saw the damage from brutal attacks on Gaza in 2008, 2014 and 2021. True, these sometimes came after extremist groups like Hamas and Palestinian Islamic Jihad (PIJ) would fire off rockets at southern Israel. But these are almost toy rockets with minor consequences and frequent backfires.

Yet the IDF policy has been that for every Israeli casualty, at least 20 Palestinian casualties would be visited upon the other side. And these were never with toy rockets of dubious capabilities but with 21st-century high-impact weapons. I know that the IDF took all gloves off in October 2023, and their calculus for casualties was no longer 20:1 but 300:1 or even 1000:1. This is well documented by multiple Israeli civil society organizations and former IDF soldiers who became whistleblowers. And there were no longer virtually any constraints on trying to minimize damage and death for women and children.

This war, more than so many others, has inflicted collective punishment on a civilian population in ways hardly ever seen or imagined. From the start, all access to food, water, power, and communications was cut off to a civilian population of over two million. And today, nearly nine months into it, with 37,000+ Palestinians (primarily women and children) killed in retribution and 10,000 more missing and presumed dead for 1200 murdered, tortured, and kidnapped Israelis, we end up either in a numbers game or blindness to what many see as the unrestrained destruction of a people.

This is not legal self-defense. Israel did not fire the first shot on October 7th and was, of course, traumatized and overwhelmed by the slaughter of innocents. But it surrendered the claim of self-defense when it proceeded to not only go after Hamas infrastructure and targets, but many times IDF committed massacres of innocent civilians and the desperate and starving. Actual intent by the IDF is not the issue but the effects.

There is no place to flee; all borders are mostly sealed. The Israeli government surrendered the claim of self-defense when it empowered, encouraged, and even financed Hamas to isolate, block, and weaken the Palestinian Authority. The Israeli government deliberately followed a practice for decades of "mowing the lawn," that is, the regular extermination of moderate or potential negotiating partners who stuck their heads up for decades, creating more and more extremists attack after attack. I saw this, I heard this, I witnessed this in Palestine. This has been freely admitted by IDF and *Shabak* sources.

When you rob a people of their past and their future, you leave them no choice but to strike out any way they can, often to soft targets and often to other innocents. When have we seen a conflict like this resolved militarily?

WHAT SPACE IS THERE FOR A SOLUTION?

The only solutions can come from discarding all our paradigms, prejudices, and paranoia of the past and remembering my former buddy Ambassador Rahm Emanuel's words decades ago: "You never let a serious crisis go to waste. And what I mean by that is **that it's an opportunity to do things you think you could not do before.**"

We must stop the insanity now, rescue Israel and the Israelis from their blindspots, and push for peace and reconciliation.

We must have a humanitarian ceasefire now. It can't be tied to the question of the hostages because, despite their suffering and that of their families, however horrible and painful, they cannot hide the fact that they've been lied to from the start by their government about the true priorities of the Israeli Prime Minister and Government. The slain and forgotten hostages cannot stand in the way of stopping the senseless killing. Few seem likely to be still alive.

Israel will never be able to erase Hamas from the Palestinians through warfare. Only a political solution can hope to liberate the Palestinians and the Israelis from further terror, extremism, and violence.

HAVE YOU SEEN ANY POSITIVE SIGNS?

It's hard to see many positives. However, despite the massive loss of life of civilians, I'm thankful it's not even more significant. It could have been even far worse already, with 100,000 or more dead. The IDF could have tried to physically drive the Gazans entirely out of Gaza into a hostile and uncooperative Egypt – a reverse Exodus! This seems cruelly ironic as we recently passed through the Jewish Passover holidays, commemorating the liberation from the bondage of the Hebrew people from Egypt under Pharoah Ramses II. That reverse Exodus might still happen if the right-wing extremists in the Israeli Cabinet have their way. We could have already been in a wider regional war to a far worse degree with Lebanon, Syria, Iran, and even Jordan.

I'm amazed that even amidst hunger and the onset of famine in some places, food has lasted as long as it has. The supermarkets and shops in Gaza before the war always amazed me. Thank God it was not as bad a winter as it could have been, but the summer heat is now here and getting far worse. I'm amazed that I can still be in contact with many former staff members and their families on WhatsApp and Facebook. I'm glad to see some efforts to speak out against the violence in civil society in Israel as well as here and from some in Congress. But I've been hugely disappointed and ashamed of the Biden Administration. Far too little, far too late.

In the coming chapters, I am going to paint a larger picture of what it meant to be in the oPt – in Gaza – before the calamities of 10/7 and the Israeli retaliatory war against Hamas. In the first chapter, I will talk about the context of Gaza and what I saw and learned. In subsequent chapters, I will talk about the needs of Gaza, the central conundrum of Palestine, Humanitarian Assistance and Development programming in Palestine, confronting the problem of persistent corruption and the lack of accountability in Palestine, the neglected open wound of Gaza and Palestine, the many lost opportunities for peace and what this all has meant for national security. I will come back to today and recent months since 10/7 and try to engage with you on options for the future, as well as the implications of the many protests nationwide to the suffering in Gaza.

There are photos scattered throughout the book. They are primarily self-explanatory with the text. Chapters II-V include ample PowerPoint slides drawn from a multicultural class I gave in 2023 before the war under the ENCORE Adult Education learning organization, which provides subscribers classes in person at George Mason University in northern Virginia or online. My classes were, of course, the latter, Zoomcast from Gaza or East Jerusalem, and included American Jews, Christians, and Muslims. They provide background and context.

For the safety of many Gazans mentioned here, I do not usually provide the last names except where they have consented or are deceased.

CHAPTER I

ARRIVAL IN GAZA AND SOCIAL CONTEXT OF GAZANS

International Medical Corps (IMC) started operations in Gaza in 2008. After years of limited emergency operations, IMC led a consortium for the USAID Gaza 2020 Health Matters Project – a major initiative intended to run from January 2016 to January 2021 and to improve the delivery of primary health care in Gaza. Partner organizations included CARE, Mercy Corps, and the Palestinian NGO Juzoor.

The Gaza 2020 project had progressed for about 18 months before it faced a sudden interruption and virtual shutdown in 2018 with the turmoil of foreign policy and funding under the Trump Administration. It was reactivated at a smaller scale and with private donations in 2020. Then, in 2021, with the Biden Administration, the USAID West Bank Gaza Mission restored funding for the project, albeit delimiting the purpose and justification only to COVID-19 protection. This was followed by emergency humanitarian assistance funding from USAID's Bureau of Humanitarian Assistance in 2021, 2022, and 2023.

IMC recruited me in late 2021 as they looked for someone with USAID experience and leadership skills. I was fascinated by the prospects. While I had been to Israel many times since the 1980s, I had never lived and worked in the country or the occupied territories. I had always felt something of a calling to it which had remained unrequited. After Peace Corps, I explored the idea of joining a group in Israel that would pair American Jews and Israeli Arabs for peacebuilding activities around Haifa. Still, in the end, it cemented my commitment for years to Latin America.

Friends in Israel were happy I was coming there and were understanding and supportive (at the time) of my planned work to support a humanitarian assistance mission in Gaza. One Israeli friend, who had served two decades before in a tank division in Gaza, let me know he thought the conditions for the Palestinians and Gazans were unjust and needed someone who could see and understand both sides. Other Israeli friends told me it would be a "mitzvah," a blessing for me to undertake the work. Virtually all hoped for a future day of reconciliation and peace.

After flying to Tel Aviv and some logistics matters in Jerusalem, I arrived in Gaza as the head of International Medical Corps oPt in late February 2022. IMC had not previously tried to launch a program on the West Bank and was one of the few international NGOs working only in the Gaza Strip. IMC had engaged a team leader from Bethlehem on the West Bank who made the complicated trip into Gaza when possible but otherwise worked remotely.

Entering Gaza was a process, running the gauntlet through different checkpoints. On the Israeli side, Erez Terminal was a large airport terminal-like structure that governed the entry and exit of Palestinians with permits to enter or work in Israel or the West Bank and those expats generally with special permits to oversee humanitarian assistance in Gaza. First, you had to enter and put your luggage up for X-ray scanning for contraband or weapons. Then, you had to go through a choreography of turnstiles each time. The first turnstile would involve sharing your passport and confirmation of your emailed permit from COGAT with an Israeli soldier on duty. They would scan you on their computer, which, for some reason, nine times out of ten, would not be able to find you in the system. You'd have to show your "FN" number, the number of your permit application, and with luck the young soldier might find it after a fifteen-minute delay. Although I assumed their computers were networked, they seemed extremely slow, rudimentary, and often unproductive. If you were lucky and they found you in whatever system COGAT was using, the soldier would have to fill out a piece of paper, like a chit, confirming you were in the system. Often, they would forget to sign, stamp, or include some vital piece of information. Of course, they would ask you, sometimes with courtesy, sometimes with belligerence, "Why are you going to Gaza? What is your job?" even though this was presumably in the system.

You would then pass to a second booth at the other end of the room and go through a similar process again. Eventually, you would probably be granted access, and they would print a pink paper chit confirming you were exiting Israel proper into the No Man's Land. Of course, the process into Gaza was much easier and quicker than the process of exiting and returning to Israel.

From that booth, you would walk through some long hallways and further turnstile gates until coming out to an open area no longer in Israel, where you would wait for a shuttle bus. This was a relatively recent accommodation. The alternative was walking about two kilometers through a fenced-in path to the first Palestinian checkpoint. Most people, of course, took the shuttle bus, which was on a constant back-and-forth run.

This first Palestinian checkpoint was in a large Quonset hut terminal, called colloquially 5/5 or Khamsa Khamsa (Hamza/Hamza), where the police of the Palestinian Authority nominal government would process you through. This was relatively easy and something of a formality, in essence serving as a midway buffer between the Israeli side and the further checkpoints about 500 meters away from Hamas, the DFA.

The Hamas checkpoints were known as 4/4 or Arba Arba and were much more serious and careful. This checkpoint also scans your luggage with an X-ray (which mostly seemed nonfunctional). It might even be a hands-on search as well for contraband, such as alcohol or sexually suggestive material. There were usually long lines for processing for the chits to wave you through. Inevitably, always on the first visit and sometimes sporadically on others, you would have to sit and wait for an interview with the DFA Ministry of the Interior officials. While you would have already received a permit to enter, they wanted to question the expat coming in further. These interviews were courteous and not at all belligerent; often, they came with invitations of small cups of coffee. Eventually, you would be waved through the checkpoint and be able to take a short taxi ride of about 500 meters to the official Gazan gate and a parking lot where organizations might have their official vehicles waiting. Going into Gaza from initial arrival at Erez might take 1-2 hours.

IMC had a reasonably large staff; when I got there, it had over 60 Gazan staff, which would eventually grow by another 20 or so. The initial reaction, while positive and warm, included some dose of initial skepticism from local staff. They had been relatively comfortable answering to an absentee supervisor in Bethlehem and were probably unsure how long I would last.

IMC had not had expat staff in Gaza for some time, with only two having arrived a few months previously. One was a Croatian director of finance and administration, and the other was a young American working as a report writer. The former had worked in Gaza ten years before and worked for IMC in Syria. I learned that both had felt barriers and resistance to their presence from several local staff members.

Our program focused on health and protection needs across Gaza. Protection issues included mental health and psychosocial services (MHPSS), gender-based violence (GBV), and child protection. Within a couple of months, we also added a disaster risk reduction component to address how to help build resilience on a local community level to either manmade disasters or that arising from the increasing burden of climate change. We worked in all five governorates of Gaza, from the northern settlements of Beit Lahia to the south and Rafah.

We were barred from contact with official institutions, such as the local Gazan Ministry of Health. I had never worked in a situation where we were not supposed to work with the local government at all. This was hardly a best practice anywhere and certainly unhelpful for program sustainability. But this was an artifact of the U.S. Government's no-contact policy with Hamas, the de facto authority in Gaza. We had to operate at arm's length, using, at times, the Palestinian institutions in Ramallah, under the control of the PA, as an intermediary and for purposes of local registration. As an international NGO founded decades before in Los Angeles but with sister organizations in the UK and Croatia (EU), we worked mainly through local partners. These included a network of Christian faith-based health facilities and over a dozen local Gazan NGOs and community-based organizations.

Here's a photo we took of the IMC staff with me grouped outside our then offices in June 2022, a few months after I arrived.

Reception in Gaza

I look at this photo with warmth, fondness, and nostalgia. It was natural that some people would be uncertain and tentative. I was patient and spent the first couple of months, which coincided soon with the holy month of Ramadan, listening, observing, and getting to know the staff. By the time I arrived, the team was also in the middle of recruiting a big increase in local staff, which would bring us to about 80 by then.

But overall, almost all showed unmistakable warmth and hospitality. Only a few seemed set in their ways, resistant to change, resistant as well to expat staff managing things. Some of the staff felt they had worked well enough for a long time without outsiders from abroad and were unnerved by my arrival and the arrival of the other two expats who had arrived a few months earlier.

Shortly after my arrival, Abu Mahmoud, one of our janitors and office helpers, invited me to join him in celebrating his son's wedding. It was an excellent way to mix with people outside the office. Abu Mahmoud spoke very little, if any, English and was a humble and modest man. Yet I always enjoyed trying to engage a little each day as he went around with office tea and occasional treats for the staff. He was surprised that I took tea with no sugar, and this became a little game each morning when he would ask with mild disbelief, "No sugar, no sugar?" and I would answer again with a smile, "Lah lah lah shukran," in fumbling Arabic confirming the point.

Our work schedule was Sunday through Thursday, as Friday and Saturday are the weekends in most of the Middle East, true in Israel and Palestine. Office hours were 8 am to 4 pm, although shortened by two hours as was the custom during the fast of Ramadan. The expats all had individual apartments in a lovely guest house apartment building in a neighborhood with many other diplomatic, UN, and NGO staff, about one street over from the seashore road of Ar Rasheed.

I learned this was relatively unusual for some IMC work sites worldwide, where an IMC guest house would typically host all the expats together in one villa. In this case, we could all have our own modest spaces, eventually coming to number eight expats from Europe, Africa, and America on the fifth and fourth floors of what was known as the Save the Children building since Save the Children had their offices on the ground floor and a subfloor basement area. Our offices then were about a kilometer away, an easy 10-minute walk. We would eventually move later than September into a larger and more friendly work environment space another kilometer away, in an apartment building across from the UNRWA compound and not far from Al Azhar University of Gaza.

I followed the advice of our IMC security staff and brought into Gaza with me a substantial amount of Israeli shekels in cash to cover my costs for close to a month. Shekels remain the legal currency in the occupied Palestinian territories. But to my surprise, keeping so much cash had hardly been necessary. A surprising number of shops and restaurants accepted and could use international credit cards for transactions. There were several Middle Eastern and Palestinian banks in Gaza with modern ATMs, where one could easily pull-out cash as needed. I'd been told in our security documentation the opposite, and I managed to update and correct this and other items for others.

Prices were also surprisingly reasonable in shops and restaurants. Fresh produce, dry goods, and frozen goods were either at or below typical Israeli prices. Produce seemed much cheaper. Meals were also quite reasonable in restaurants. Like everywhere, there were high-end restaurants that catered to a more exclusive clientele and more reasonable ones. I was surprised to see pizza shops, gelato places, and the more traditional falafel places.

Walking around Gaza was very safe for both male and female staff. There was far less accosting of foreigners as sometimes happens in other Middle Eastern cities or other parts of the world. While foreigners were a relative novelty in Gaza, Gazans were friendly and inviting. The coastline was lovely to walk along: kilometers and kilometers of relatively undeveloped beachside, unfortunately not the cleanest in central Gaza City as Gaza's sewage was not well treated and litter and trash were all too common. The reasons for this were no doubt complex; because of the blockade, there were limitations on mechanical equipment and the entry or prioritization of things like waste disposal trucks. You could sometimes see the picking up of trash and garbage in open-air horse-drawn carts, which would then dump the food waste, plastic, and other garbage from one unsanitary place to another.

Undeniably, there were social issues affecting this. There wasn't a visible culture of public hygiene and trash and waste management, at least in urban concentrations. A few kilometers south, things got cleaner along the coast, but this was probably due to the reduction in population concentration. Gaza as a city and its northern refugee camps, which had evolved into permanent squatter settlements of various degrees, had almost New York-style concentrations of people living and pressing in on each other. Still, there were relatively few buildings that would go above several stories. Though more of these were coming, some impressive commercial and residential high rises reached ten stories or more. However, electricity cuts and constant shortages could also be problematic for the environment and building access.

There was a healthy array of coffeehouses everywhere. Gazans, like so many Arab countries, certainly had sweet tooth fancies. Many of these coffeehouses, which might also have nargileh or waterpipes for smoking if that was your thing, also had many desserts and Arab or Turkish pastries.

Gaza was famous for its seafood, fish market, and marina. Palestinian friends elsewhere, such as in Jordan, would frequently recall with nostalgia when, years before the blockade by Israel, they could drive down to Gaza and eat the fish freely. The fish market was just a couple blocks away, next to the impressive *Masjid Al Hassina*. It was also a short walk to the Gazan marina to see the fleet of Gazan fishing boats.

Driving down to eat fish in Gaza from the outside had long not been possible in a bottled-up Gaza; the Israeli blockade was not just on land but extended out to sea, with Gazan artisan fishermen not allowed to go beyond 6-10 kilometers distance by Israeli warships in the Mediterranean. This hugely cut into the fishing capacity of the Gazans and limited the catch, but for the most part, they made do until, of course, 10/7 changed everything.

During the first several weeks, I remained exclusively in Gaza as I had to wait for the DFA Ministry of the Interior officials to process a six-month residency permit that would enable me to come and go. That gave me plenty of time to begin to visit our partners in Gaza and different communities in Gaza where we worked and a chance to gain insights into the unique circumstances there.

Several families invited me to their homes for meals, which gave me more ways to learn about family life. I was amazed in many cases by the remarkable sophistication of some of the family members. Sometimes, family members and spouses had been successful Palestinian professionals in Europe, Egypt, and Türkiye. Still, they had decided to return to Gaza to make their home there despite the challenges and periodic conflicts with Israel.

Here are some photos of Gaza to further humanize it and make it recognizable. Many are from last year's Ramadan fasting period, and some from the Iftar dinner International Medical Corps hosted for our local Palestinian staff and their families. As you can see in the following photos, these were far happier days. The yellow salted fish is a bit of a tradition for Gazans as we approach the Eid holidays at the end of the holy month of Ramadan.

The photos below of myself with the women at lunch were taken last year to celebrate International Women's Day.

One of the things that impressed me so much on my arrival in 2022 was how, despite the scarcity and limitations of some things, the markets had a remarkable abundance of fruit, vegetables, and greens. There was frozen food – even vegan products! – from Türkiye, Egypt, and industrial concerns from the UAE and elsewhere in the region. Of course, in the bigger supermarkets, many of those products were beyond the reach of the less affluent and poorer Gazans, particularly those living outside Gaza City.

If you can believe it, Gaza City once held much beauty. Despite the conflicts in 2008, 2014, and 2021, there was extraordinary resilience and pride in what was shaping up to include some lovely architecture in the newer parts of Gaza City. Gaza City had a few modest malls and an enormous mall called the Capital Mall, which had juice bars, restaurants, clothing stores, and even a food court, with modern escalators between floors.

There were multi-story buildings, some reaching up to fifteen floors, and residential and office towers. New clinics and hospitals were expanding. The Anglican Ahli Arab Hospital, once the first modern hospital in Gaza known in the early twentieth century as the "English Hospital," had increasingly modern equipment, including a new soon-to-open cancer diagnostic and treatment center, with the help of the Augusta Victoria Hospital from Jerusalem. With funding from the USAID West Bank/Gaza

Mission, International Medical Corps had recently equipped a new PCR lab in the summer of 2023 to help support pandemic preparedness and a training laboratory at the Al Azhar University of Gaza for healthcare workers—all this funded by American taxpayers, with little or nothing remaining in the relentless bombings.

During my time there, I and other expats lived in the more protected and secure neighborhood of Remal, also known as the diplomatic quarter. Outside our apartment building was a lovely garden with a koi pond. We were one street from Ar Rasheed

Street, which followed the beach and the Mediterranean coast. It wasn't hard at times to completely forget the insularity of Gaza and the scope of the Israeli blockade for a moment.

Friends from Israel, as well as other nationalities, wondered inevitably what the reaction of the Gazans was to the fact I was from an American Jewish background who also professed the Baha'i Faith. The reactions were, without exception, gentle and friendly curiosity. People wondered about whether I could speak and read Hebrew. They were surprised to hear me admit that I had studied Hebrew as a boy but had forgotten so much from its lack of use since my teenage years. I could read the Hebrew alphabet, and make out or sound out words, but I had forgotten so much vocabulary I would joke that all I could remember were the words "ani, atah, anachnu, machberet" (I, you, we, notebook). Why I remembered those was puzzling. I vaguely remembered some basic Jewish prayers. We had never been observant when I was growing up, and we hadn't kept kosher (kashrut) at home or been diligent with Jewish holidays. However, I remembered years of Passover seders with my grandparents and Rosh Hashanah, the Yom Kippur fast of the High Holidays, and the gifts and Hanukkiah menorah lights from Chanukah.

Gazans – at least at that point before the nightmare of 10/7 and the Israeli response - emphasized that they didn't hate or detest Israelis. On the contrary, many even admired the pluck and entrepreneurship of Israel. But the IDF and the actions of the right-wing Israeli governments were another matter.

While I sincerely appreciated and valued our work in Gaza, I was keen to see how we might diversify our program in the occupied Palestinian territories and start some pilot programming on the West Bank. In this, I found a ready potential ally in the very experienced and thoughtful Palestinian country director of International Orthodox Christian Charities (IOCC), George Malki, who hailed from Bethlehem but had a permit to live in Jerusalem. George was a profoundly intuitive development expert with whom I worked closely on the EXCOM of AIDA. He had passed the usual time for CDs who rotated on and off the EXCOM. Still, he had such an institutional history and memory of AIDA's history and invaluable connections with the Palestinian National Authority that he was asked by acclamation to remain on board as a voting member and critical anchor. On a body usually heavily expat-weighted, George was a consistent Palestinian presence and fount of common sense.

With George's help, I could travel to Ramallah, the Palestinian capital, and consult with the Palestinian Authority Ministry of Health. I met Dr Rand Salman, the head of the National Palestinian Public Health Institute, who shared an understanding of local health priorities and challenges with me. These included notably a severe and increasing problem of colonic and gastrointestinal cancer. In addition, I saw that pandemic preparedness efforts were mixed with a need to upgrade awareness.

The West Bank had a pretty good network of primary healthcare facilities, but professional training and supervision at the secondary and tertiary health facility levels were uneven. This also deteriorated due to the softening of previous cooperation and support from Israeli hospital facilities like Hadassah Hospital. I also met with the Palestinian Minister of Health herself, Dr. Mai Al Kaila, a Palestinian public health physician, diplomat, and politician. I looked up her biography and saw she had spent training and clinical time in Spain and Chile. So when I was ushered into her offices with George, I offered a few jokes and humorous asides in Spanish. This elicited a warm response from her in Spanish, and we bantered briefly. I explained in English a bit of the work of IMC in Gaza and our desire to help the MOH in those ways that might be possible. She appreciated our work in Gaza, which, despite the existence of Hamas, was nominally under her concerns for the broader Palestinian public health. She encouraged me to look for ways of helping the MOH to meet needs on the West Bank, recognizing the needs in underserved areas away from population centers and those cut off by the Israeli Barrier or Wall.

A little over three months into my arrival, I learned that IMC would hold a global country director conference in Dubai, United Arab Emirates. This was the first such meeting IMC had been able to hold since before the COVID pandemic. I attended with our senior Palestinian program lead, who lived in Bethlehem.

It was symbolic of our circumstances that each of us had our own ways of traveling. As an American, I had no problem leaving Gaza through the Erez Terminal in the north into central Israel. From there, I would take a car or taxi to Tel Aviv, an hour north, or Jerusalem, about 90 minutes to the northeast, if there was no traffic. I could fly out of the country from Ben Gurion Airport and take a direct flight to Dubai, about a four-hour trip.

In the case of my Palestinian colleague, she was not allowed to use Ben Gurion nor dawdle in Israel when leaving Erez Terminal, although she had, in effect, a transit permit to do so. She would have to take a taxi to the West Bank for Bethlehem. She would have to take a cab to the Allenby Bridge crossing on the West Bank to Jordan. This involved different transactions and arrangements, which could take several hours. From the Jordanian side, with coordination from our IMC Jordan office, she would have to travel either to Amman or the Amman airport, which would involve at least another 1-2 hours. She could then take a flight from Amman to Dubai. It was, in total, a multi-day effort each way to travel. For years, the Israelis had blocked Palestinians from flying in and out of their airport, clearly to add to the nuisance value and burden for them. This was true even for American or EU citizens of Palestinian origin.

The IMC conference allowed me to meet many IMC HQ and regional staff I had only encountered by Teams or Skype. It was an excellent opportunity to reconnect with an organization I had some professional contact with at their HQ many years earlier. Unfortunately, Dubai in mid-June was a bit overwhelming for some, particularly HQ staff from Los Angeles. In my case, I was well-adapted. My internal thermostat was altered after my experiences in Baghdad a decade before.

Returning to Jerusalem and thence to Gaza, I worked with my Palestinian colleague to share excitement and engagement about our work as part of the larger global community. A few people had pitched in to help me develop a PowerPoint slide deck about Gaza and our work there. While this was not ultimately used in the way expected in Dubai, it did give me the idea to widen our circle among the local Palestinian staff and begin a process of strategic visioning and planning for our program. True, the shadow of the war in May 2021 was in the background for many. There were still destroyed building sites around Gaza and deep trauma memories from the ten days of conflict and losses. I wanted us to try to overcome that and think beyond the year-to-year emergency funding we were receiving from the U.S. Government through USAID's Bureau of Humanitarian Assistance. So, I mobilized a steering committee of volunteers, and we began planning a stock-taking and strategic visioning workshop in late August.

We decided to try to mount this workshop outside Gaza, in one or more possible sites in Israel. We would link it with team-building activities. We secured a modest budget from HQ to cover the expenses, and I contacted Israeli authorities to cultivate them and encourage the granting of permits for our local Gazan staff. We looked at different alternatives. The most economical involved a self-led workshop in East Jerusalem. I polled my Gazan colleagues, and going to Jerusalem was the most popular. While a few had been able to get short-term work permits to go to Jerusalem in the past to reach vendors or purchase supplies, few had any familiarity. And most deeply valued the idea of being able to visit Jerusalem, a holy city for Muslims, because of the presence of the mosque (or masjid) at the Dome of the Rock, the *Haram i Sharif*, at the top of the Temple Mount above the Western Wall in the Old City. Many Gazans wanted to be able to go there in the evening and pray and commune there. Many also wanted to be able to walk the streets and markets of the Old City.

In my back and forth between Israel and Gaza, I had made it a point to connect with the Israeli military that made up the Coordination Liaison Authority (CLA) of the Coordinator of Government Activities in the Territories (COGAT), a branch of the Israeli Ministry of Defense that managed oversight and administration of assistance to the occupied Palestinian territories. They had offices at Erez Terminal, this large airport terminal-like structure that mediated entry into Gaza on the Israeli side of the border.

I coordinated outreach early on with the Director of AIDA, Joseph Kelly. Joseph was an opportune American local hire available in Israel because his wife was the Country Director for Catholic Relief Services oPt. He served with distinction for several years with AIDA, energetically applying his enthusiasm, humor, and common sense to many complex problems along the way.

Joseph led a small local staff for the AIDA secretariat, a team that was both customer service-oriented and positive in their outreach to the many NGO members. Managing an NGO network like AIDA is no small feat. It's akin to the proverbial herding of cats, requiring much running around to bring people together. It demands perseverance and patience to encourage participation. It's not uncommon in a network of roughly 80 NGOs to have only a quarter participating in the monthly or quarterly meetings. Depending on the program's size of the affiliated organization, the different dues levels might also include a few "freeloaders" taking advantage of membership benefits without consistent contributions.

The AIDA secretariat included Rima Shahin, a profoundly committed administrative assistant I always found helpful and responsive. AIDA also had a capable Palestinian advocacy coordinator and writer in Ruba Awadallah, who effectively managed the advocacy expectations of different members with a range of priorities. Sadly, she moved on too soon because she got a competitive offer to join the UN in that area. Finally, Dr Moner Mourtaja was the AIDA Gaza Coordinator, generally on the ground in the Gaza Strip. He was a key lieutenant for Joseph in program and logistics operations in the oPt. Through crisis and escalation, he was a valuable networker and communicator, a Gazan "schmoozer," perhaps. He regularly convoked the AIDA staff leads in Gaza for exchanges and coordinated with the UN and other international interlocutors. Occasionally, he annoyed others with his voluble and creative license with tasks. But his heart always seemed to me to be in the right place. He had returned to Palestine voluntarily after a long time in Europe in different positions, including that of a university vice president for program and European affairs. He had worked first with a French INGO, PUI, then came to the AIDA secretariat. The secretariat staff was small, but it was not uncommon for some to work until late at night, past midnight.

In any case, Joseph Kelly and I got an appointment to meet with the CLA head and deputy head of international relations. The former was an Israeli Captain in the IDF; her deputy was a lieutenant. Both had rotated into these positions for 18 months. The captain was a transplant; she had been an American Jew who had made "aliyah" when younger and migrated to Israel, and thus, she was still somewhat bicultural. This was not unusual, I found.

We visited their offices adjoining Erez Terminal. They were courteous and friendly and invited us to coffee, which reminded me of their Arab counterparts in other circumstances. Joseph and I explained our respective organizations and the scope of our programs in Gaza. (a different CLA office outside Ramallah, the Office of Civilian Administration for the Military Government, managed West Bank international NGO activities.) They wanted to know about funding sources and the level of contact with the DFA. They pumped us gently for any information we could provide about details of life in Gaza, which we mostly avoided to stay away from giving anything that could be considered intrusive intel.

They also, of course, had their agendas. They wanted to assure us they were there to be as helpful and faciliatory as possible to our work in Gaza. They wanted us to understand that they, as individuals and as part of the CLA international relations office, were aware and appreciative of the need for humanitarian assistance in the Gaza Strip. We shared contact information. They also were a bit amazed at my Jewish background and wanted to confirm that I had never had any problems in Gaza. I assured them I had not.

Remembering this and other conversations with Israeli officials is, of course, bittersweet. No comparison exists between how many of them thought and spoke, at least for my benefit, before the 10/7 attack and the war. I'm not naïve about their agenda, their priorities, as well as their concern for the image of Israel as being cooperative and helpful, at least then. Joseph and I thought there was also probably a bit of self-selection within the IDF. Recruits and career officers are more inclined to be sympathetic to the cause of Palestinians often sought these types of assignments, and likely, the IDF processes also favored that.

Still, there was value added to putting names and faces to contacts on both sides. I explained my plans for an IMC staff retreat and strategic planning workshop, and they took notes. I suggested that it would not be a "retreat" in the classical sense but rather a "forward" since we were envisioning a way forward for us all.

After completing online applications with COGAT, eventually, we would indeed be able to secure permits for over two-thirds of the Palestinian staff. A few were rejected outright. Others were notionally called back for interviews. Why the rejections were never quite clear; it seemed that COGAT would analyze cellphone numbers and make judgment calls on some degree of separation of family members and contacts from identified terrorist or DFA elements. But most of our staff were approved.

In the end, we conducted a two-day training for 45 local employees and three expats from the Gaza office to East Jerusalem in late August 2022, followed by a one-day team-building exercise in the Golan Heights and northern Israel. We also called it an "IMC Forward" for HQ because we would look ahead to the future and not be mired by the past.

With the threats of repeated escalation of violence and associated trauma for the Gazan people, IMC sought to provide the Gaza team a break outside the office, some transformative shared experiences, and a chance to restore energy elsewhere to keep building up the skills and knowledge needed for work requirements.

The training was about defining IMC's mission, vision, and strategic goals to better implement USAID-funded humanitarian assistance work. Its significance for IMC's local staff cannot be overstated: for the vast majority of them, it was the first time in their lives to leave Gaza. It was the first time to be able to walk the streets of the Old City of Jerusalem in the evening and go to pray at Al Aqsa, the Temple Mount, and the first time to participate in this sort of empowering activity. It was, for many if not most, the first time they had ever seen a river with their own eyes, not to mention getting into it.

We included games, icebreakers and other exercises to maintain interest and energy levels. We even closed the second day of the Forward workshop with a simulation of the popular TV show SHARK TANK, with staff dividing up into four competing teams to vie for the attention, favor, and support of judges for the most persuasive and compelling pitches for new products, services or initiatives.

The staff included a cross-section of all departments and teams of IMC, including Health, Child Protection, Gender-Based Violence (GBV), Mental Health, Psychological Support, Communication and Grants, Logistics, and Operations. With about 20 employees recently joining IMC, the Forward workshop also provided for socialization and the chance to talk to older colleagues, share experiences and knowledge. It also helped employees to cope with significant changes in the organization. We also discussed ethical questions and safeguarding the people under our care and assistance.

Since the success of organizations usually depends on the training and development of the workforce, and the ability to communicate effectively, analyze critically, and solve problems are the skills that employees need to develop, the necessity for this type of training was urgent. The training helped employees grow as individuals and increased their productivity and efficiency. It helped them understand IMC policies and procedures, which would boost morale and help with employee retention rates. For employees, it is important to know to what degree management is aware of their well-being. Regular training helps them keep a positive image of the organization and boost employee morale so that they can perform even better.

Most of participants expressed the need for redoing this kind of activity periodically, since it motivated them to do the work they do, and they felt so honored to participate in the strategic visioning and planning exercises for IMC.

The formal objectives of the Forward for the IMC Gaza team, designed to enhance performance under the USAID BHA grant:

- *Mapping Out Our Competitive Space;*

- *Clarifying USAID/USG Regulations and Unique Gaza Requirements;*

- *Redefining a Vision, Mission and Strategic Directions;*

- *Improving Work Coordination, Communication and Collaboration;*

- *Enhancing Employee Morale and Motivation;*

- *Localization and Cultural Grounding for Gaza and Palestine;*

- *Improving Social Communication and Outreach.*

We sought to steer a "Forward" visioning exercise to help us move collectively ahead to advance and persist. We saw those days as a pause, reflection, and brainstorming space outside the office. We saw it as a positive and useful tool to significantly enhance performance for the USAID grants. We also saw it as a way of helping to consolidate the onboarding and commitment to IMC of new staff and perhaps shaking up some assumptions and paradigm boundaries of older hands.

I told our staff that we wanted to be mindful of what we learned in the past but focus on the future. We wanted to encourage some guided brainstorming about the future. What kind of organization did we imagine we could generate or create two or more years down the line? What strengths would we want to enhance? What weaknesses do we need to overcome? What vulnerabilities do we want to try to erase? What opportunities might be out there, and what might we create?

Following the two-day workshop at a local hotel in East Jerusalem, we hired a bus to bring the staff on a day trip up to the Golan Heights in northern Israel, or as some referred to it, half-jokingly and half-seriously "occupied Syria." Indeed, this land, won by Israel during the 1967 Six-Day War, was annexed unilaterally by Israel in December 1981. While rejected formally by the UN, it is almost always shown on Israeli and most American maps as de facto Israel.

We hiked by the Baniyas waterfalls for about five kilometers. Then we went down to Ha Gosherim to indulge in a team-building exercise in inflatable river rafts called kayaks [sic] by the Israelis. It was amazing how virtually every person, with one exception, got into those inflatable rafts, including the women. Everyone had great fun splashing around on a course near the River Jordan for a couple of hours.

Feedback from the staff was over the moon. All emphasized that IMC staff cherished spending quality time together and making recollections to take with them to dazzle others in Gaza. It was the first time many had seen a river, not to mention jumping into one to kayak! Kayaking as a team-building effort genuinely satisfied everyone because it gave team cooperation lessons and a peaceful encounter with the breezy greenery and bliss that fed long-term recollections. It also brought many into direct contact with vacationing Israelis and allowed them to see the "Other" in a very different family way. Afterward, as evening approached, we arranged a sunset lake cruise on Kinneret, the Sea of Galilee, to enjoy the water one final time before departing back to Jerusalem and the next day to Gaza. I'll share some photos here.

Special thanks to my former Communications Officer, Yasmeen, for compiling the original collage. I'm leaving off the last names of those from Gaza.

45

"It was more than wonderful experience at the right time, which allowed me to get rid of negative feelings."

Mervat

Health Program Officer

"I was so happy joining the activity. I used to do work, work, work. It was a different experience to me to know more about strategic goals of IMC in the future and participate in decision making."

Isaa

Compliance Officer

"FORWARD was just wonderful. It was a quantum leap in place and time. We were together a team, and this is the wonderful thing."

Amal

Health Program Officer

"We need this to be done every three months. Thank you, IMC!"

Nadeen

GBV Manager

"Some people give it all they have – I appreciate that you always go above and beyond to find even more ways to contribute to the team."

Mohammed

Grants Manager

"You never do just a good job when you can do a great one. Thank you for the time and effort you put into everything that made this succeed."
Abdallah
Human Resources
HR Officer

"On this earth what is worth living for!"

Ibrahim

MEAL Officer

"No one's contribution is considered too small or unimportant for recognition. After receiving the out-of-office hours, it's no wonder employees are now more motivated to do their job and do it well, too!"

Amal

HR Manager

"If you could read my mind, then you'd know how grateful I am for you at this very moment. Thank you, IMC!"

Yehia

Finance Manager

"I found my pot of gold at the end of the rainbow and that is my beautiful IMC family here in Gaza. This experience will be one of my top favorite memories which I will cherish deeply until the end of time."

Suzan

Procurement Project Assistant

"We need this more frequently to be done. Two days are not enough. It was fun for me. People wanted to talk and share experiences more in depth, but this needed more than just two days."

Dr. Shamil Kalyayev
Medical Coordinator

"Every moment lasts for a second but gives a memory that is cherished forever, and we will never forget what we experienced during this day"

Hussam

Warehouse Officer

"We can always count on you for top-notch work. Thank you for the splendid FORWARD activity you had for us."

Mohammed

Procurement Lead

"FORWARD inspired me to look at everything in a more positive light. I can't thank you enough for your uniquely optimistic attitude in such activity.

Omar

Procurement Officer

"A light mood makes for a light load. Thank you for making that happen."

Ayah

MHPSS Counsellor

"It is the first time for me to be allowed to see my country."

Duaa

Health Program Officer

"Everyone in this office appreciates everything you did to make FORWARD happen. Allow me to express mine to you now."

Yasmeen
Communication
Officer

The best thing that happened is that my participation in FORWARD provided us the opportunity to visit and pray at Al-Aqsa, and the training was fruitful and so beneficial for me to achieve my career goals.

Wafaa
MEAL Assistant

"Away from the constraints of time and place and the constraints of boring office work was our trip to Jerusalem.

The bus was writhing between hills and valleys, not even stopped by the singing, and babbling of the passengers at times.

The Soul finally settles between the streets of the old city, reaching its mosque and its golden dome, and performing three prayers in its precincts. That was a remarkable and unforgettable event."

Methqal
Technical Coordinator
for Emergency Response

"Because of you, work at IMC became the dream of everyone. I could not be more grateful. Thank you."

Reem

GBV Facilitator

Look at their faces and humanity. It's essential to absorb this, personalize it, and internalize it. This was a seminal experience for so many, and we became the envy of other organizations that had not had the success we had in securing permits for the Gazan staff to enter Israel. It certainly didn't hurt our recruitment efforts.

We did a follow-up workshop for Gazan staff in mid-January 2023. This was held inside Gaza; we weren't in a financial position to try to retake people off-site. We used the facilities of a local sporting club in Gaza and had one day with all hands and one day with the senior staff for stocktaking and to see what further changes we might want to try to undertake. The central portion of our USAID Mission funding was ending, and we didn't know if BHA funding would be delayed.

I had exploratory contacts with some members of that Bureau who suggested there might well be a plus-up increase in funding available for Gaza and IMC. I was even asked if we could develop a satellite program in the West Bank, which had shown a significant increase in political violence in recent months.

While Gaza was quiescent primarily at that point, Jenin in the north and Hebron in the south were showing many protests and actions by extremist elements as well. In Jenin, a new group had appeared, the Lion's Den, which was claiming credit for some lone-wolf attacks on Israeli civilians as well as IDF units. In response, the Israeli Army and Airforce had gone on and launched major retaliatory attacks, which would come to include both missile attacks against encampments by helicopter gunships and even for the first time in over 20 years, fighter jets had conducted strikes near Ramallah and East Jerusalem.

Over the last two decades and certainly since the Second Intifada, 2022 had been the most violent in Israel and Palestine. UN officials had come out repeatedly condemning the high level of death, injuries, and arrests of Palestinians in the West Bank and East Jerusalem. This included children. 2023 would quickly prove to be even worse, long before 10/7. The number of mass arrests of Palestinians increased. Protests broke out near Ramallah and other places across the West Bank. Some began to speculate that a Third *Intifada* had begun.

The spark for this was undoubtedly Israeli settler violence across the West Bank. I saw this repeatedly in the local news. Israeli settler encampments and colonies became increasingly emboldened, swooping down and conducting unprovoked attacks on neighboring Palestinian villages. They sent out bulldozers, often accompanied by IDF soldiers, to uproot hundreds and then thousands of Palestinian olive tree groves, a crucial part of their sustenance. They destroyed water systems, demolished homes and schools, and perversely seemed to deliberately target schools and classrooms built by U.S. government and EU donor funds. This brought only mild protests from the respective embassies and virtual silence from the Member State capitals.

In classic bully scenarios, unanswered violence and aggression just encourage more of the same. Settler groups swooped down with drones and dropped leaflets with intimidating messages on surrounding Palestinian lands. Drones carried loudspeakers, telling the Palestinian villages horrible things: "You are all cattle. We will come down in the middle of the night to brand you like the animals you are."

Settlers dressed in paramilitary uniforms carrying guns and often followed at close quarters by IDF units that were there to "protect them" and "maintain order." The soldiers would do nothing if settlers would arbitrarily kill Palestinians on the roads near the encampments; people who were unarmed and had done nothing to possibly deserve this.

This happened over and over again, fueling the extremism of the settler caucus in the Israeli Knesset, which would pressure the government for more funding to expand illegal settlements and thoroughly marginalize the Palestinians. I have driven by and into some of these settlements and seen them across the West Bank. In many cases, it seems like these Israeli adventurers would go with some caravans and cars and claim the strategic high ground on some ridges and then secure massive subsidies to build up what can only be called colonial outposts above and between Palestinian villages. This is not on Israeli land. This is on land seized temporarily during the 1967 Six-Day War from Jordan. Despite international demands, indeed clear statements in the past from the U.S. government as well, the Israelis held onto the land.

In the year 2000, there were perhaps 100,000 settlers in the West Bank; after aggressive government expansion programs and subsidies for resettlement, and political theater calling this Palestinian territory Judea and Samaria, there may be now close to 800,000 Israeli settler-colonists holding the best land, the best water supplies, and the best road access in the occupied Palestinian territories.

This also represented a clear abrogation of the Oslo Accords and other agreements Israel had previously signed. The West Bank land was temporarily carved into three general areas or subdivisions in the Oslo II Accords. Area A was marked with vivid red signs, signaling that holders of Israeli passports were not allowed and that this land was under the direct administration of the Palestinian Authority with full control over civil and security matters. Area B was also a Palestinian enclave, but the Palestinian Authority only had civil control and not direct security control. Area C, which represented about 60% of the West Bank, were areas where there was temporary Israeli military control and no real civil administration, including the Jordan River valley area.

In late October 2022, I was encouraged to visit Amman, Jordan. I was there in part to see the IMC program and had a great exchange getting to know Ahmad, the Country Director, and his staff. Ahmad and I had become friendly, becoming a bit of a jocular trio with the IMC Yemen Country Director Wasim, who was himself a Gazan Palestinian.

The primary purpose, though, was to meet with potential donors from a Saudi-origin foundation. I prepared some presentation materials, and with the help of our IMC Middle East regional development director, I joined the meeting and made the pitch to discuss our program. I talked about our work in Gaza and our hopes to start a program up on the West Bank. They seemed to appreciate the pitch and asked lots of questions. They were a donor for IMC in other countries in the past.

It was instructive to me to see their reactions and thoughts about funding assistance programs for restive Palestinian populations. They were reluctant to fund programs in Gaza because of their sensitivity to a volatile situation.

About the West Bank, and my statements that the neediest areas included Area C, which had no access to services from the Palestinian Authority, they paused. They considered Area C as probably too problematic as well as this time since they might be seen as in a situation of confrontation with the Israelis. They wanted to avoid political controversies or visibly standing out front regarding the occupied territories' social conflicts. They left open the possibility of some support in the future with Area A but were nervous about Area C.

Unfortunately, there seemed to be little I could do to convince them otherwise. I offered a menu of options for things we might try to undertake on the West Bank, including a possible initiative to develop mobile outreach services together with one of our Gaza partners, Saint John Eye Hospital. Saint John Eye Hospital also operated a smaller clinic facility in Anabta without surgeries, supported by its main hospital in East Jerusalem. But they decided to postpone engagement.

In November, my wife came out to visit Jerusalem. We went first on an R&R trip to Tashkent Uzbekistan for two weeks. It was a fascinating and rewarding trip to a new Central Asian Turkic country, clearly with heavy historic Russian influence, and we travelled by train and the local airlines to far flung historic towns like Samarkand, Shahrisabz, Bukhara, Urguench and Khiva. These Silk Road stops showed us a remarkably hospitable and friendly people, relatively new to tourism, nominally Muslim but with an incredible history of ancient Jewish settlements and synagogues, and with an easy-going tolerance of religion that belied Muslim stereotypes. While Tashkent itself was modern and showing a bit of a boom in new construction slowly supplanting the Soviet era history, the towns outside the capital had a surfeit of thirteenth and fourteenth-

century mosques, universities, shrines, and markets, much of it the legacy from Amir Temur, or Tamerlane of the Mongol conquests. In Samarkand, we saw the ruins of an ancient observatory built by the astronomer polymath Uluggh Beg, grandson of Amir Temur, to track the sun's and stars' movement. The Islamic architecture was gorgeously elaborate. And we had the chance to visit two of the ancient Jewish synagogues of Central Asia in Samarkand and Bukhara, the latter now reduced to a few dozen mostly elderly Jewish families as almost all had migrated to Israel with the fall of the Soviet Union.

On our return to Israel, I made arrangements with Israeli and DFA authorities for my wife to join me in a short visit to Gaza so she could see it with her own eyes. She saw for herself the hospitality and warmth of the Gazan local staff. This was a rare opportunity since civilians very rarely get approved to enter Gaza.

As 2023 opened and took shape, what was seen across the West Bank as well as Gaza was the repeated Israeli practice of collective punishment and collective deportation of Palestinians. These are practices forbidden under international law. Yet they were hallmarks of the Netanyahu Cabinet in Israel and particularly of the most right-wing extremists in that group. What do these phrases mean?

Collective punishment is when a military or occupying power chooses to indiscriminately punish an entire civilian population because of the acts or crimes committed by individuals or a few. No court, no tribunal conducting an assessment of guilt. It is a pressure tactic, really a terror tactic, intended to force a civilian population to give up the militants resisting the forces of the occupying power.

Collective deportation is similar. It also violates several UN and international agreements and the Geneva Convention. It refers to the massive and indiscriminate uprooting of an entire population to seize their land and leave them dispossessed, homeless and stateless. It is considered as well as a war crime. And it has been happening regularly, long before 10/7, across the occupied Palestinian territories.

In fact, as AP's Joseph Krauss recently noted, "Palestinians mark 76 years of dispossession as a potentially even larger catastrophe unfolds in Gaza. Palestinians [are marking] the 76th year of their mass expulsion from what is now Israel, an event that is at the core of their national struggle. But in many ways, that experience pales in comparison to the calamity now unfolding in Gaza. Palestinians refer to it as the *Nakba*, Arabic for catastrophe. Some 700,000 Palestinians — a majority of the prewar population — fled or were driven from their homes before and during the 1948 Arab-Israeli war that followed Israel's establishment." This *Nakba* has now been repeated once again in slow motion across the West Bank, with many Palestinian communities in the occupied territory being broken up, demolished, and further dispersed and dispossessed.

In March 2023, IMC held another global meeting of HQ staff with the country directors and senior program leaders in Dubai. March was seen as a better option since it was cooler than June. But it also meshed up nicely with the Dubai International Humanitarian Aid and Development Conference, which drew participants and speakers not only from around the Middle East but Europe as well.

I met Mukesh Kapila there, a senior humanitarian who had been the head of British humanitarian assistance and conflict aid for years, had held senior roles with the UN and had witnessed the terrible disasters and genocides of Rwanda and Darfur in Sudan, and had served as Under Secretary General of the International Federation of the Red Cross and Red Crescent societies, later received a CBE from Queen Elizabeth II. Coming out of Gaza, with the sense of something ominous brewing there, it was alarming and enlightening to have the chance to talk with him over dinner and gain his perspective on the consequences of remaining silent.

I returned to Jerusalem to hear the disappointing news from USAID's humanitarian assistance bureau that due to the earthquakes in Türkiye and Syria and congressional budget cuts, USAID would not in fact have much in the way of additional resources for our program in Gaza, nor to expand to critically tense locations in the West Bank. We could still submit a revised application for funding, but it would be for fewer resources than originally hinted at. Other INGO programs in the occupied Palestinian territories were also cut back; I learned from colleagues at AIDA that EU resources were coming up short compared to what had been expected. UN colleagues told me that pledges for addressing the humanitarian fund needs were dropping off from the needed levels to address Palestinian emergency assistance.

We were also receiving modest funds from a variety of regional sources, including the King Salman Humanitarian Relief Fund and the Shefa Foundation Fund. But USAID was by far the 800-lb. gorilla in terms of development and humanitarian assistance resources, and we were hugely dependent on its outcome. This was also very politically vulnerable, as our organization and others had seen abrupt funding cutoffs under the Trump Administration.

Overall, it seemed like, politically and financially, donors were getting tired of assistance needs in the Middle East and Palestine in particular. This was the toxic blend of donor fatigue and political policy apathy from essential countries like the United States, which had made no genuine efforts to push for any sort of strategic or diplomatic progress on the creation of the Palestinian state and protecting the legitimate aspirations of the Palestinian people for years. Neither the Obama, Trump, nor Biden presidencies had made more than what had seemed cursory efforts.

The provocative news all around was about an inevitable and impending reconciliation between Saudi Arabia and the Gulf States with Israel. Initiated under the Trump administration as the Abraham Accords, the focus under the Biden Administration seemed to be to ignore the case and cause of the Palestinians as well and push for the Arabs to make common cause with Israel as part of a bold new package of economic agreements what would eventually link trade between India, Israel and Europe. This seemed to be wishful thinking, believing that the Palestinian condition could be easily swept under the rug and ignored to pursue the chimeric economic and national security benefits of a normalization treaty and alliance. Yet according to credible sources, despite some hesitancy, Saudi Arabia was clearly dipping its collective toes into the tub of normalization, testing the waters through its Persian Gulf neighbors to see how it might work.

When I was in Dubai for the March 2023 visit, there were many indications that the Emiratis were promoting tourism from Israel. Israeli bankers and investors were visiting Dubai, and even the Ultra-Orthodox Jews could be seen on the prosperous streets and at the UAE tourist sites like the Burj Khalifa and the Burj al-Arab. There was talk of the opening of a synagogue in Dubai. I had to admit, I was surprised and pleased to see this on some level as an American Jew. But deeper down, I wondered and thought, "This will not end well."

I had also been developing potential partnerships with Boston Children's Hospital. BCH's Global Health Program strategically partnered with IMC, focusing on emergency trauma care. It was becoming increasingly obvious that this area needed improvements in Gaza and the West Bank.

I also developed good relations in exchange visits and meetings with the Palestinian Red Crescent Society (PRCS) leadership staff in Ramallah. Over the course of several months from late 2022 into the spring of 2023 I invested time and enthusiasm in promoting possible partnerships and exchanges. PRCS was a very respected organization, and in Ramallah they had a very impressive infrastructure, along with a network of clinics in hospitals across the occupied Palestinian territories as well as in the neighboring Palestinian diaspora in refugee settlements of Jordan, Syria and Lebanon. PRCS had been a sort of proto–Palestinian Ministry of Health in the days of the PLO in exile before the creation of the Palestinian Authority. They were connected and affiliated with the global International Federation of Red Cross and Red Crescent, as was Magen David Adom in Israel, as both were national chapters.

The PRCS had a budget of nearly $100 million, partially from the IFRC and partially from European donors. This was a large budget, but by means sufficient for all that they were taking on across Palestine. Unfortunately, they did not seek or accept money from the U.S. Government because of a legal requirement from the U.S. Congress that they sign a document known as the Anti-Terror Certification (ATC). The ATC was a symbolic thorn and hurdle for many Palestinians, which was frustrating to deal with.

It's not that PRCS supported terrorism. They didn't. But post 9/11 legal requirements like the ATC were seen as offensive by many Palestinians because they frequently saw what they considered as the legitimate rights of self-defense against an occupying power (Israel) as characterized as terrorism. Conversely the actual acts of terrorism committed against Palestinian villagers by Israeli settler colonists in different parts of the West Bank, as well as arbitrary arrests, detentions and demolitions committed against Palestinians that were decried globally were never described as such by either the United States or the European Union.

Despite this hurdle, I managed to set up a series of Zoom video calls between BCH in the United States, IMC in Palestine and the PRCS, and this led eventually to some brainstorming about the needs of the PRCS Hospital in Hebron (Khalil), in the southern West Bank and a planned visit by Global Health Program leadership to Israel and Palestine in May. BCH hoped that we might be able to identify private donors willing to support an emergency trauma care program for Hebron Hospital and possibly more. I hoped that I could get IMC resources to complement this as well in partnership. I drove to Hebron carrying the BCH staff, and we visited the facility which was already in the midst of a major expansion and upgrade. We were received very cordially by the PRCS hospital leadership and we walked through the old hospital and the adjacent and adjoining new construction.

Rather brilliantly, PRCS' Hebron Hospital had leveraged a $10 million grant from a Dutch donor, intended to fund renovations for two floors of the existing hospital and had been able to match it with other monies to allow for the construction and equipment of four new floors to substantially increase the capabilities of their hospital. They had succeeded in luring back to Palestine a number of very skilled Palestinian doctors and surgeons, to help in building out a wide array of new subspecialties to address the needs of Palestinians in the Hebron region.

Back in Gaza, I participated in a regional phone call with the IMC Middle East colleagues, and we received further instructions to develop new multi-year country strategic plans. This had been initially raised in Dubai, but on the call, we were given clearer guidance about developing a first draft for our respective programs by July, with a process of high-level headquarters review to commence by September 2023 of the final versions.

I provided the feedback to our senior staff, and we decided to build on the products from the small group discussions of the IMC Forward meetings we had held in recent months, as well as collate input from other sources including what we could use from AIDA. AIDA had hired some very thoughtful consultants who had done constructive research about what had come to be known as the shrinking space for humanitarian and development assistance, really a steadily shrinking environment increasingly closing off options, opportunities, and potential solutions to the open wound of the Palestinian people.

We also received some support from the IMC HQ to help us assess next steps. Dr Jill John-Kall, the IMC Senior Health Advisor, visited for two weeks in late June and worked with our Medical Coordinator and Health Team staff. She was amusing and quite capable; South Asian Indian family transplanted to South Texas. She had valuable perspectives from what she had observed in Gaza over years past, visits to other IMC programs, and shared experiences in Afghanistan with other organizations.

Before Dr Jill's visit we also had a visit from Eoin, our Irish Mental Health and Psychosocial Services Regional Advisor. His Irish was at times not the easiest to understand. Yet, he kept calm and avoided getting his "Irish" up when in flying to Tel Aviv from his residence in Barcelona, he found himself dreadfully harassed by Israeli security, which mysteriously refused to let his small suitcase on board the flight. They had seemingly arbitrarily forced him to dispossess himself of the bag and dump all his stuff in one of these vinyl plastic carryall soft-sided bags. He was told he could recover the suitcase back in Barcelona on his return. We never found out what the Israelis were terrified of from his innocuous bag. Eoin worked intensively with our MHPSS Coordinator from Gaza, Jasem, the Technical Supervisor, Ahlam, and Team Manager, Mohammed.

We hired a Palestinian consultant to help with the process and conduct some donor mapping. Unfortunately, he proved unable to travel from Ramallah to Gaza since his Israeli permit had expired the week before. We held a strategic planning workshop to agree on possible priority areas for IMC to work on, but the local consultant who supported that was also not the most effective.

2023 was a year of visits for sure. A month later, we also received a visit from our then-desk officer from London, Livinia Mouries, who worked with our staff and me to assemble a first draft of the proposed strategy. I had tried to lead a process as participatory as possible, but as things would play out unhelpfully with the local consultants, I had to pick up the lion's share of conceptual work and writing.

Liv's visit coincided with the wedding of one of our younger Gazan staff members, Hassan al Ramlawi. A 24-year-old logistics assistant who could be goofy at times but was so enamored with new AI technology tools like Chat GPT, he effusively talked up how it could be useful to project and program staff to my wife and me.

Liv and I were invited to Hassan's wedding on a Saturday. I was determined to stay for it, since I had been out of the country for the wedding two months before of Suzan and Ibrahim from the office. We stayed over in Gaza, and both of us attended. It was such a joyous event, segregated by gender, of course, as per the Muslim customs. Liv went with the women, and I stayed with the men. While Liv had what I learned was a much more involved and rich experience over many hours

of the day and night, I too spent a couple of hours with the groom's entourage going from house to house of different relatives and in-laws and dancing on the streets to general merriment. Eventually we all went to the coastal strip of Ar Rashid, along the beach, where a half dozen or more wedding halls dotted the area, each filled with one or more wedding parties celebrating in the uniquely Gazan ways.

After the wedding, I escorted Liv out of Gaza to Jerusalem, and from there, we made our way one morning to Bethlehem on the occupied West Bank before her return flight to London. Bethlehem was the home of our local program team lead, and we came through Israeli checkpoints to stop for coffee, coinciding with another joyous day, the celebration of the release of the secondary school grade scores and passing lists.

It was a veritable street festival down several of the central Bethlehem arteries; so many families paraded in their cars with fireworks, silly string blasts, and noisemakers up and down the street.

After watching this fun vicariously, we also stopped by the notable "Walled Off Hotel," an incredible museum and hotel across the street from the imposing and forbidding Israeli Wall, which cut much of the ancient Palestinian city in half. The Palestinian side was adorned with caricatures and graffiti of resistance calling out the Israeli occupation, including some stunning award-winning artwork from Banksy. The owner's daughter gave us a tour of the hotel after visiting the well-done Museum of the Occupation, which detailed in careful exhibits, dioramas, and interactive displays the burden of the Occupation and what it had meant for decades. It ended somewhat on a hopeful note by showcasing all the accomplishments and talents of the Palestinian people

in the occupied territories and the global diaspora.

Bethlehem was one of the most significant places to see the wall and its effects. The Walled Off Hotel, right across from a corner of it, had the tagline "The Worst View in the World" for its visitors, and this was indeed the case. You could see what this behemoth represented for the people, cutting off a key section of the town and interrupting the flow of traffic, commerce, and daily lives for thousands of people.

My daily routine in Gaza and Jerusalem was of course usually far more prosaic. I would make my way to the Gaza office, about a 20-25 minute walk if I was on foot, sometimes alone and sometimes accompanying our expat Azerbaijani Medical Coordinator. On a great day, I would go out with some of our staff to visit with different local partners either in the Gaza City area or more afield across the Gaza Strip.

Other times, I would be in our well-equipped offices, sometimes visiting with different teams or the senior staff meetings, often having to cut through the inevitable barrage of emails from outside or inside the organization while reviewing and approving payment transfer requests prepared by our finance team. Occasionally, we would have on-site meetings with different project partners, but for a larger group, often using the rooftop conference room of the Phoenix Hotel, one of the few approved hotels for  visitors and which was pre-cleared by the U.S. government funding vetting restrictions. If I had to go to another location by car, it would always be by an official IMC-branded leased vehicle in Gaza with one of our several professional drivers, who had colorful stories to tell and share about their families and past work histories. I couldn't self-drive in Gaza, due to legal and liability issues. Outside Erez Terminal, back in Israel proper, I could and would drive often and to different towns and villages on the West Bank.

We had two IMC-rented guesthouse apartments in Sheikh Jarrah, East Jerusalem. One was set up as a guesthouse for expat staff cycling in or out of Gaza, and the other was the Mission Director apartment, with a small, improvised office space. I could easily walk from there to the UN OCHA offices for periodic meetings, to the AIDA offices at NRC, or to the Ambassador Hotel, which was a famous historic meeting spot for many in the diplomatic and humanitarian assistance community.

I could also easily walk a few blocks to the relatively new Jerusalem Light Rail, traversing the old Bar Lev line bisecting East Jerusalem from West Jerusalem. With the divisions long gone after Israel conquered and annexed the Palestinian side, it was now just a principal avenue connecting Highway 60 up north of Jerusalem towards Ramallah and the West Bank checkpoints near there and south towards the Old City and then on to Hebron Road and the southern part of the West Bank.

The Light Rail or tram ran north from the Damascus Gate of the Old City, Shimon HaTzadek and Ammunition Hill to the East Jerusalem neighborhoods of Shu'afat, Beit Hanina and Jewish settlements further north. It went south and west towards Jaffa Street and the City Center, the Central Bus and Train Stations all the way to Mt. Herzl, on the edge of the Jerusalem Hills. The USAID offices were in commercial space in the Mamilla Mall, just off the City Hall tram stop, a high-end open mall built on space adjoining the Old City's Jaffa Gate to the Jewish Quarter. The U.S. Embassy Office of Palestinian Affairs, the unofficial consulate to the Palestinians, was also near there.

By September 2023, things were humming along quite well. In mid-July, we had shared with HQ a draft of the new IMC oPt strategy and updated it in a revised version by early September. I tried to mesh the input of my local staff, our HQ technical support, and my own sense of what was needed and what was feasible in Palestine.

I won't go into the strategy itself in any big way to avoid proprietary and confidential details from it. The document reached about 30 pages plus annexes. I received word from IMC HQ that each of the roughly 20 country directors would be asked to offer

PowerPoint presentations and oral arguments to a large senior HQ group online, to lay out the vision and resource requirements for the new country strategies. IMC oPt, the Gaza program, was a small to mid-sized program, but one with hopefully great potential to grow. We would be among the first initial oral presentations, in mid-September.

I wanted to paint a complex picture of Gaza in the space and time window available for us. Gaza, for many, seemed to be monochromatically dismal and opaque. I wanted participants and listeners from HQ to learn more about the importance of Gaza and to encourage greater private, unrestricted fundraising for resiliency work in Gaza and Palestine. I also wanted to get people to think outside the box regarding new and unorthodox partnerships that could support our efforts in the troubled land. Gaza was not at all an easy place to work in, but it was important and required keen awareness of the mix of humanitarian needs and diplomatic imbroglios as well as the ever-present potential for violence.

Outbreaks of violence in Gaza during several months in 2014, May 2021, August 2022, and May 2023 had increased people's aid dependency and their reliance on negative coping strategies to address basic needs. The escalations, along with the closure of Israeli-controlled border crossings, exacerbated the fragile state of Palestinians and resulted in immediate needs, notably related to mental health and psychosocial support services (MHPSS), Child Protection, Gender-based Violence, shelter, food security, livelihoods, WASH, education, and cash assistance and essential medicines and supplies.

In the West Bank, including East Jerusalem, Israel's military occupation continues to impede basic human rights of Palestinians. The ongoing conflict, including excessive use of force, demolitions, evictions, settlement expansion, and settler-related violence, all drive insecurity, block and prevent socioeconomic progress.

Overall, 2022 and the first half of 2023 saw an almost unprecedented increase in conflict-related Palestinian casualties in the Gaza Strip, West Bank, including East Jerusalem, and in settler-related violence against Palestinians and their property. The restrictive and discriminatory planning regime applied in Area C and in East Jerusalem continues to prevent Palestinians from addressing basic housing, livelihood, and service needs, with continuing high rates of demolitions and seizures of Palestinian structures, including "self-demolitions" in East Jerusalem, on the grounds of a lack of Israeli-required building permits. Demolitions, evictions, and Israeli settler violence are some of the ongoing Israeli policies and practices, many linked to the presence of Israeli settlements, which intensify the coercive environment on vulnerable communities in Area C, East Jerusalem, and the Israeli military-controlled part of Hebron City (H2). H2 was an eyesore and open wound in the southern West Bank. It was a blatantly provocative and illegal Jewish settlement in the middle of ancient Hebron (Khalil), completely disrupting the city and its Palestinian community.

The Israeli authorities, citing security reasons, continued to impose physical and administrative restrictions on humanitarian programs, including constraints on the delivery of materials needed for humanitarian projects and limitations on the implementation of projects that involve building, expanding or rehabilitating infrastructure in the Gaza Strip, Area C, the H2 area of Hebron and in East Jerusalem.

Civic and humanitarian space in the oPt has long been limited by restrictions imposed by Israeli and Palestinian authorities, which can hamper a principled approach to aid delivery. These restrictions take several forms, such as bureaucratic hurdles to registration and denial of legal facilities (including visas and permits), access restrictions to the West Bank and Gaza, and excessive security-related measures preventing the free movement of humanitarian personnel and goods. As a result, humanitarian actors find it increasingly difficult to provide relief and protection to Palestinians throughout the West Bank and Gaza. This is unlikely to relent in the coming years.

Direct limitations imposed by Israeli authorities include the restrictions on the movement of people and goods in and out of the Gaza Strip, the permit system for Palestinians in the West Bank and the building restrictions in Area C, which make it difficult for aid organizations to provide housing, infrastructure and basic services. The previous Israeli government enacted in 2022 new procedures governing entry to and residency of foreign nationals in the West Bank.

Amending a less restrictive 2016 procedure, this new policy adversely affects general Palestinian freedom of movement and standard of living while also having far-reaching and detrimental effects for a range of sectors, including Palestinian academia, civil society, and national and international humanitarian and development operations. For INGOs like IMC, restricted nationality issues for expats coming to Israel and the oPt, the unfavorable assumptions on quality of deployment life and military escalation risks in the Gaza enclave, complex GOI visa regime and approval process and limitations on time in Gaza and Jerusalem make it challenging to recruit and retain senior and specialized staff.

Restrictions on movement between the West Bank and Gaza have been in place for over 20 years. Entry or exit—including for national staff of humanitarian organizations—requires approval, which is commonly denied by Israel for opaque or arbitrary reasons.

Though in 2022, Israel allowed the highest number of exits from Gaza since 2004, this figure still constituted only nine per cent of the monthly average in 2000, before the imposition of access restrictions. As discussed above, obtaining visas and permits for international staff to access the Gaza Strip and the West

Bank remains challenging, time-consuming and sometimes impossible for staff of many nationalities. The Palestinian authorities—in both Gaza and the West Bank—also impose restrictions on humanitarian aid and civic space, through bureaucratic delays, onerous reporting requirements and lack of timely coordination with humanitarian organizations.

The then-new Israeli government (GoI) coalition agreement stipulated that the government has 180 days from the time of its swearing-in to pass a law imposing a tax on donations from foreign governmental and intergovernmental entities to non-profit civil society organizations registered in Israel, including annexed East Jerusalem. That timetable had passed by then.

A draft bill tabled by the opposition and likely to receive support from coalition parties provides for the re-classification of Israeli NGOs upon receipt of foreign governmental funding and would impose extensive reporting and public disclosure requirements, as well as the introduction of a 60% tax on financial contributions from a foreign entity. Globally since the 1940s, official humanitarian and development assistance has generally been exempted from taxation.

A 2018 survey in 47 developing countries showed that all afforded exemptions to providers of aid assistance from a range of different taxes, including income, property, and indirect taxes. Implementing agencies, including international and national NGOs, were similarly exempted. The introduction of taxation of this sort by Israel would, therefore, stand apart from state practice and act as a disincentive for donors to support Israeli and Palestinian civil society. Should this come to pass, the resources of organizations critical to the provision of humanitarian relief and human rights protection would be depleted.

This obstruction of aid funding is coupled with draft bills and policy measures intended to deny entry to Israel and the oPt to officials of the International Criminal Court, the International

Court of Justice (ICJ), and the Human Rights Council special procedures, as well as individuals suspected to engage in legal or policy proceedings perceived to affect Israel negatively. These attempts to restrict humanitarian advocacy and human rights monitoring are combined with proposed criminalization of such engagement—directly or indirectly—by Israeli nationals, punishable by up to seven years' imprisonment.

Likewise, the GoI indicated its intention to act against organizations engaged in ICJ proceedings, equating that with the "promotion of terrorist activity." Many humanitarians and civil society activists felt with reason this might lead to an arbitrary "terrorism" designation of international, Palestinian, and Israeli NGOs under Israel's 2016 counterterrorism law and the draconian 1945 Defense Emergency Regulations.

Efforts to promote policy debate and undertake critical public advocacy have also been stifled and mischaracterized. In oPt, measures being imposed by Israeli and Palestinian authorities have served to impair longstanding access restrictions in place for vulnerable communities, as well as for the humanitarian and development actors.

The combined impact of attempts to delegitimize and politicize aid provision and providers, shrinking physical and normative space for humanitarian action, and the complexity of counterterrorism measures and their possible abuse render principled humanitarian action increasingly difficult in the oPt. In what has long been a hostile and complex operating environment, principled humanitarian action and unimpeded access in oPt face increased scrutiny and pressure.

The living conditions of people in need across the oPt have been severely undermined, as a result of conflict, military occupation, and blockade, as evidenced by high rates of unemployment, poverty, and food insecurity. The dire conditions of people in oPt are mainly attributed to the Israeli occupation and blockade, which continues to disempower and disenfranchise the local population. The current situation further increases restrictions to Palestinians' mobility and access to basic needs while creating a progressively more hostile operational environment for humanitarian, development and human rights organizations. State actors, primarily the GoI, are the architects of this regime of restrictions and are certainly complicit in the reputational attacks designed to delegitimize actors and undermine humanitarian and human rights action. Space for civil society, human rights, development, and humanitarian action continues to shrink in oPt, with public and legal attacks against NGO and UN actors escalating.

The increasing use of counter-terrorism legislation (CTL) to constrain NGOs and civil society organizations' activities and advocacy creates a further chilling effect, particularly in relation to implementing programming in Gaza. All of this further exacerbates the humanitarian crises and impedes the impartial delivery of aid.

The increased politicization of assistance has further intensified the crisis, with vulnerable communities in the oPt suffering mounting negative consequences. The pressure to vacate this space is as real as it is intentional, as aid actors have seen increasing efforts to obstruct aid, hemming in operations, and hamstringing programming. A significant downward trend in the available operational space for civil society organizations and national and international humanitarian and development actors demonstrates this.

I talked briefly about our partners in Gaza. These included CARITAS Jerusalem, the local branch of CARITAS International under the Jerusalem Catholic Archdiocese, which supported us in primary health care. We also worked with Ahli Arab Hospital, under the oversight and management of the Episcopal Church, for secondary health care, gender-based violence, and mental health psychosocial services and the Saint John of Jerusalem Eye Hospital Group, for life-changing ophthalmic care.

Ahli Arab Hospital was historically one of the oldest in Gaza, and had originally been the English Hospital in the last years of the Ottoman Empire and the post WWI mandate of the British Empire. Indeed, it was notable that so many of the hospitals in Gaza originally were Christian Mission hospitals and clinics from different Christian denominations in this now predominantly Muslim land.

Saint John of Jerusalem was supported for over 100 years by the Priory St. John and the Anglican Communion, which had a presence in the region dating back to the time of Crusaders. IMC had helped equip and train staff at the Main Eye Hospital in Sheikh Jarrah, East Jerusalem. In addition, IMC with USAID support had helped equip an eye hospital in Gaza with essential equipment, and the Qatari government had helped Saint John construct the facility.

Discussing the logistics and supply chain available in Gaza, I wrote that INGOs faced unique challenges within the Gaza Strip political and socio-economic context. Gaza was a semi-autonomous component of the occupied Palestinian territory administered by a DFA on proscribed sanction designation lists for the USG, EU, and UN, although the latter two have special operational flexibility.

The DFA itself has a near-hostile modus operandi with the formally legitimate Palestinian Authority, which administers West Bank territory from Ramallah under sharp civil and military occupation controls. Gaza is under a 16-year blockade by the occupying power military, the Israeli Defense Forces, which sharply curbs commercial shipping and entry through the Kerem Shalom checkpoint near the Egyptian border, as well as transit of persons through the Erez Terminal checkpoint.

The Erez barriers, virtually the only point of exit from the Gaza enclave except for the perilous Egyptian-managed Rafah border crossing, have sharply reduced the flow of Gazan citizens into Israel for humanitarian needs or economically driven job-seeking from 200,000 in the year 2000 to 17,000 in 2023. This has drastically reduced income and economic prospects. I noted that the Rafah crossing is a dangerous and hugely expensive pressure valve that permits the exit of perhaps 50,000 more Gazan citizens but at exploitative risks of corrupt Egyptian predatory practices.

NGO programs funded by the U.S. Government must obey USG Treasury OFAC controls and conduct purchases in the cooperating country, understood to mean either Gazan, West Bank Palestinian or Israeli vendors. Within Gaza, there is a surprising local availability of many products from a limited group of vendors, but some supply chain needs, such as for large pharma or equipment purchases require looking to vendors outside the Gaza strip enclave. Procurement imports into Gaza involve time-consuming approvals by GoI Defense Ministry, CLA and *Shabak* intelligence authorities who conduct their own exhaustive vetting to verify end users and to de-conflict problems by items classified as potential "dual-use" by combatants if diverted to the wrong hands.

We had a history of ties and partnerships with over 15 community-based organizations and local NGOs. These groups, which would all be "vetted" under U.S. government rules, worked with us in Gaza to address needs in health care, gender-based violence, child protection and care for handicapped and less abled and others. They often had better inroads with local leaders and Islamic clergy and knew how to ensure local buy-in to our activities.

Most of these organizations operated on a shoestring. A few had significant budgets at times from European donations but that was a minority. Many of them had willingly come on board during the COVID-19 pandemic project funded by the USAID Mission as a limited attempt to resurrect in part the halted Gaza 2020 health project. But they all faced challenges when public interest and concern about COVID had faded and the perceived threat receded.

Luckily Gaza's isolation and blockade from Israel had helped in part to minimize the effects of the pandemic. Meeting with the staff and organizers from these groups could be challenging. They saw large and varied needs, particularly with the most marginalized and isolated of communities. But as can often happen with donor funded projects and programs, you fight with the army you have, not with the army you want. It requires more than a little creativity to try to find ways to meet the identified needs and gaps at least in part, when the donor is limiting closely what funding can be spent on.

I was always impressed with the women. Many of these organizations had strong women leaders, who did not fall in line with all the stereotypes of conservative Islamic societies. They were mindful of conservative mores and traditions, but also willing at times to push the envelope a bit and defend the rights, resources and concerns of women. I was intrigued to learn in Gaza that unlike some Muslim societies there was a tradition in some localities of women as community faith leaders, even if not formal clergy.

One INGO program which particularly made an early impression on me for innovation and creativity was the Mercy Corps International Gaza SkyGeeks program. I had the chance to visit it at the MCI offices in Gaza in April 2022, about two months after arrival. They were close to our offices in Gaza City. Kudos to the MCI staff that helped make this happen. They had begun with a series of innovative startup hubs, promoting practical business skills.

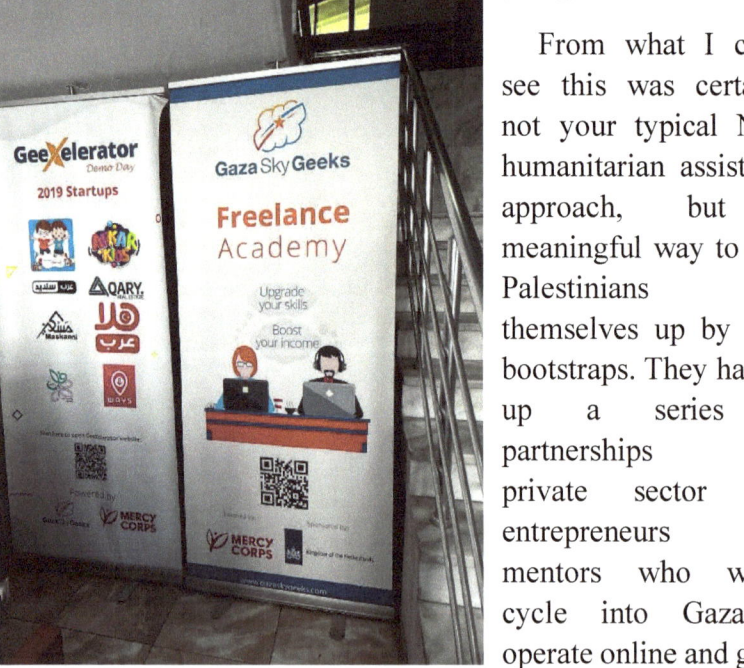

From what I could see this was certainly not your typical NGO humanitarian assistance approach, but a meaningful way to help Palestinians pick themselves up by their bootstraps. They had set up a series of partnerships with private sector tech entrepreneurs and mentors who would cycle into Gaza or operate online and guide the development of IT and computer coding skills for a large and growing cohort of young Gazans. By the time I had visited, I believe over 10,000 had passed through code trainings and many had been able to translate their practice into tangible soft and hard skills for jobs and incomes for their families.

Many had been able to find jobs offshore online where they could earn significant incomes – an incredible and flexible approach to human development. Even more, some had been able to launch their own businesses and companies, which was truly remarkable in Gaza for the effects of the Israeli siege and blockade on the territory, which sharply limited who could go in or out. Kudos to Alan al Kadhi who I came to know as a key energizing spirit behind the initiative. As a longtime global development executive and trainer, I always respected this melding of private sector and nonprofit sector approaches to community development, to reduce dependence and boost income and self-respect. Alan argues these days that tech skills and access like this, for now on the West Bank and hopefully some day soon again in Gaza, are crucial and essential for a Palestinian economic kickstart.

The PowerPoint presentation of our new strategy, including a brief film clip with images from around Gaza, was a big success. It stirred very positive feedback from IMC leadership and the HQ technical units. In fact, we heard from several that we had "knocked the ball out of the park" and had delivered one of the best presentations, setting a new bar or standing for upcoming ones. Our Gazan local staff were proud, and it fueled a strong sense of appreciation for being valued and recognized.

I had hoped to address within the new strategy presentation the topic of new alternative partnerships, including Israeli organizations that had either special credibility to work in Gaza and the West Bank or had a profound social purpose in terms of addressing in a proactive and positive way Palestinian needs and services. I had made several contacts over the past several months with some potential partners and had enjoyed very amicable discussions.

It was admittedly a controversial question for most of my Gazan staff. Yet there was an element of practicality and pragmatism that I discussed with them as we explored the availability of funding from sources like the USAID West Bank/Gaza Mission, which had funded the original IMC Gaza 2020 Health project in 2016, and then had used funds from the U.S. COVID 19 American Rescue Plan to support a temporarily revived COVID 19 project for care, prevention and pandemic preparedness from late 2021 to early 2023.

One of the largest pools of money available for funding at the USAID Mission was the Congressionally authorized Middle East Peace Partnership program (MEPPA). It had been created a few years before under the leadership of Congresswoman Nita Lowey. This account had several tracks for application and had been organized in a well-meaning way of trying to boost people-to-people interactions between Jews and Palestinians. The theory of change was that the peace and reconciliation process could be furthered by breaking down barriers and stereotypes that people held about each other and support channels for mutual assistance. There were different emphasis areas: they included infrastructure, economic development as well as social concerns such as health services.

Some groups had been able to develop grants to support medical and health training exchanges between Israel and the West Bank. Groups like Project ROZANA, under the able leadership of Australian implant to Israel Ronit Zimmer and with lean organization chapters in the United States, Geneva, Australia and Israel, had been able to cultivate relationships with sophisticated Israeli hospital and medical training institutions such as Hadassah Hospital, Wolfson Hospital and others to bring groups of Palestinian nurses and physicians for retraining and skills improvement. There were of course cultural issues and hiccoughs, but overall, they had had good success at boosting skills and improving patient referral access despite the difficulty of working with Palestinian institutions such as the Ministry of Health in Ramallah under the program.

U.S. government rules would stymie any assistance perceived as providing a benefit to the Palestinian National Authority. This was unhelpful and counterproductive and increased tremendously the difficulty of these efforts while limiting the potential scope. However, ROZANA and other groups had succeeded to some degree, but they had not been able to penetrate Gaza. Among many issues, there was also a palpable feeling among Gazan health professionals that any benefits or training perceived as coming from the "enemy" would be seen by DFA authorities as potentially treacherous and the equivalent of consorting with the enemy and espionage.

Despite these challenges, I met with ROZANA a couple times and toyed with proposing a possible partnership or linkage. I found the idea of people-to-people partnerships very appealing, and something that had to be done somehow to break through the distortion fields of noxious government authorities on both sides.

Another promising potential civil society partner I met with on the Israeli side was Physicians for Human Rights – Israel (PHR-I). This was a left-leaning progressive committed advocacy group in Israel that was totally opposed to the Israeli occupation of Palestine, and very concerned and creative in addressing a host of health issues for marginalized peoples both in Israel and Palestine, including refugee and minority population groups that had slipped through the Israeli safety net, such as Bedouin Arabs, African or Syrian refugees, LGTBQ individuals etc. They had hired some years back a Palestinian Israeli Arab public health doctor living in Israel, Dr. Salach, who had been a leader in addressing the often-neglected problem of Diabetes and obesity within the Palestinian people, as well as care for the elderly.

With Dr. Salach's help, PHR-I had been able to negotiate an arrangement where periodically several times a year he would lead medical missions of Israeli Arab physicians and nurses into Gaza from Israel proper, and conduct multi-day sojourns where they would both help address the needs of Gazan patients who needed more sophisticated medical care than was easily available in Gaza, but without the means of a hospital transfer to an Israeli or West Bank facility. This would include cardiac, cancer and orthopedic surgeries as well and would involve partnerships with Gazan health facilities to train the Ministry of Health staff.

I met with Dr Salach first for coffee one evening in Beit Hanina in east Jerusalem, and later went to their offices in Tel Aviv. They also hoped to expand work in mental health psychosocial services to address trauma. They had secured the full authorization of the MOH and DFA as well as support from the Israeli COGAT which authorized the periodic medical missions and provided the needed permits. Ideologically and practically, PHR-I had focused on Gazan public sector facilities under the control of the Gazan MOH.

This would be forbidden with any U.S. or European funding but made perfect sense as that was where the poorest of the poor went to and where the greatest need lay.

We met multiple times, once with the help of Dr. Jill during her field visit in June 2023, and we slowly kicked around the idea of a pilot program which could be proposed under the USAID MEPPA funding which would try to extend this to one or more Gazan NGO or non-profit hospitals, without direct links to the government. We discussed whether we might also try to develop a pilot to work with some of their Israeli Arab and Palestinian health practitioners on the West Bank, to expand the MHPSS services in critically difficult areas such as Jenin. None of this would be easy to develop or undertake, but we shared a common interest in expanding access to services and breaking down barriers.

A third group of interest that I had conversations with was the Israeli NGO IsraAID. Despite the name, they were unconnected with the Israeli government and while maintaining a less political stance than PHR-I they were quite opposed to the policies of the Israeli government with the needs of the Palestinian people. They had started up some years before to project Israeli voluntary non-governmental humanitarian assistance to crisis and hot spots around the world, with modest private funding and small projects.

The IsraAID CEO, a young Israeli enthusiastic visionary leader Yotam Polizer, surprisingly had some ties to Nancy Aossey, the CEO and leader of IMC in LA, consorted in similar fundraising circles and this seemed to me to be very promising. He and his colleagues, which included about 50 staff in Tel Aviv and working remotely, had built up IsraAID from a $15 million per year to a $50 million per year program, without direct governmental assistance. Though an Israeli NGO, they had recently boosted their registration in the U.S. and were also qualified to receive tax free contributions from private donors there. They had even collaborated already with IMC some years before on an Ebola humanitarian assistance effort in Sierra Leone West Africa.

Yotam and I discussed potential partnerships and collaborations, again with the assistance at one point of Dr. Jill. IsraAID indicated that they had good connections notwithstanding with the Israeli COGAT and could also help IMC in terms of facilitating Israeli approvals for the importation into Gaza of donated medical equipment, which had proved to be a headache on repeated occasions.

I had planned to lay this out as one element of our new IMC Palestine strategy, by reaching out to these new partners. However, it had also proved controversial with some back in the IMC HQ. While the concepts were sound, and the potential for fundraising and joint grant writing efforts seemed promising and a valuable way to try to diversify and broaden our funding base for services in Gaza as well as the West Bank, there was hesitation about the optics of collaboration with Israeli organizations.

I felt there were several things we could do to mitigate these concerns, and create, if necessary, some distance which would also protect our Gazan staff. Given the worries though, I did not overly emphasize the details in my pitch deck on the new strategy but did reference these as opportunities we wanted to explore. I had hopes that we could be creative and innovative in taking an important step to furthering some level of social reconciliation across the border.

Our Regional HQ expert on gender-based violence arrived from Milan Italy to support the local GBV team and our Kenyan GBV Coordinator, Joy Mashedi. Laura Canali was a recognized expert in the field, with over ten years of experience with IMC and about another five years with other organizations. She approached fieldwork with evident enthusiasm and was kind and approachable to the local staff. Joy brought ample experience of her own from different countries in Africa and had the most peaceable and serene outlook of almost any professional I knew.

My boss, the Senior Director for Middle East and Europe, came to visit for the first time in September. He seemed surprised with what he saw. I sensed he got impatient with some of the bureaucracies required with running the Israeli gauntlet and entering Gaza. Unfortunately, a family emergency cut short his trip then, and I had to scramble to find a way to get him out early to Israel proper through Erez, and on to the airport outside Tel Aviv. He promised to come back for a more proper visit. It would be sooner than both expected.

In early October I received word in Gaza that USAID was calling a meeting for AIDA's Executive Committee members with USG funding in Jerusalem. I was a little disappointed; I had planned to remain in Gaza over the weekend to join Joy, Laura and some of our local staff to visit historic places in Gaza City and outside. In the old city of Gaza, near the Souk (market), there were ancient Christian Eastern Orthodox and Catholic rite churches dating from Byzantine times and mosques from Ottoman empire days, coexisting without problems or challenge.

South of Gaza City, there was a remarkably well-preserved World War I cemetery from the British Empire days, with careful protection of the graves of thousands of dead British, Australian and Canadian soldiers who lost their lives during WW I battles. Further south, there were the ruins of the Monastery of Tell Umm Amer, believed to be the birthplace of the fourth century theologian Saint Hilarion. It has been under excavation for twenty years with the help of the French government and different international NGOs. We had planned to go out on Saturday over the weekend. I'd been before, taking some of our other visitors. So this time I would have to miss it.

Tuesday night after dinner, I joined Joy and Laura for a post-prandial walk along Ar Rasheed, the avenue that fronted the

Mediterranean coast. We were picked up by our Gazan colleague Nabil Mousa, who was the manager for the Monitoring and Evaluation (MEAL) team. I thought we were just going to walk for an hour, but we ended up walking over 12 kilometers, for a couple hours, all the while engaged in all sorts of conversation about Gaza and its future.

For much of that time Nabil and I walked together and talked while Joy and Laura followed a distance behind. We ended up all being fairly fast walkers, but Nabil and I were faster. We talked about his family outside of Gaza in the Gulf countries, and his aspirations for the future.

Nabil asked me about U.S. politics and its direction in the following year. We talked about possible futures for Palestine and Palestinians, and whether there might be a hopeful one for reconciliation with Israel if as seemed increasingly likely, Israel and Saudi Arabia were to go forward with a normalization of relations. Would that possibly prove better in the end or were Palestinians at risk of being forgotten people once again? It was a deep and meaningful conversation.

We eventually caught up with Laura and Joy on the walk back, watching in some spots so many Gazan families with their children, following the typical evening practice of late-night decompression on the Gazan shore and beach. Quite a few kids were circulating around on the sidewalk in the evening in these colorful illuminated go carts with the kids using the sidewalk as their own promenades. Gazans were typically up very late even with small kids. They drank coffee into the nighttime, far later than I really could or should. And yet they would also arise very early in the pre-dawn hours for the Fajr prayers. The significance of Fajr lies in its role as a transition from the stillness of night to the vibrancy of day. I couldn't help but wonder, when do Gazans sleep? Do they ever manage eight hours a night?

I left Gaza that Wednesday afternoon for the Thursday meeting, unaware of the terrible things about to happen two days later on 10/7, and how much all that I had known for two years would be destroyed in the Israeli offensive to come shortly after.

Figure 1Photo of Joy, Laura and Eyas post 10/7

THE CONUNDRUM OF PALESTINE

Let me digress here and share some discussion I raised just before 10/7, about the situation we faced in Palestine and what the world at large seemed to be insistently ignoring before the Hamas attack.

The occupied Palestinian territory (oPt) is one of the most complex and challenging environments in the world. The oPt remains a protracted political crisis characterized by over 55 years of Israeli military occupation. This crisis is exacerbated by a lack of adherence to international humanitarian and human rights law, internal Palestinian divisions, and the recurrent escalation of hostilities. The results are chronic protection concerns and humanitarian needs which will continue in the absence of a sustainable political solution and opportunities for further development. In Gaza, the Israeli occupation, and over 16 years of an Israeli imposed land, sea and air blockade/movement restrictions and recurrent escalations have contributed to Gaza's dire living conditions.

Outbreaks of violence in Gaza during several months in 2014, May 2021, August 2022 and May 2023 have increased people's aid dependency and their reliance on negative coping strategies to address basic needs. The escalations along with the closure of Israeli-controlled border crossings exacerbated the fragile state of Palestinians and resulted in immediate needs, notably related to mental health and psychosocial support services (MHPSS), Child Protection, Gender-based Violence, shelter, food security, livelihoods, WASH, education, and cash assistance and essential medicines and supplies.

In the West Bank, including East Jerusalem, Israel's military occupation continues to impede basic human rights of Palestinians. The ongoing conflict, including excessive use of force, demolitions, evictions, settlement expansion and settler related violence all drive insecurity, reverse, and prevent socioeconomic progress.

Overall, 2022 and the first half of 2023 brought an almost unprecedented increase in conflict-related Palestinian casualties in the Gaza Strip, West Bank, including East Jerusalem, and in settler-related violence against Palestinians and their property. The restrictive and discriminatory planning regime applied in Area C and in East Jerusalem continues to prevent Palestinians from addressing basic housing, livelihood, and service needs, with continuing high rates of demolitions and seizures of Palestinian structures, including 'self-demolitions' in East Jerusalem, on the grounds of a lack of Israeli-required building permits. Demolitions, evictions, and Israeli settler violence are some of the ongoing Israeli policies and practices, many linked to the presence of Israeli settlements, which intensify the coercive environment on vulnerable communities in Area C, East Jerusalem, and the Israeli-controlled part (H2) of Hebron city. The Israeli authorities, citing security reasons, continue to impose physical and administrative restrictions on humanitarian programs, including constraints on the delivery of materials needed for humanitarian projects, and limitations on the implementation of projects that involve building, expanding or rehabilitating infrastructure in the Gaza Strip, Area C, the H2 area of Hebron and in East Jerusalem.

Civic and humanitarian space in the oPt has long been limited by restrictions imposed by Israeli and Palestinian authorities, which can hamper a principled approach to aid delivery. These restrictions take several forms, such as bureaucratic hurdles to registration and denial of legal facilities (including visas and permits), access restrictions to the West Bank and Gaza, and excessive security-related measures preventing the free movement of humanitarian personnel and goods. As a result, humanitarian actors find it increasingly difficult to provide relief and protection to Palestinians throughout the West Bank and Gaza, with the oPt scoring 4/5 in the ACAPS Humanitarian Access Index. This is unlikely to relent in the coming years.

The living conditions of people in need across the oPt have been severely undermined, as a result of conflict, military occupation, and blockade, as evidenced by high rates of unemployment, poverty, and food insecurity. The dire conditions of people in oPt are mainly attributed to the Israeli occupation and blockade, which continues to disempower and disenfranchise the local population.

The situation even before 10/7 increased restrictions to Palestinians' mobility and access to basic needs, while creating a progressively more hostile operational environment for humanitarian, development and human rights organizations.

To understand the operational context of IMC and other INGOs in the oPt, it is essential to understand the governing authorities over the oPt and the political dynamics that the mission has to observe as part of its presence in the area:

Israel, as primary duty bearer: Israel, as the occupying power, has a duty to ensure the human rights, protection, security, and welfare of the Palestinian population living under occupation and to guarantee that they can live as normal a life as possible, in accordance with their own laws, culture, and traditions. In practice, Israel fails to comply with its international law obligations. However, given the preponderance of economic and security dominance of Israel over the oPt, its tight control over access of good and people to and from the Gaza strip and the limited and tightly controlled labor market which pursues employment and income in Israel, it is impossible to ignore its influence and presence over humanitarian and development assistance activities.

State of Palestine (Palestinian Authority), as secondary duty bearer: The Palestinian Authority (PA) has obligations under international law toward the protection of human rights and the welfare of the Palestinian population within its territory, or subject to its jurisdiction, within the limits of its effective control and powers, considering the obstacles placed by the occupation. Palestinian authorities could improve conditions for communities in Areas A, B and C of the West Bank and in Gaza through the sustainable provision of essential services. However, corruption concerns (some of which may be overblown by the media) have sharply curtailed available donor resources, along with economic strangulation and unilateral denial of customs and other tax resources by the GOI and USG legislation such as the Taylor Force Act have brought the PA to the brink of bankruptcy. The PA has limited governing authority in the West Bank and exercises curtailed influence over the DFA Hamas in Gaza. The PA can also direct advocacy towards the international community to highlight Israeli international law violations that contribute to a coercive environment, settlement expansion, and forcible transfer. The PA must also be understood as responsible and cognizant for the restrictions they place on access for aid actors, and the barriers and lack of transparency that are often associated with coordination.

Gaza authorities De Facto Authorities (DFA), as secondary duty bearer in the Gaza Strip: Like the PA, authorities in Gaza need to be understood as responsible and cognizant for the impact of the restrictions placed on the delivery of aid and protection in the Strip on people in need's access to assistance. While the formal no-contact policy of the USG (as defined in the USAID WB/G Mission Order 21) and the EU sharply limit contact by INGOs like IMC beyond that which is unavoidable and essential for aid operations, the USAID license from the U.S. Department of Treasury Office of Foreign Assets Control (OFAC) does provide some latitude for the operational necessities for health and humanitarian assistance in Gaza. There is a noticeable challenge created by INGOs which self-censor and over-restrict contact with DFA lower-level employees beyond that demanded by law and regulation. This has occurred in part due to worries over the U.S. False Claims Act even with belated U.S. government action against nuisance unsupported suits; it's important that IMC coordinate with collective actions that push back against this threat to humanitarian and development assistance and other aid obstruction challenges.

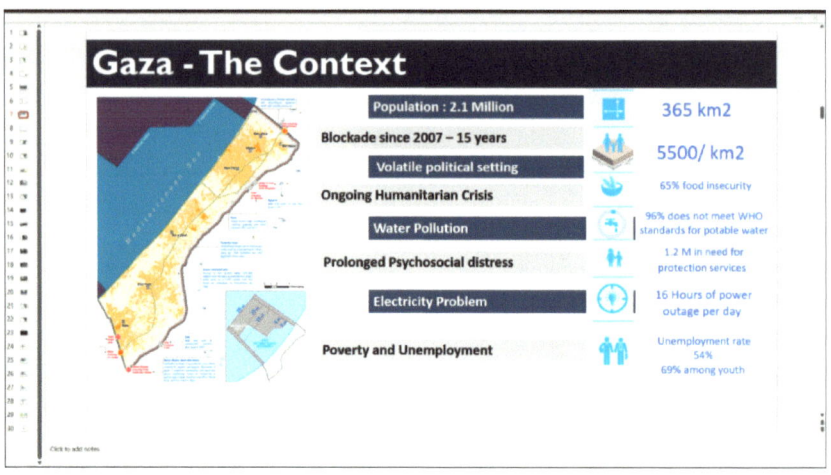

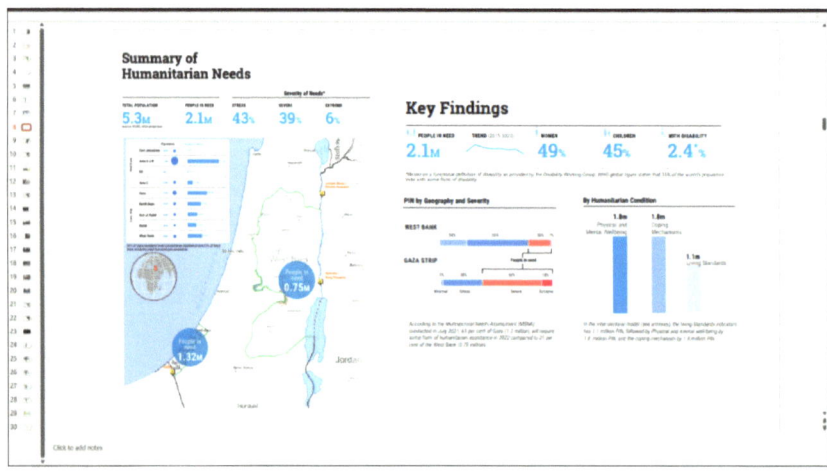

Conundrum of Palestine or How we Got Where We Are (1)

- The legacy of the Occupation from 1967
- "They never fail to miss an opportunity to miss an opportunity." Abba Eban
- **1978: Camp David Accords:** Potential Palestinian peace proposals were discussed, but never carried out.
- **December 1987: First intifada** A Palestinian uprising, or intifada, brings clashes and protests in the West Bank, Gaza and Israel. Unrest continues for years, with many killed or injured on both sides.
- **1993: Oslo Accords** The first of two pacts, known as the Oslo Accords, are signed between Israel and the Palestine Liberation Organization (PLO), setting out a peace process based on previous U.N. resolutions. (A follow-up accord was signed in 1995.) Agreements created the Palestinian Authority to oversee most administrative affairs in the West Bank and Gaza. PLO is recognized by Israel and the United States as a negotiating partner. Left unresolved are key issues such as Israeli settlements in the West Bank and the status of Jerusalem, viewed by the Palestinians as the capital of any future state.

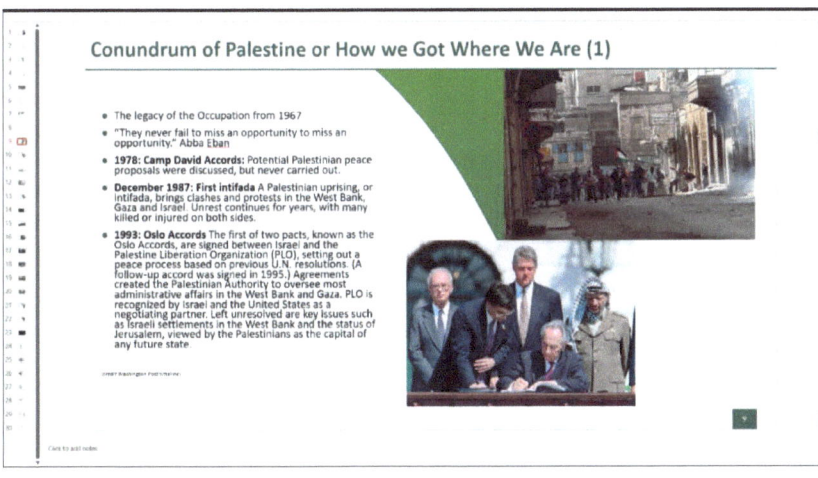

Conundrum of Palestine or How we Got Where We Are (2)

- **2000: Second intifada** The second intifada, or Palestinian uprising, begins after riots broke out following a visit by right-wing Israeli political figure Ariel Sharon (and later prime minister) to a compound in Jerusalem venerated in Judaism, Christianity and Islam. Clashes and other violence continue until 2005, leaving hundreds dead on both sides.
- **2006: Hamas elected in Gaza** The Palestinian militant group Hamas wins elections in Gaza, leading to political strains with the more moderate (but hugely corrupt) Fatah party controlling the West Bank.
- **December 2008: Israel attacks Gaza** Israel begins three weeks of attacks on Gaza after rocket barrages into Israel by Palestinian militants, who are supplied by tunnels from Egypt. More than 1,110 Palestinians and at least 13 Israelis are killed.
- **November 2012: Israel kills Hamas military chief** Israel kills Hamas military chief Ahmed Jabari, touching off more than a week of rocket fire from Gaza and Israeli airstrikes. At least 150 Palestinians and six Israelis are killed.

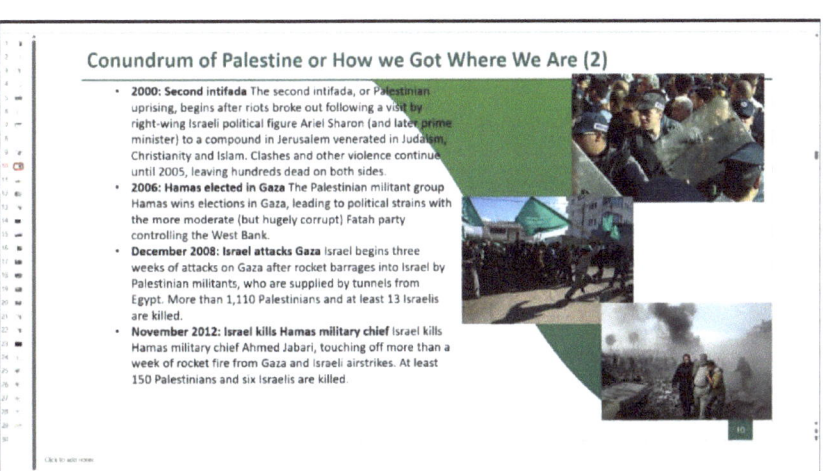

101

Political Transition (2005-2006)

- Israel withdrew soldiers and settlers from the Gaza Strip by September 2005.
- In the 2006 PA parliamentary elections, Fatah lost to Hamas, prompting sanctions by Israel, the United States and the European Union.

Fatah Emblem

Israeli-imposed Siege (2007)

Hamas took control of Gaza; Israel reacted, imposing a blockade, or siege.

Conundrum of Palestine or How we Got Where We Are (3)

- **Summer 2014: Hamas kills three Israeli teenagers** kidnapped near a Jewish settlement in the West Bank, prompting an Israeli military response. Hamas answers with rocket attacks from Gaza. Seven-week conflict leaves more than 2,200 Palestinians dead in Gaza. In Israel, 67 soldiers and six civilians are killed.
- **December 2017: Trump recognizes Jerusalem as capital** of Israel and announces that it plans to shift the U.S. Embassy from Tel Aviv, stirring outrage from Palestinians.
- **2018: Protests in Gaza** Protests take place in Gaza along the fence with Israel, including demonstrators hurling rocks and gasoline bombs across the barrier. Israeli troops kill more than 170 protesters over several months. In November, Israel stages a covert raid into Gaza. At least seven suspected Palestinian militants and a senior Israeli army officer are killed. From Gaza, hundreds of rockets are fired into Israel.
- **May 2021: Israeli police raid al-Aqsa Mosque** after weeks of tension in Jerusalem, one of the holiest sites in Islam, Hamas fired rockets toward the city for the first time in years, prompting Israel to retaliate with airstrikes. The fighting, the fiercest since at least 2014, saw thousands of rockets fired from Gaza and hundred of airstrikes on the Palestinian territory, with more than 200 killed in Gaza and at least 10 killed in Israel.

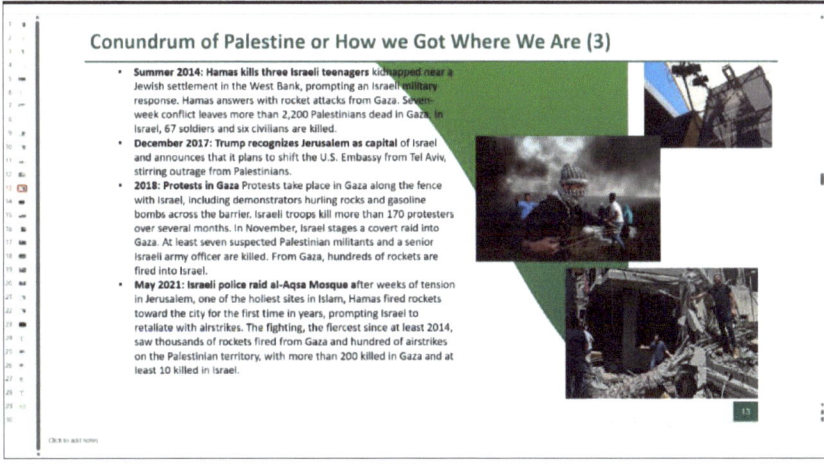

13

Click to add notes

"Great March of Return" (2018-2019)

200 Palestinians killed and 29,000 injured

Gaza still addressing physical and mental repercussions from this and the May 2021 war

Photo Source: Ishtah 2016

103

Israeli Offensives – Disproportionate Retaliation?

Neighborhood destroyed in Israeli attack (2014)

- 2008 - 1,400 killed, 5,300 injured
- 2012 - 175 killed, 1,000 injured
- 2014 - 2,250 killed, 11,000 injured

Palestinian girl mourns little brother killed in Israeli attack (July 2014)

Photo Source: https://theglobepost.com/2018/05/15/gaza-digital-economy/ (Fitton 2018)
https://www.mcclatchydc.net/news/local/united-states/israel-war-crimes-gaza-embody

---

Cross-Border Escalations lead to May 2021 War

- 19 health facilities destroyed
- 261 Palestinians killed and more than 2,200 injured
- 113,000 temporarily internally displaced persons

Photo May 2021 Reuters/xdaz

Photo: MaanNEWS.org

Photo: May2011 TheGuardian.com

Palestinian child celebrates ceasefire after home destroyed (May2021)

When I look at pictures like this, I can't help but worry about the horrific mental health burden that has been created for the survivors. It's not only about 10/7 and the incomparable trauma that has arisen from that for millions of people. It's about the constant repetition of a cycle of violence from repeated escalations and clashes, with nowhere to go to escape.

- The escalation of hostilities in 2022 and early 2023 heightened risks and exacerbated the vulnerabilities of young people in Gaza, resulting in high rates of anxiety, depression, and post-traumatic stress disorder, all of which may increase high-risk behavior. How much more now?

- The OPT has one of the highest burdens of mental health issues and psychological disorders in the Eastern Mediterranean Region, with 54% of Palestinian boys and 47% of Palestinian girls aged 6 to 12 years presenting emotional and/ or behavioral disorders.

- There's a compounding effect of the long-term exposure to violent conflict, financial precarity, and a lack of freedom and opportunity apparent in the 40% of households in Gaza that reported at least one member of their household experiencing signs of psychosocial distress or trauma in the year prior to the 2022 MSNA data collection. With some of the highest observed rates of psychosocial distress and trauma reported in localities near the access restricted areas (ARAs), these households are particularly vulnerable to human rights concerns and potential displacement, and face restricted access to services.

- In Gaza, approximately 57,000 households reported that at least one child in their household demonstrated signs of psychosocial distress.

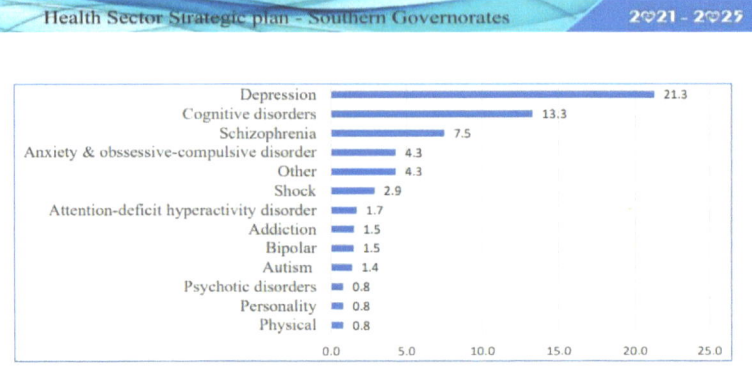

Figure 7: Incidence rate of mental illnesses by diagnosis per 100,000 population

- Symptom-levels of depression differ across areas and are particularly high in Gaza. 71 percent screened positive for depression in Gaza, compared to 50 percent (SE=3.05) in the West Bank.

- About 7 percent of adults in WB&G screen positive for PTSD. This share varies only very slightly between areas, with 6.9 percent for Gaza compared to 7.2 percent for the West Bank.

- Adults in Gaza have a higher risk of mental health problems and a lower level of life satisfaction, while aggression levels are higher in the West Bank than in Gaza.

- For residents of Gaza, the highest levels of PTSD symptoms are among the youngest age brackets (between ages 18 and 29) and tend to decrease with increasing age. For residents of the West Bank, symptom levels are significantly higher in older age groups (older than 40) compared to those younger than 30.

- Lower education levels are associated with higher prevalence of depression and PTSD.

- According to a recent study conducted by Save the Children and War Child – Holland in 2022 children and young people reported living in a perpetual state of fear, worry, sadness and grief, waiting for the next round of violence to erupt, and feeling unable to sleep or concentrate.

Other key findings in 2022 included:

- Children are feeling less safe when away from their parents (90% in 2022 compared with 60% in 2018).

- Children are experiencing higher levels of emotional distress (on average an increase from 55% to 80%).

- Children reported feeling fearful (84%), nervous (80%), sad (77%) and grief (78%) in 2022 compared with fearful (50%), nervous (55%), sad (62%) and grief (55%) in 2018.

- Children's distress is exhibited by more worrying behaviors, such as bedwetting (79% in 2022, 53% in 2018) and reactive mutism (59% in 2022, 42% in 2018.

- Children reported feeling less supported by their family and friends; their belief in their parents' and siblings' ability to support them dropped by 9% and 12% respectively.

• Children are showing lower levels of positive thinking and resilience; 48% of them reported having difficulty concentrating and 78% of caregivers reported that their children rarely complete tasks.

• Caregivers are also experiencing higher levels of emotional distress with 96% reporting feeling sad and constantly anxious. Nearly two-thirds (63%) of caregivers feel they are not useful and 61% reported an inability to overcome difficulties. More than one-third (39%) of caregivers reported a lack of self-confidence.

• The May 2021 conflict directly affected many frontline workers such as case managers, and protection professionals who are also in need of support. This was further exacerbated by the stressors from the August 2022 escalation, and during Ramadan 2023 a series of additional strikes and tensions.

Gaza Needs Assessment, War Child and Save the Children, 2022

Multisectoral Needs Assessment (MSNA) 2022

These studies were from the year before 10/7 and the three escalations which preceded the Hamas attack and the war. Can you possibly imagine what the damage to mental health, the encouragement of deeper levels of violence and extremism must be, for those survivors of the current war? We focus a lot on the basics of food, water and shelter…but mental health resilience is just as hard if not more unlikely to come by.

Conundrum of Palestine or How we Got Where We Are (4)

- **Spring 2022: String of terrorist attacks in Israel** A spate of violence on Israelis by Palestinians marked the deadliest string of terrorist attacks in Israel in years — with 14 people killed in a handful of individual Palestinian attacks between March 22 and April 8. Israel clamped down on militants and activists, and launched "Break the Wave" military operation in the West Bank, making 2022 the deadliest in many years. Israeli forces killed 146 Palestinians in the West Bank in 2022 (UN says over 200), a death toll higher than in any other year since the UN began keeping records in 2005. Israel's Foreign Ministry said Palestinians killed 29 Israelis that year.
- **August 2022:** Sealing the "Envelope of Gaza," barring entry or departure of intl humanitarian staff as well as locals. Renewed escalation of one week with repeated "surgical strikes."
- **December 2022: Netanyahu sworn in again** as Israeli prime minister, after winning an election that gave him his sixth term and elevated a once-fringe bloc of far-right, extremist (some say terrorist) politicians into powerful seats. The most far-right government in Israeli history, which critics say has already begun to eliminate any prospect of a two-state solution. And began to upend democratic institutions.

Conundrum of Palestine or How we Got Where We Are (5)

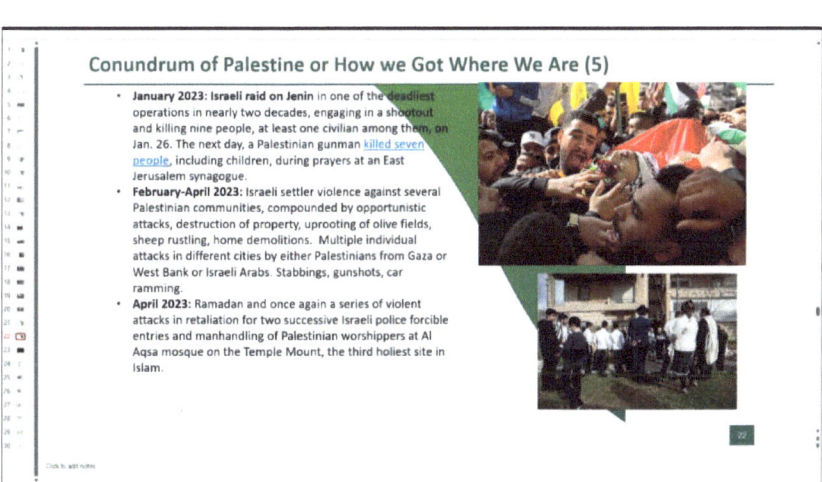

- **January 2023: Israeli raid on Jenin** in one of the deadliest operations in nearly two decades, engaging in a shootout and killing nine people, at least one civilian among them, on Jan. 26. The next day, a Palestinian gunman killed seven people, including children, during prayers at an East Jerusalem synagogue.
- **February-April 2023:** Israeli settler violence against several Palestinian communities, compounded by opportunistic attacks, destruction of property, uprooting of olive fields, sheep rustling, home demolitions. Multiple individual attacks in different cities by either Palestinians from Gaza or West Bank or Israeli Arabs. Stabbings, gunshots, car ramming.
- **April 2023:** Ramadan and once again a series of violent attacks in retaliation for two successive Israeli police forcible entries and manhandling of Palestinian worshippers at Al Aqsa mosque on the Temple Mount, the third holiest site in Islam.

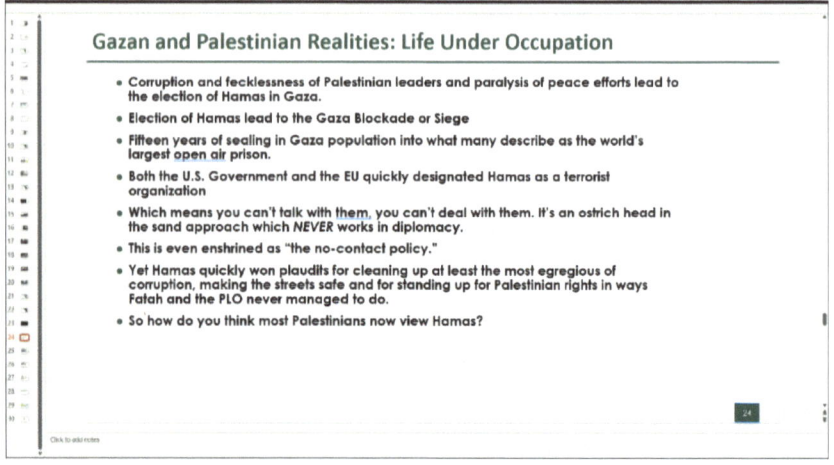

Gazan and Palestinian Realities: Life Under Occupation

- Corruption and fecklessness of Palestinian leaders and paralysis of peace efforts lead to the election of Hamas in Gaza.
- Election of Hamas lead to the Gaza Blockade or Siege
- Fifteen years of sealing in Gaza population into what many describe as the world's largest open air prison.
- Both the U.S. Government and the EU quickly designated Hamas as a terrorist organization
- Which means you can't talk with them, you can't deal with them. It's an ostrich head in the sand approach which *NEVER* works in diplomacy.
- This is even enshrined as "the no-contact policy."
- Yet Hamas quickly won plaudits for cleaning up at least the most egregious of corruption, making the streets safe and for standing up for Palestinian rights in ways Fatah and the PLO never managed to do.
- So how do you think most Palestinians now view Hamas?

Of course, that was then and now is now. There was another escalation again in August 2023, and then the ferocious attack October 7th last year. That was the attack from which there was no going back, with the vengeful retaliation days later of the Israeli Defense Forces, which had been knocked on their collective behinds and taken completely by surprise. Even though they had been warned, and young female officers had detected the training exercises preparing for the attack.

With the focus of course on the war, and the 10/7 attack, the narrative most hear now largely ignores the ongoing grind and burden of Palestinian life under occupation.

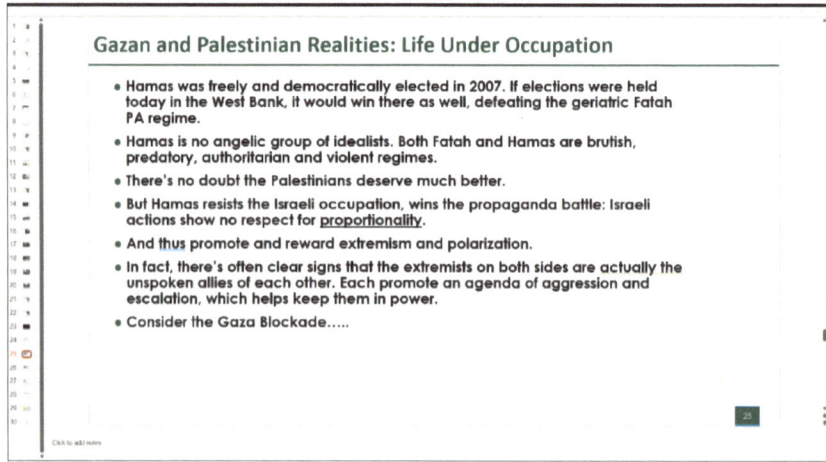

Gazan and Palestinian Realities: Life Under Occupation

- Hamas was freely and democratically elected in 2007. If elections were held today in the West Bank, it would win there as well, defeating the geriatric Fatah PA regime.
- Hamas is no angelic group of idealists. Both Fatah and Hamas are brutish, predatory, authoritarian and violent regimes.
- There's no doubt the Palestinians deserve much better.
- But Hamas resists the Israeli occupation, wins the propaganda battle: Israeli actions show no respect for proportionality.
- And thus promote and reward extremism and polarization.
- In fact, there's often clear signs that the extremists on both sides are actually the unspoken allies of each other. Each promote an agenda of aggression and escalation, which helps keep them in power.
- Consider the Gaza Blockade.....

Gazan and Palestinian Realities: The Blockade

- In 2002 Over 200,000 Gazans were able to work in Israel, earn and support their extended families. A huge percentage of Gaza benefited.
- With the adoption of the Blockade and no contact policy those numbers dropped to no more than 10,000 or less.
- This has huge impact on livelihoods and economic security. Which we will likely go into more depth in subsequent classes.
- The Gaza Blockade by Israel supports a narrative of oppression, apartheid and aggression which suits the political needs of Hamas. It justifies an authoritarian approach and its retention of power.
- It paints Gaza inevitably as the aggrieved and the marginalized. The victim of arbitrary exclusion.
- https://youtu.be/yd-PHoWSmRA

Gazan and Palestinian Realities: The Blockade, Occupation and International Humanitarian Law

- The blockade and related actions by the Government of Israel against Palestinians and Palestine are clear examples of "collective punishment".
- The UN Special Rapporteur for the occupied Palestinian territories, Dr Francesca Albanese has noted (as well as her predecessors:
  - The Palestinian people, both in Gaza and the West Bank are utterly blocked from freedom and self-determination.
  - Diplomats even from the UN attempt at times to counter weigh the rights of Israel and Israelis against those of the Palestinians; they attempt to draw a false equivalence of normalizing the escalations, violence and responses as justifications.
  - Yet this ignores the reality of proportionality: Palestinians protest and throw stones and weapons of very limited scope. Israel responds with 21st century weapons and may wound, maim or kill 100 Palestinians for every Israeli hurt or killed.
  - Each generation has faced greater despair and hopelessness of any sort of political or social solution. within a climate og systematic violence.
  - However ugly the term, and however controversial it is in some circles, it is hard to avoid the international legal definitions of the crime of apartheid
  - This is fueled by the indiscriminate use of martial law to support wholly illegal settlements, and a narrative that seems to increasingly fuel the idea of outright illegal Israeli annexation of Palestine.

Gazan and Palestinian Realities: The Blockade, Occupation and International Humanitarian Law

- The ugly and tragic picture of apartheid is amplified by the wholesale embrace of what can only be called Settler Colonialism. Again this is also not just a polemic term but one rooted in Human Rights Law and International Humanitarian Law.

- Settler colonialism is a reflection of the wanton and indiscriminate extracting and exploiting of water and other natural resources, all for the benefit of Israel, none for the benefit of the Palestinian people.

- It includes the criminalizing of human rights organizations, and the shrinking space of operations for civil society as a whole both that of Palestinians as well as international groups.

- In future classes we will try to examine how humanitarian assistance and response fits within development policy and architecture. We will consider what USG assistance from USAID and State has effectively meant or not. We will look at the influence of corruption, accountability and further impacts of the No Contact Policy.

- We will discuss critiques and national security implications: for Israel as well as for us.

Click to add notes

CHAPTER III

HUMANITARIAN AND DEVELOPMENT ASSISTANCE

Let's turn to the question of International Development and Humanitarian Assistance in Gaza and indeed the occupied Palestinian territories, the oPt. Let me describe the key agencies involved, including the role of American foreign aid. In so many ways, for better or worse, funding from the U.S. Agency for International Development is the 800 lb. gorilla among donors, hard to ignore. And the rules it enforces can take all the oxygen out of the room as far as many other donors are concerned.

Development and Humanitarian Assistance – the Agencies

- US Government Foreign Aid generally can be broken down to several key areas. But the usual rules as followed across most of the world don't easily apply here in the occupied Palestinian territories and Gaza.

- In most developing countries, the U.S. Agency for International Development, under the oversight of the State Department, administers a broad based development assistance program focused of several key strategic objectives.

- Under former Administrator Mark Green, an unusually capable and competent Trump appointee, many countries were grouped into different categories following the "Journey to Self Reliance." Mark Green argued that the purpose of foreign assistance was to bring an end to it, by ending the need for it. Supporting greater competence and capability and transparency- accountability. Countries were respectively scored on some key universal indicators.

- Among the poorest countries, or those facing natural or human-made disasters, humanitarian assistance ruled, at least temporarily.

- Among the richer developing countries, a focus was made on trade and infrastructure improvements, through the new U.S. Development Finance Corporation.

Development and Humanitarian Assistance – the Agencies (2)

- Yet Palestine is unique – a semi autonomous occupied territory of a rich and capable economic power. And one with an almost permanent and unbreakable line of credit and support in many billions of dollars in economic and military assistance.

- Foreign Aid for Palestine became a key USG focus as part of the Oslo Accords. USAID opened up a West Bank/Gaza mission in Israel in 1994.

- Reportedly over $4 billion in aid have been programmed in the intervening 28 years.

- Superficially USAID points to big investments in a range of different sectors, largely on the West Bank.

- USAID focused on these sectors and areas. In theory....

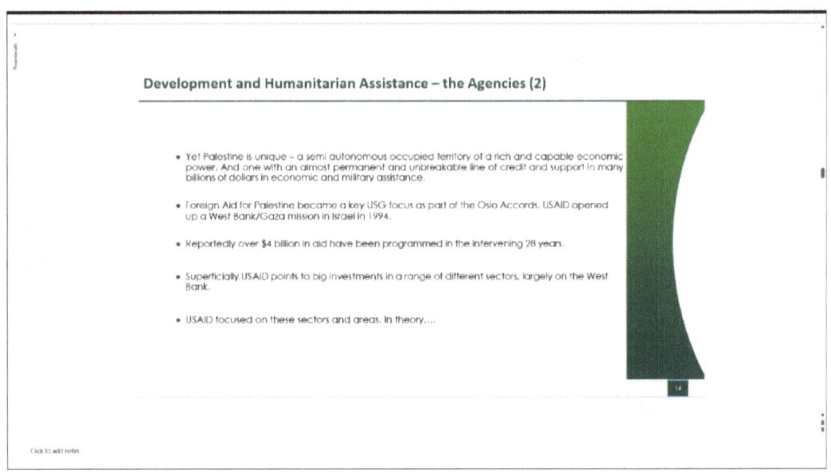

Development and Humanitarian Assistance – the Agencies (3)

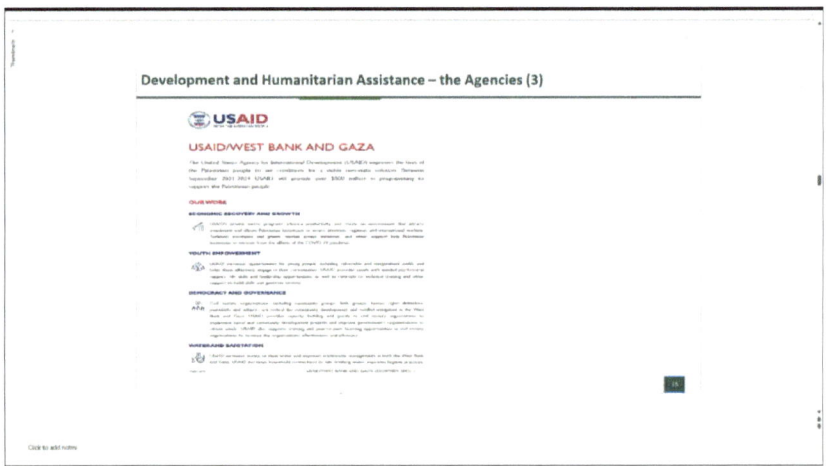

Development and Humanitarian Assistance – the Agencies (4)

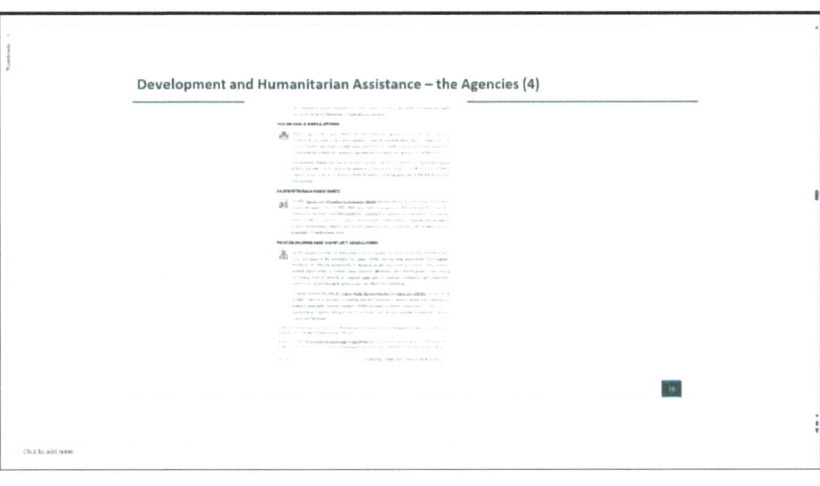

Development and Humanitarian Assistance – the Agencies (6)

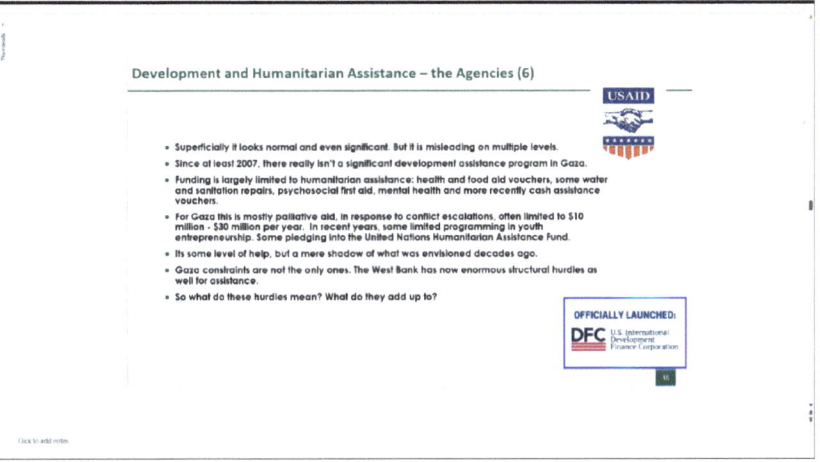

- Superficially it looks normal and even significant. But it is misleading on multiple levels.
- Since at least 2007, there really isn't a significant development assistance program in Gaza.
- Funding is largely limited to humanitarian assistance: health and food aid vouchers, some water and sanitation repairs, psychosocial first aid, mental health and more recently cash assistance vouchers.
- For Gaza this is mostly palliative aid, in response to conflict escalations, often limited to $10 million - $30 million per year. In recent years, some limited programming in youth entrepreneurship. Some pledging into the United Nations Humanitarian Assistance Fund.
- Its some level of help, but a mere shadow of what was envisioned decades ago.
- Gaza constraints are not the only ones. The West Bank has now enormous structural hurdles as well for assistance.
- So what do these hurdles mean? What do they add up to?

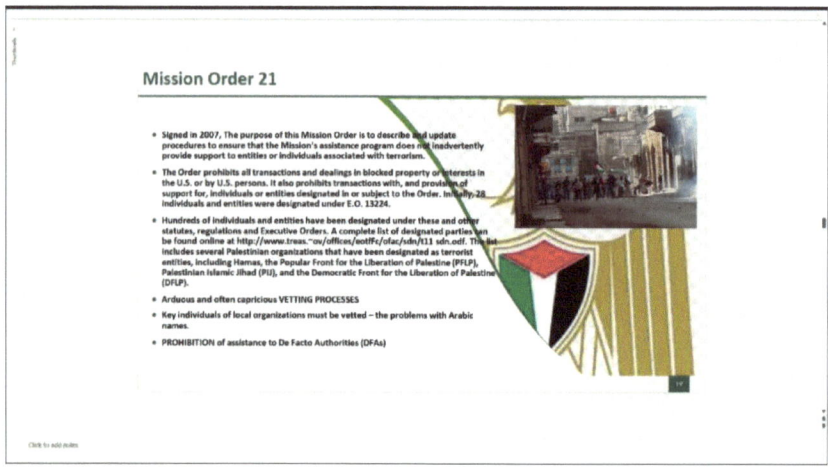

Mission Order 21

- Signed in 2007, The purpose of this Mission Order is to describe and update procedures to ensure that the Mission's assistance program does not inadvertently provide support to entities or individuals associated with terrorism.
- The Order prohibits all transactions and dealings in blocked property or interests in the U.S. or by U.S. persons. It also prohibits transactions with, and provision of support for, individuals or entities designated in or subject to the Order. Initially, 26 individuals and entities were designated under E.O. 13224.
- Hundreds of individuals and entities have been designated under these and other statutes, regulations and Executive Orders. A complete list of designated parties can be found online at http://www.treas.~ov/offices/eotffc/ofac/sdn/t11 sdn.odf. The list includes several Palestinian organizations that have been designated as terrorist entities, including Hamas, the Popular Front for the Liberation of Palestine (PFLP), Palestinian Islamic Jihad (PIJ), and the Democratic Front for the Liberation of Palestine (DFLP).
- Arduous and often capricious VETTING PROCESSES
- Key individuals of local organizations must be vetted – the problems with Arabic names.
- PROHIBITION of assistance to De Facto Authorities (DFAs)

Mission Order 21 is at the heart of much of the distortions that arise with American foreign aid. Like many comparable regulations it arose with good intentions – there had been bad examples of some foreign aid dollars previously going to organizations with dubious if not downright hostile intent, groups that supported violence or extremism. The absolute dollar amount was small, and the percentage of overall U.S. government assistance was even smaller. But regulators and appropriators wanted a zero-tolerance management of that to ensure that not one single dollar of American aid goes to someone it should not go to.

There are a number of problems with that approach. The first is that one really should look critically at how much you are spending to deal with what is at worst a limited problem. When you create a very fine filter, a sieve that is almost impenetrable to deviation, you sharply raise the cost of compliance. It might end up costing you $1000 to save $100, or even just $10. Where do you draw the line?

When you raise the cost and difficulty of vetting and compliance, you also guarantee that many well-purposed and useful ideas get filtered out as well. It becomes extremely difficult for smaller organizations with little in the way of management infrastructure or capacity, but lots of good ideas, to make it through the reviews, the paperwork and the interminable vetting process. That's essentially the cost of doing business, and you no longer have a level playing field but one that is sharply tilted in favor of the bigger groups with the resources and means to survive the demands of vetting and clearances.

There is another problem as well. As expressed in Mission Order 21, it is absolutely forbidden with very few exceptions that organizations have any sort of contact with the de facto authority in Gaza, Hamas.

So, let's consider this. Hamas is a nasty organization with brutal credentials. But effective and responsive grassroots activity in Gaza make it almost impossible to avoid all contact with the group that is in fact in charge of the territory. Before the war, even the Israelis were dealing with Hamas, albeit through third parties. They were helping to fund Hamas. This was a deliberate policy to undermine the less extremist Palestinian Authority and al Fatah, in nominal charge of the West Bank and ruin the chances of any peace with Palestine and a two-state solution.

Take for example the area of health. How can you meaningfully and effectively implement a health program in a country and refuse to talk to technical staff of the Ministry of Health? Or coordinate what you propose to do with a country's health plans and facilities? Where do you draw the line?

The problem here is that Congressional appropriators may make rules, but then those rules are interpreted and operationalized by the agency lawyers. One can't help to remember the dictum from Shakespeare's *Henry IV Part II* – "The first thing we do, we kill all the lawyers." With all due respect to the legal profession (where my niece is headed) there's a problem of a failure of common sense in how these rules are put into effect.

Surely if you make the choice to not be talking to anyone in the military wing of a group like Hamas, that should give you leeway to deal with political types. And if you make the choice that you also don't want to talk to the political representatives, then perhaps you can cut things off at the Minister level of a government, but still avoid restrictions on interactions with people assuming technical functions, and allow groups to work with ease with doctors, nurses, hospital and clinic administrators etc. But that is not allowed.

There's a further dimension I also can't help but question: what do we as the United States gain in terms of a no contact policy at all? Diplomacy and influence with international groups, agents and countries should in fact be all about talking to your enemies, talking to your adversaries. That's what diplomacy should be all about.

We don't need our U.S. government personnel or program grantees and implementing partners talking only to friends. They're our friends, they don't generally need to hear too much from us other than a Christmas card at the end of the year. But to have and expand our influence, we need to persuade, we need to cajole, we need to gain influence and use that influence to chip away at extremist views and hostilities.

As it bears repeating again, Hamas is virtually the only group that we put in this category of No Contact. Lots of other bad guys and disreputable types are reachable and accessible so we can find ways of working with each other, on whatever is possible.

The Taylor Force Law below also fits into this category of counter-productive bludgeons that hurt our influence and ability to change things for the better.

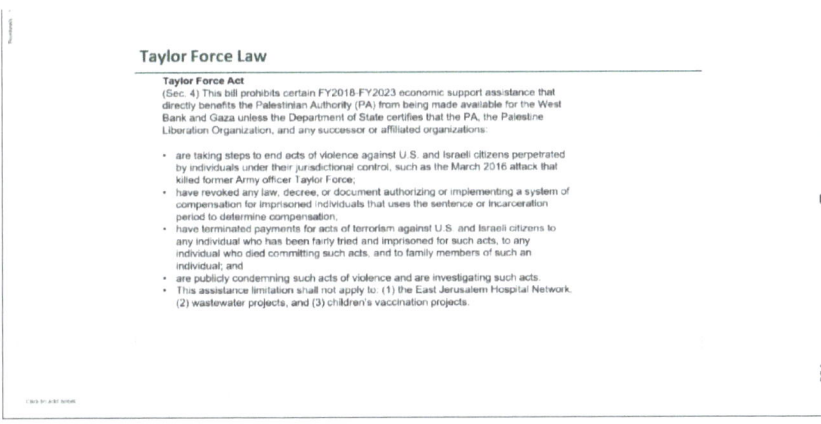

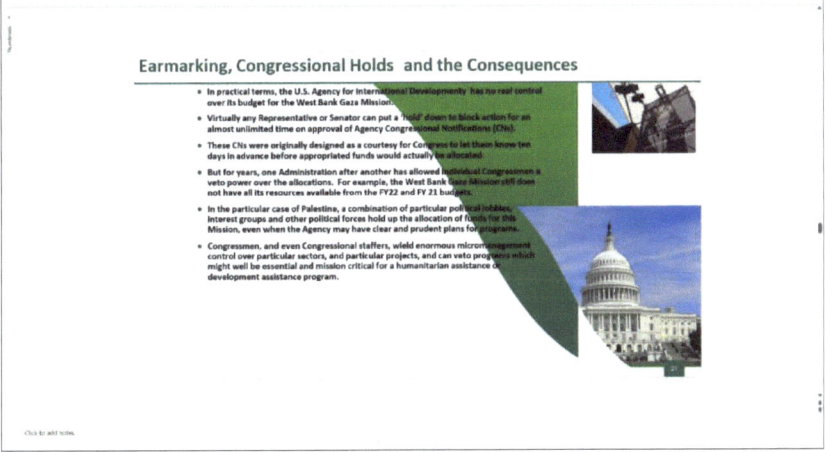

MANAGING AND AVOIDING DIVERSION OF AID

So many of the directives, regulations and policies were
structured as feverish attempts to avoid, reduce or mitigate the
diversion of aid, the potential waylaying of foreign assistance to
the hands of the DFA. This was in part to placate U.S. government
legal boundaries about any benefits accruing to designated Foreign
Terrorist Organizations. It was also about placating the Israelis,
since Israel maintained zealous control over what went in and what

went out of Gaza, or at least so they thought they did before 10/7. The Israelis were particularly exercised even before 10/7 over anything that could possibly be considered a 'dual-use' item, that is something that would be provided which the DFA could take advantage of to use for its own militancy and extremist purposes. There are international oversight rules which define and delimit dual-use but the Israelis would frequently take this to an entirely different level. Even before the war it was very burdensome and delayed the entry of many innocuous items.

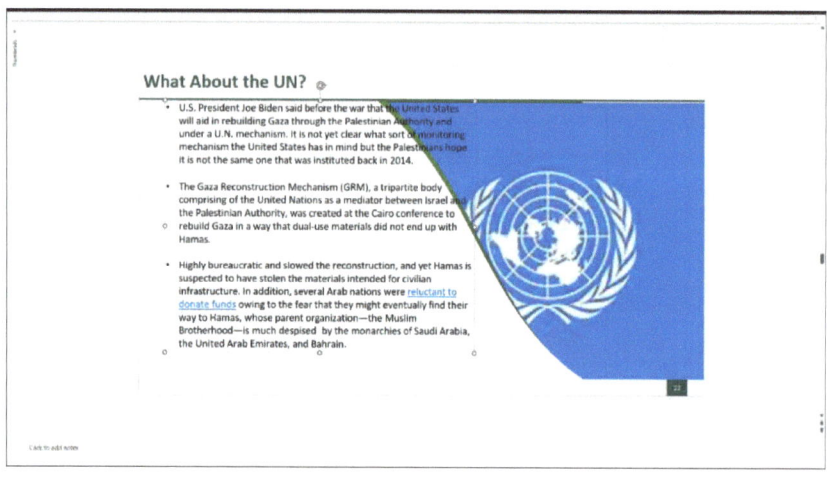

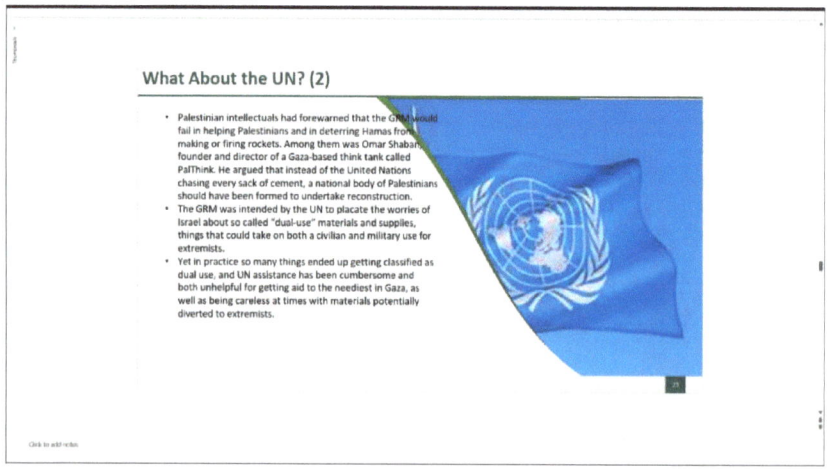

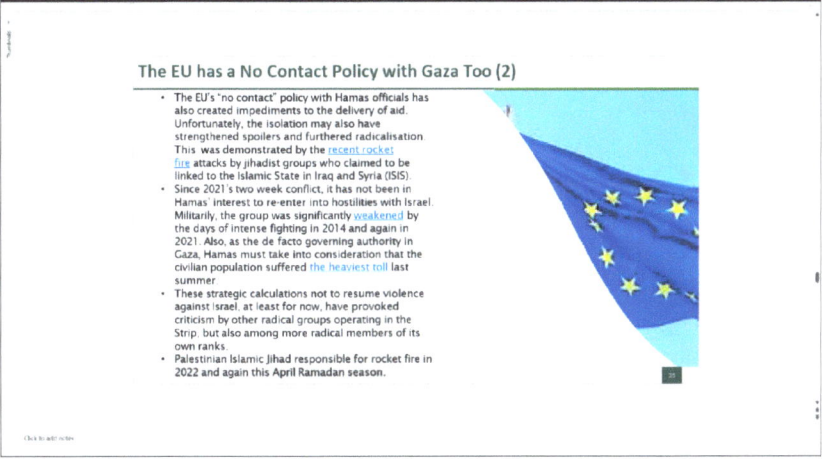

Of course, as we know today, the world changed forever on 10/7. The attack then and in subsequent days is most remembered for the brutality, murder and rape of young people at the Nova Music Festival and the kibbutz and moshav villages bordering the western fence of Gaza. But less remembered was how Hamas was able to also fire round after round of rockets, including some more sophisticated ones than in the past, not only to nearby targets in southern and central Israel but even north to Jerusalem and further away. It shocked and stunned not just the Israeli Defense Force but the entire population.

EU efforts had supported the Quartet for years. But the Quartet accomplished virtually nothing, in the face of intransigence from both the Palestinians and the Israelis. They do still have lovely offices and an impressive building in Sheikh Jarrah, but surely the organization has a zombie existence well beyond its original purpose and intent.

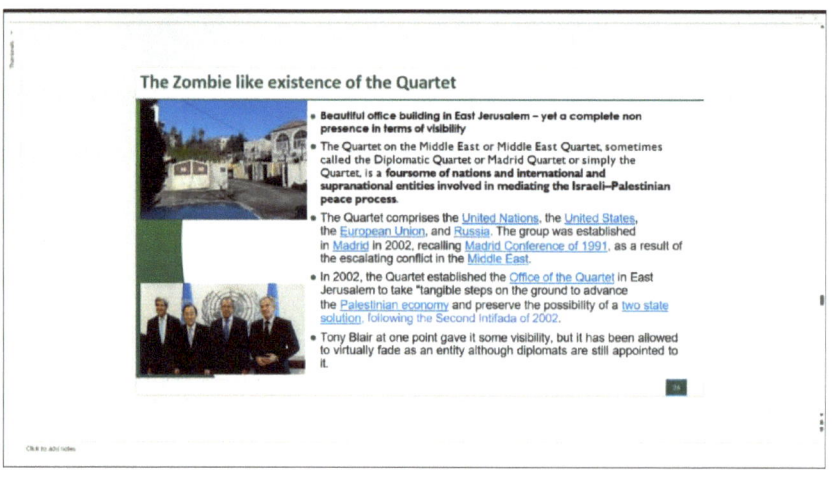

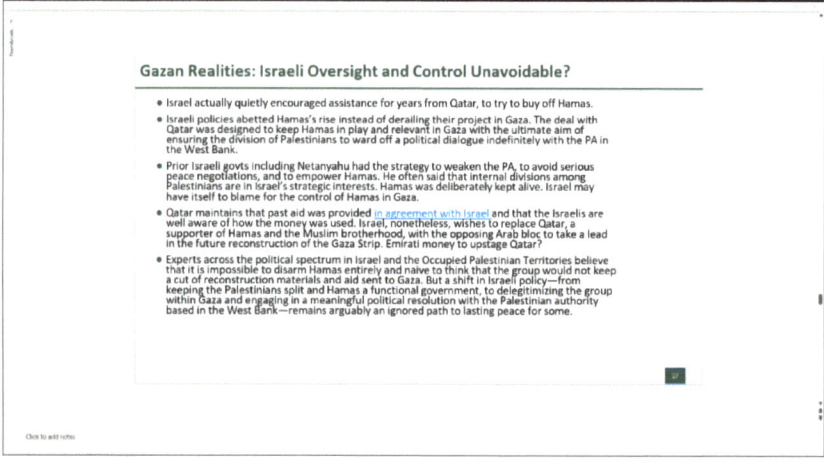

We know this even better now with the stories that came out from both Israeli and Western journalism after 10/7. As I mentioned earlier, the Netanyahu administration had been quietly helping to channel funds to Hamas – without control or restrictions – for years. They believed in totally unfounded idea that they were buying peace, but in fact they were very intentionally working to strengthen Hamas to weaken the Palestinian Authority and any hope of a credible partner for peace negotiations as originally envisioned under the Oslo Accords.

And yet Gaza is not and never has been the only flashpoint. Even in the heart of East Jerusalem, Israeli religious and right-wing extremists played a heartless game in seizing through any means possible Palestinian land and homes. This included the tragic neighborhood of Sheikh Jarrah in the heart of the occupation, where my apartment and UN offices were.

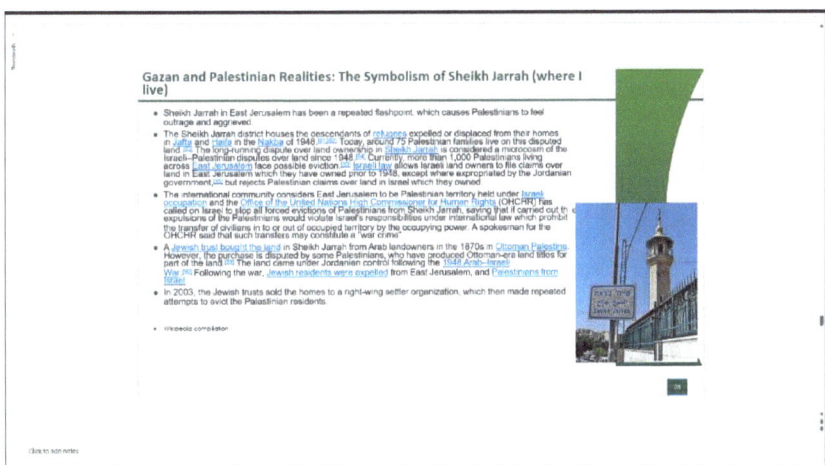

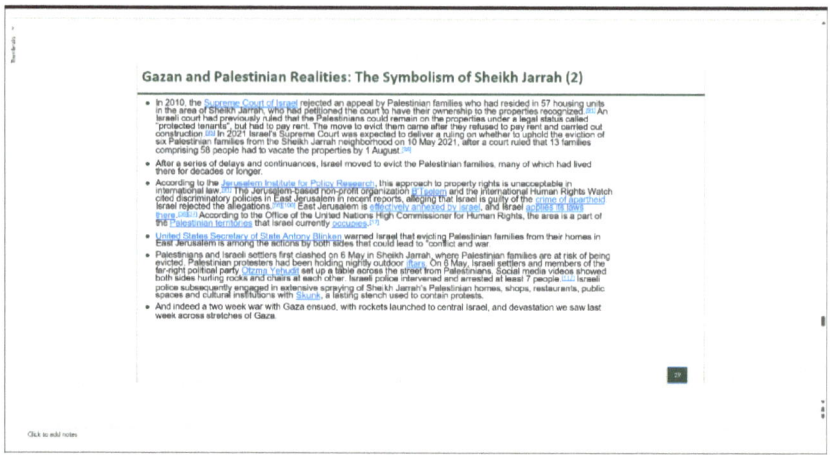

Gazan and Palestinian Realities: The Symbolism of Sheikh Jarrah (2)

- In 2010, the Supreme Court of Israel rejected an appeal by Palestinian families who had resided in 57 housing units in the area of Sheikh Jarrah, who had petitioned the court to have their ownership to the properties recognized. An Israeli court had previously ruled that the Palestinians could remain on the properties under a legal status called "protected tenants", but had to pay rent. The move to evict them came after they refused to pay rent and carried out construction. In 2021 Israel's Supreme Court was expected to deliver a ruling on whether to uphold the eviction of six Palestinian families from the Sheikh Jarrah neighborhood on 10 May 2021, after a court ruled that 13 families comprising 58 people had to vacate the properties by 1 August.
- After a series of delays and continuances, Israel moved to evict the Palestinian families, many of which had lived there for decades or longer.
- According to the Jerusalem Institute for Policy Research, this approach to property rights is unacceptable in international law. The Jerusalem-based non-profit organization B'Tselem and the international Human Rights Watch cited discriminatory policies in East Jerusalem in recent reports, alleging that Israel is guilty of the crime of apartheid. Israel rejected the allegations. East Jerusalem is effectively annexed by Israel, and Israel applies its laws there. According to the Office of the United Nations High Commissioner for Human Rights, the area is a part of the Palestinian territories that Israel currently occupies.
- United States Secretary of State Antony Blinken warned Israel that evicting Palestinian families from their homes in East Jerusalem is among the actions by both sides that could lead to "conflict and war.
- Palestinians and Israeli settlers first clashed on 6 May in Sheikh Jarrah, where Palestinian families are at risk of being evicted. Palestinian protesters had been holding nightly outdoor iftars. On 8 May, Israeli settlers and members of the far-right political party Otzma Yehudit set up a table across the street from Palestinians. Social media videos showed both sides hurling rocks and chairs at each other. Israeli police intervened and arrested at least 7 people. Israeli police subsequently engaged in extensive spraying of Sheikh Jarrah's Palestinian homes, shops, restaurants, public spaces and cultural institutions with Skunk, a lasting stench used to contain protests.
- And indeed a two week war with Gaza ensued, with rockets launched to central Israel, and devastation we saw last week across stretches of Gaza.

Sheikh Jarrah was a constant symbolic flashpoint for clashes. It is in part the heart of the traditionally Arab East Jerusalem, part of the territory that Israel conquered in the 1967 Six Day War and eventually annexed as part of Greater Jerusalem, an act that was never accepted under international law or the UN without the resolution of the greater problem of the occupied Palestinian territories.

Nablus Road runs through the center, what the Israelis call Shechem Road. Virtually all the street signs are in Arabic with Hebrew and English accompanying and indeed most of the population are Palestinians. While a few gave up or sold their properties to real estate brokers and Israeli expansionists the majority of Arab Palestinians still hang on to it. Some have seen their titles, which may date back to the Ottoman Empire, challenged and overturned by Israeli courts and their old style Jerusalem stone houses demolished or seized. There is a nearby Jewish shrine to Shimon Hatzadek (Simon the Just or Simon the Righteous), who reportedly lived in the time of 300 BCE and met Alexander the Great during his conquest of Jerusalem. Given this proximity, many ultra-Orthodox Jews and Haredim have moved into the neighborhood.

I lived on Dalman Street, just off of Nablus Road. Every Friday afternoon around 4 PM local there would be a perfunctory protest from a mix of Palestinian and often European protestors who would chant slogans for the liberation of Palestine, the protection of Palestinian lands, the end of the occupation, etc. Occasionally there would be clashes or near clashes with a few Israeli Jewish counter protestors but usually peaceful albeit noisy for an hour. Sometimes Israeli police would push them down the street where I lived where there might be other clashes, because an Israeli Member of the Knesset had a satellite office nearby as is the metropolitan police HQ.

These demonstrations always saddened me because I sensed a sense of fatalism from the Arab residents of East Jerusalem, a sense that there was no real protection against their constant losses. They were often outnumbered by some young people who seemed like European protest tourists, around for the periodic noisy demonstrations. But none of it solved anything.

As an outsider, I could have some degree of distance to see that while this was definitely part of the Arab East Jerusalem and listed by the United Nations as part of the much larger occupied Palestinian territories, the oPt, Israeli Jews had some basis for their claims and their own sense of belonging. And indeed, this is what fuels the conflict overall. Neither side can afford to acknowledge any legitimacy to the claims of the other, and neither side will be willing to negotiate any sort of settlement that addresses these claims. Certainly not in the particularly inflammatory East Jerusalem, but also not in the wider West Bank lands which adjoin and adjacent to these precincts.

In Sheikh Jarrah you can find the compound of the United Nations Office of Coordination for Humanitarian Assistance (OCHA), which attempts to manage fundraising appeals to deliver resources to support projects to ease the neglect, marginalization and lack of social services of the Palestinian people throughout the oPt, including Gaza. It has been routinely but increasingly harassed by the Israeli government for years, particularly under the Netanyahu administration. Even before the war, the Humanitarian Coordinator and other UN diplomatic staff were constantly threatened with losing their visas and their ability to remain in country, a level of harassment of UN personnel unparalleled elsewhere.

Despite this harassment, OCHA has tried since the beginning of the war to keep a laser eye on the question of protecting innocent civilians and demanding access for humanitarian assistance, including food, water, medical aid and shelter for the huge number of Gazans displaced by the war. They have published regular situation updates for global attention on the conditions of Gazans and Palestinians as a whole. For example, a recent update from them shared the following data and maps:

2.3 Million
Population of the Gaza Strip

Source: PCBS, 2024

34,622
Reported fatalities

Source: MoH Gaza, as of 3 May

77,867
Reported injuries

Source: MoH Gaza, as of 3 May

254
Aid workers killed

492
Health workers killed
(including at least 15 also counted as aid workers)

1.1 Million
People experiencing catastrophic food insecurity (IPC 5)

Source: IPC projection for 16 March - 15 July 2024

1.7 Million
People displaced in Gaza

JLOTS (Joint Logistics Over-The-Shore): A 550 m long floating dock and compound for the delivery of humanitarian cargo (under construction).

JLOTS compound, 3 May 2024

Al Rasheed coastal road: A lengthy and overcrowded route designated for the passage of humanitarian aid trucks by the Israeli authorities

No Access Zone
1.5 Nautical Miles
April (N)

ACCESS PROHIBITED

Erez
Open for pre-approved goods only since 1 May

Gaza North

Gaza

Israeli Military Road

JLOTS

Al Rasheed checkpoint

Salah Ad Din checkpoint

Nahal Oz
Closed since 2010
Karni
Closed gradually between 2007 and 2011

Wadi Gaza

Gate 96
Open for pre-approved goods via Israeli fence road

Deir al Balah

GAZA STRIP

Salah Ad Din road

Israeli military fence road: only accessible after dark for pre-approved goods

Salah Ad Din Road: Main road to cross between North and South (risk of congestion)

Khan Younis

Al Rasheed coastal road

ISRAEL

Philadelphi corridor
Bad road conditions

No Access Zone
1 Nautical Mile
April (N)

Rafah

Israeli evacuation orders on 7 May, followed by military operation

Rafah
Closed since 8 May

Sufa
Closed since 2008 (except Mar-Apr 2011)

Number of drivers and trucks cleared by Israel to use fence road is insufficient to meet demand, causing delays and fewer aid deliveries than planned

EGYPT

Kerem Shalom
Currently no safe access from within Gaza and not logistically viable since 6 May

Kerem Shalom crossing, 3 May 2024

Military zone or military operations

Passage of humanitarian aid requires coordination with Israeli military

Accessible for humanitarian aid

Military road

Bad road conditions

Holding point is the waiting point to request coordination with Israeli military before heading to the checkpoint

Israeli checkpoint (long delays, congestion and frequent closures)

Currently closed

Open for pre-approved goods and/or people

Permanently closed Crossing

JLOTS: Joint Logistics Over-The-Shore

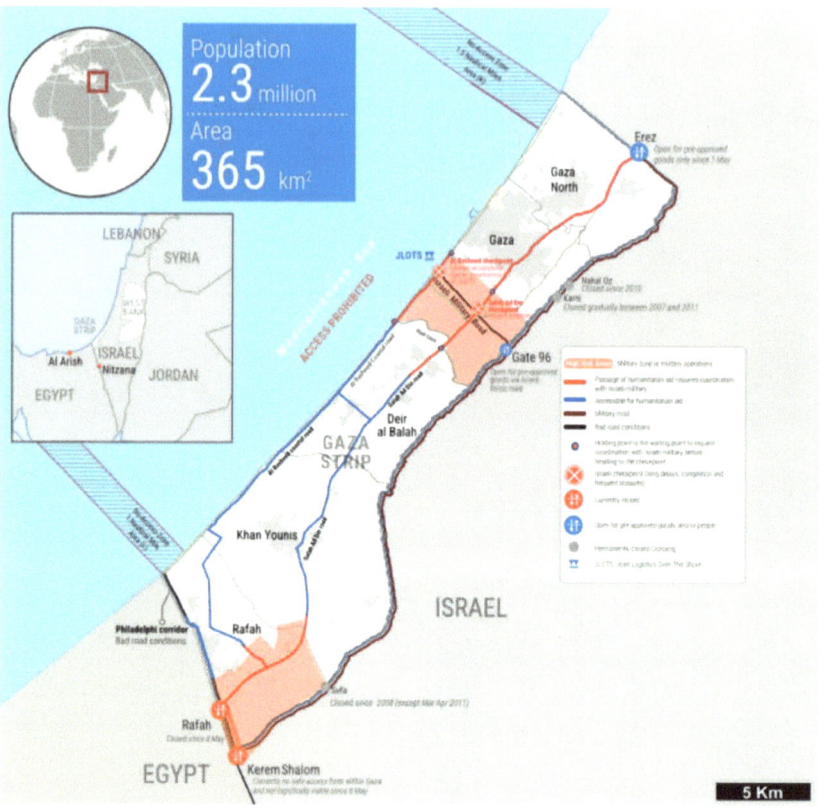

OCHA also made it a point of trying to keep the world community at large aware of the effects of the Wall, the Barrier that Israel has built over the last ten or fifteen years surrounding virtually all of the West Bank. From Israel's point of view, the Wall, built almost entirely on illegally occupied Palestinian land, was an effective means to separate itself from the concerns of the restive occupied Palestinian population, and reduce the chances for lone wolf terrorist attacks in Israel proper. And from their point of view it has succeeded. But for the Palestinians it meant also the creation of a tool for a total lockdown on their population and an apparent attempt to suffocate any aspirations of statehood for the Palestinian people, despite international agreements like the Oslo Accords and the repeated demands of the UN General Assembly and the UN Security Council to end the occupation since 1967.

OCHA has published valuable analyses of the Barrier such as this, showing how the Palestinians have lost access to valuable agricultural lands and the means to provide sustenance for their families:

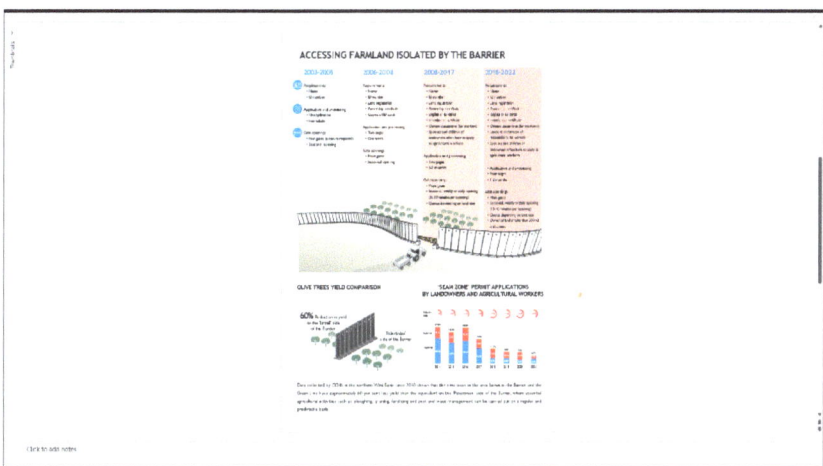

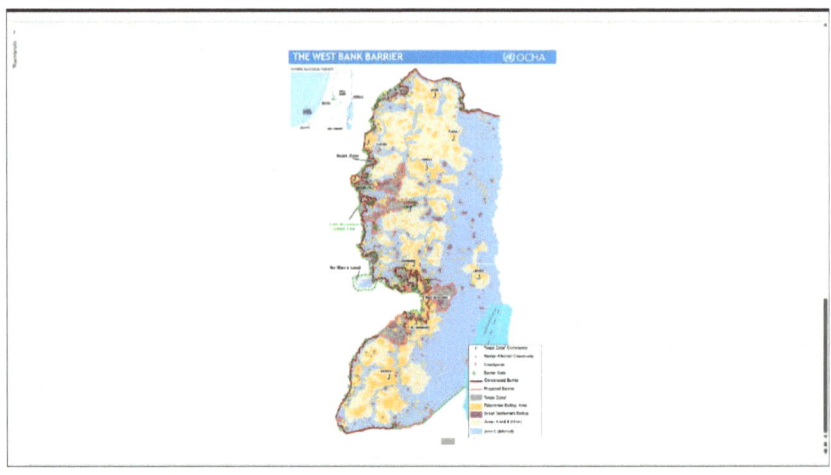

Sheikh Jarrah was also the neighborhood for different Western embassies and consulates, the UN World Health Organization (WHO) branch office and the offices of the Association for International Development Agencies (AIDA) under the then-auspices and hosting of Norwegian Refugee Council (NRC), a humanitarian nongovernmental organization established in postwar Europe to help refugees. AIDA is now under the hosting of OXFAM, a similar international group with global headquarters in the Netherlands and major offices in the UK and USA. AIDA is itself a grouping and network of now over 90 international NGOs based in Europe, Asia and the USA with programs in Palestine, either the West Bank, Gaza or both. I was elected to the Executive Committee of AIDA during the two years I was there.

AIDA for many years has helped to coordinate in Palestine the different humanitarian and development programs trying to mitigate the effects of the Israeli occupation for the Palestinian people. They would look at nuts and bolts issues for how to improve programs, how to evaluate programs, and to share resources and talent. But importantly they evolved as a significant advocacy voice for the legitimate needs and aspirations of the Palestinian people.

Slide 1

Gazan and Palestinian Realities: INGO – AIDA position on the Blockade, Occupation and International Humanitarian Law

- The Association of International Development Agencies in the oPt(AIDA) believes that all parties must refrain from using the civilians in Gaza as leverage for political gain. Palestinians' fundamental rights to life and health must not be made conditional on anything, and particularly not on political concessions.
- The security narrative is used as justification to violate the rights of civilians and is stifling sustainable development and economic sovereignty of the Palestinian state.
- The dual-use list must continue to be challenged, and vital items that support health, water, and livelihood sectors should be allowed to reach populations in Gaza where they are urgently needed.
- Items directly under the stewardship of the MoH and Humanitarian community should receive unimpeded access into urgent care facilities within Gaza. While there are divergent views on how to secure an efficient and reliable safe passage between the Gaza Strip the West Bank and the broader region, the Government of Israel, Palestinian Authorities, and third States, including in their capacity as donors to international aid, should actively work on reintroducing a safe passage

 **Association of International Development Agencies**

20

Slide 2

Gazan and Palestinian Realities: INGO – AIDA position on the Blockade, Occupation and International Humanitarian Law (2)

The Government of Israel should:

- **End the siege,** including the maritime and air blockade and land closure that collectively punishes the vast majority of Palestinians in Gaza. Recognize the detrimental consequences for this continued punitive policy, its adverse impact on achieving any sort of lasting peace, and seek political and diplomatic solutions to resolving the conflict and the question of Palestine.

- **Allow for the unimpeded entry and exit of goods and people,** with the exception of armament, as a necessary prerequisite to meet humanitarian needs and to ensure sustainable economic recovery and development. As an urgent step toward completely ending the blockade, immediately remove from the dual-use list building materials and other items that are necessary for humanitarian and development projects.

- Comply with its obligation to respect the rules laid out in international humanitarian law regarding Palestinians' human rights, including the right to move freely within a territory, and to choose one's place of residence.

- **Recognize that the Palestinian economy requires direct access to international markets** and increased access to the entire national market. In this context, sea and air facilities in Gaza are of significant importance and should be introduced and operate under agreed guidelines, placing the right to movement of people at the center of any policy changes.

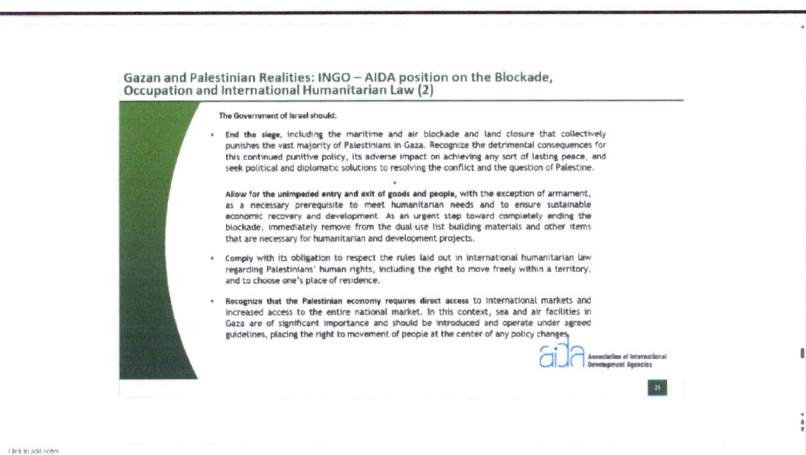 Association of International Development Agencies

21

Gazan and Palestinian Realities: INGO – AIDA position on the Blockade, Occupation and International Humanitarian Law (3)

- **Initiate** a process of redress for Palestinians who claim to have been improperly prevented from choosing their residency, including those who have been forcibly removed from the West Bank to Gaza or handed criminal penalties for residing in an area of the oPt in which they were not formally registered as residents.
- **Allow full access without fear of reprisal or harm** to the internationally recognized fishing zones and agricultural and living areas near the separation fence as part of Palestinian rights to movement and to earn a livelihood.
  - **Stop the use of indiscriminate lethal force.**
  - **Stop** intentionally causing **damage** (spraying, flooding, etc) to Palestinian lands, subjecting Palestinians to unnecessary health risks and financial injuries (from loss of livelihoods).

- **THE INTERNATIONAL COMMUNITY:**

  - **Support a transformative approach to Gaza**, considering the scale of humanitarian challenges, underpinned by a political commitment to the territorial integrity and political independence of a Palestinian state, and the non-admissibility of the maritime and air blockade, and the land closure imposed by Israel.

aida Association of International Development Agencies

Gazan and Palestinian Realities: INGO – AIDA position on the Blockade, Occupation and International Humanitarian Law (4)

- **The International Community should:**
  - **Increase efforts and pressure** on the GoI to establish a time-bound plan to end the siege, including benchmarks and accountability mechanisms to respond in case of failure to make progress. Promptly develop a common response to the GoI if immediate progress is not made in ending Israeli-imposed restrictions, for example by conditioning bilateral agreements and/or the deepening of diplomatic relations on adherence to international law.

  - **Prioritize the development of an independent Palestinian economy in Gaza.** Donors and the UN can leverage humanitarian investment to support the recovery of livelihood assets and boost private sector investments in order to support longer-term economic development. It is critical to maintain and restore the connection between Gaza and the West Bank (including East Jerusalem) to guarantee the viability of a future Palestinian state.

  - **Focus humanitarian diplomacy** regarding assistance and relief in Gaza on **Israel's duty to ensure the right of safe passage** between Gaza and the West Bank and to remove all current decrees and policies preventing this. Demand Israel to end the physical separation policy and support the establishment of a physical corridor facilitating the movement of people and goods in the oPt.

  - **Advocate for a broad stakeholder discussion on the future of the GRM**, as it was set up as a temporary mechanism and should not become a permanent mechanism, across all sectors.

  - **Increase political and diplomatic support for Palestinian unity** leading to national reconciliation and unity processes and ending the no-contact policy with Hamas. This includes applying pressure on all parties to overcome obstacles which may threaten the scheduled national elections.

aida Association of International Development Agencies

134

Gazan and Palestinian Realities: INGO – AIDA position on the Palestinians

- The Palestinian Authorities should:

- Prioritize political reconciliation and elections; fulfill its commitment for free, fair and inclusive national elections; ensure a conducive environment for elections to guarantee it is a true reflection of the will of the people. All parties should seek common ground to establish a unity government to administer the Gaza Strip.

- Fight and reverse decades of corruption, brutality and mistreatment of people and resources.

- Improve and invest in economic policy and the creation of suitable opportunities for its citizens, in particular women and youth and Palestinians living in Gaza

- Continue to support **quality public services** with **increasing investments** in health, WASH, and livelihoods.

- In future classes we will try to examine how corruption, accountability and a blind eye to try democratic institutions has damaged Gaza and the West Bank and increasingly imperiled Israel.
- We will also discuss critiques and national security implications: for Israel as well as for us.

aida **Association of International Development Agencies**

24

CHAPTER IV

CORRUPTION AND ACCOUNTABILITY

Fighting corruption is not just good governance. It is self-defense. It is patriotism and it's essential to the preservation of our democracy and our future.

– President Joseph R. Biden Jr. June 3, 2021

Even before the war, the Palestinians were very accustomed to suffering from the old game of "blame the victim." And it is somewhat of a complex picture as is often the case. I don't want to fuel that narrative any more than is justifiable, but I must also recognize that at times the Palestinians, particularly their leadership, have been their worst enemies, and this has undermined hope for resolution of their suffering. It does NOT justify by any means continued violations of international humanitarian law, the continued and merciless effects of the Israeli occupation, nor the widespread disaster and conflict fatigue that seemed to have gripped many international donors and stakeholders, even before the war.

The problems of corruption and the shirking of accountability are, of course two-sided in this jaded and exhausting conflict. The corruption of Palestinian leadership has been hugely detrimental in both the West Bank and Gaza. But Israeli corruption, both at a petty and grand scale, has also been very detrimental and an obstacle to peace.

I'll circle back to the latter to at least summarize how I understand the impact and consequences after talking with many Israeli friends. But I will first drill down a bit on the global implications from corruption and cronyism and how it manifests on the Palestinian side.

The discussion here draws liberally from different sources including the excellent book *Thieves of State: Why Corruption Threatens Global Security by Sarah Chayes* (2015). The author recounts the familiar experiences of the kleptocracy in Kandahar and Afghanistan as a whole under the Karzais, something I came to be passingly familiar with when I served in Kandahar in 2011. I also found valuable the book *The Enablers: How the West Supports Kleptocrats and Corruption - Endangering Our Democracy by Frank Vogt* (2021). I reviewed in addition the podcast "*The Ambassador and the General*" available on most platforms and a variety of discussion roundtables on corruption from the Center for Strategic International Studies and the Center for Global Development.

Dirty money is a noxious corrosive. Across the world, authoritarian leaders and their cronies rob their people. Kleptocrats are pocketing staggering sums of cash. Kleptocracies are perpetuated in Russia, China, Iran, Egypt, Hungary, Nigeria and many more countries. The U.S. Government and other Western powers are often complicit in the corruption and turn a blind eye. All too often our institutions and societies act as enablers to allow if not encourage these thieves of state that impoverish their citizens.

Western law enforcement may sometimes call out one or another bank or dictator, but the punishments imposed are meaningless and not disincentives or brakes to the corruption. The big shots are virtually never called to account. Only the small fry. When fines are applied they are minor and seen as just a cost of doing business.

Some efforts to publicize the most egregious exploits by the press and civil society: the Panama Papers, the Luanda Leaks, etc. But these pass from the headlines quickly with the vanishing attention span that exists. Yet corruption completely undermines the link between development, economic growth and prosperity.

Major banks, giant multinationals, even many governments play roles in enabling and permitting corruption and the diversion of resources. Threats have grown so large that finally countering the kleptocrats is a priority – for now! – of the Biden Administration, Congress, the EU Commission, the UK govt and other public authorities.

There is more being done now to fight illicit finance than any time over the last 20 or 40 years, particularly after the nightmare of the Trump Administration trying to upend, defang or repeal the Foreign Corrupt Practices Act of 1976. But the numbers show that the combined impact of enforcement efforts and accountability aspirations remain small in the face of the massive toll of corruption on foreign aid, foreign investment and transnational finance.

Broad public awareness and understanding is an essential starting point – focusing on where the problems are actually the most acute. The flow of illicit international finance is without parallel. A former IMF deputy managing director states that private wealth hidden at offshore financial sanctuaries amounts to at least $7 trillion, about 8% of global GDP. Much likely comes from illicit activities.

According to Global Financial Integrity (GFI) total dark money from trade is over $800 billion/year representing trade payments outside normal banking channels between 135 lower income countries and 36 advanced nations, often imports of luxury items for the elites.

Total cash stolen and shipped by kleptocrats, oligarchs and organized crime suggests total illicit finance as over $2 trillion per year. For example, Putin's cliques are the tip of the iceberg, but they are indicative of the class. These cliques exist everywhere leaders have amassed power, manipulated justice ministries, oversight and national audit mechanisms and enjoy absolute impunity.

The theft of public funds and promotion of corrupt practices reward and compensate those most loyal, enriching them and their families. They strive to keep ordinary citizens in the dark, block social media on the internet, censor mainstream media, jail, exile or kill uncooperative journalists and repress civil society activists.

Western governments frequently connive with and justify turning a blind eye. The treatment of the Azerbaijan dictator and criminal family the Aliyevs is a case in point. For years the West ignored the flow of huge amounts of petroleum based illicit funds from Baku into Western financial markets and the luxury circles of London and the U.S. This was justified by the excuse that Azerbaijan was an ally keeping an eye on neighboring Iran's activities. But Azerbaijan, in its actions over Iran and in the attacks against Armenian territory, often danced to the tune of the Kremlin.

Bankers were the most active enablers and money launderers for the dictator and his family, but Western countries consciously turned a blind eye to this. As well with many other countries. Corporate kickbacks of course continued to flow even after the U.S. Foreign Corrupt Practices Act and after the UK and EU slowly introduced similar legislation.

• Airbus finally paid over $4 billion in fines to settle belated charges about their global bribe paying arrangements for contracts.

• Siemens, the huge European engineering firm, created a special office to manage bribes internationally.

• Odebrecht, the huge Brazilian mining and construction company, ran bribery schemes up and down Latin America, Africa and Europe.

• Walmart was fined for massive bribery in Asia and Latin America.

Sadly, this crony corruption has been known to penetrate the Palestinian National Authority and its leadership for years. I've heard outrageous claims of the amount of cash Mahmoud Abbas and some other PLO stalwarts might have stashed away. And no doubt this is true for Hamas as well. Yet these open secrets that undermine governance and accountability are conveniently set aside all too often.

The next and previous slides again come from a class I taught online from Gaza City last year for the ENCORE adult education program, linked with George Mason University. The class had numbered about 50 who subscribed, including Jews, Palestinians and others.

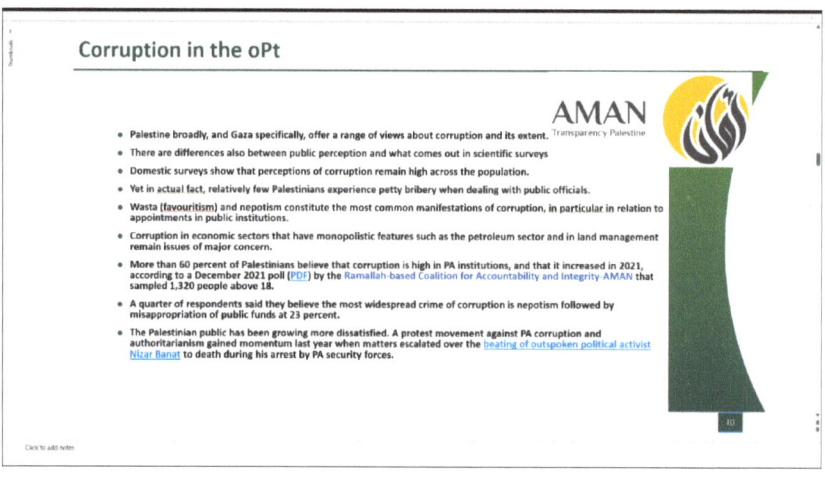

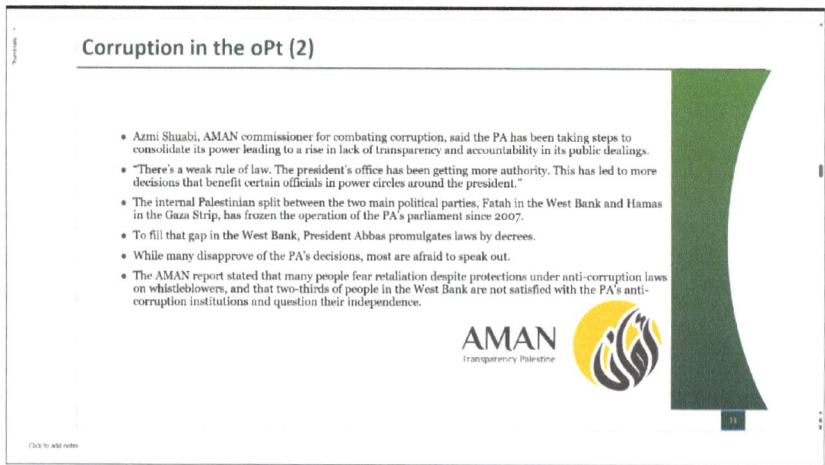

Corruption in the oPt (3)

- Shuabi, head of Aman, explained that President Abbas hires the head of the anti-corruption commission and the head of the judicial council, which makes it hard to guarantee their independence from the PA.
- The main challenge remains the lack of political will to fight corruption, says Shuabi.
- Case study of PA plans to build a specialised Khaled Al-Hassan Cancer Hospital in the town of Surda near Ramallah, which never came to fruition. This has happened many times.
- Many shared pictures of the proposed building on social media with a hashtag asking "Where's the hospital?".
- Businessmen and philanthropists donated about $10m to build it, but the site of the proposed hospital stands as an empty dug-up piece of land. Plans for the 15-storey building with more than 200 beds were changed multiple times and the public was kept in the dark, activists say.
- On January 14, the Ministry of Health announced that the project had been frozen due to a lack of funds.
- "We started with the first phase, but didn't have enough donations to cover the construction cost of $160m," Prime Minister Mohammed Shtayyeh said days later, and that the donations allocated for the hospital have been placed in a separate bank account. The PA, however, has given no proof that the money has been kept in a bank.

12

Corruption in the oPt (4)

- AMAN notes that President Mahmoud Abbas recently encouraged investments for cancer departments in public and private hospitals in the West Bank, where the healthcare infrastructure is bursting at its seams due to decades of Israeli occupation.
- Head of the Ramallah-based Bisan Center for Research and Development, Ubai Aboudi, said mismanagement is worse than financial corruption.
- "A whole project has stopped. If you spend a huge sum of money digging up for a project and you don't have the cash flow, then who benefitted from that money," he told Al Jazeera.
- The PA has been struggling with deep financial woes; unable to pay civil servants' salaries in full.

13

Corruption in the oPt (5)

- According to Transparency International, since its inception, the Palestinian National Authority (PNA) has faced major internal and external threats and challenges.
- Stalled its efforts to develop and implement effective anti-corruption policies. Still PNA is credited with significant progress in strengthening public governance systems, from various corruption surveys and governance indicators.
- The PNA has made efforts to strengthen its legal and institutional framework against corruption.
- A number of anti-corruption laws have been enacted and institutions have been created:
    - the Anti-Corruption Commission and Corruption Crimes Court,
    - an external audit bureau,
    - the Economic Crimes and Support Unit within the Attorney General's office.
- But efforts remain fragmented. Need for better coordination of anti-corruption efforts and institutions.
- Lack of an access to information law also prevents civil society organizations and the media from fully playing watchdog role.

14

Click to add notes

Corruption in the oPt (6)

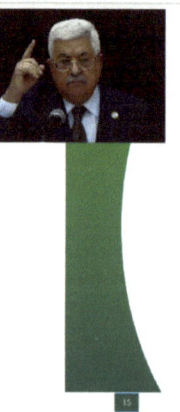

- For years, the AMAN coalition of Palestinian nongovernmental organizations (NGOs) founded in 2000 focused on issues of administrative and financial corruption.
- However, the Palestine chapter of Transparency International decided in 2021 to tackle a much more controversial issue: political corruption.
- Eroding integrity of the current Palestinian leadership forced the local Transparency International to tackle a corrupt political system that among other things canceled an already long-overdue national election and allegedly ordered harming a critic in Hebron by the Palestinian security forces, an act that led to his death and the violent crackdown of demonstrations calling for accountability.
- In their anger at the deterioration of the Palestinian political system, many repeated a statement made by Palestinian President Mahmoud Abbas that he would resign if 50 or more Palestinians call on him to step down. Abbas, 86, is now in his 12th year in office after long passing his four-year term and appears to have consolidated all powers in his hands.
- Read more: https://www.al-monitor.com/originals/2021/09/palestinian-ngos-begin-campaign-against-political-corruption#ixzz805Vjo5bK

15

Click to add notes

Corruption in the oPt (7)

- In a 10-point manifesto, AMAN called on Palestinians to reject this anti-democratic slippery slope and made a special plea to civil society organizations to "fight this political corruption by creating a coalition that can contribute to making a change toward a more honest governance structure."
- Azmi Shuibi, a former member of the Palestinian Legislative Council, produced the first-ever anti-corruption study in 1996, which resulted in an angry reaction from President Yasser Arafat and the arrest of a Palestinian journalist that broadcast the report.
- Shuibi, now an adviser on the issue of corruption, said that the situation is very serious and must be addressed with the efforts of all involved. "We need to raise the red flag and make a loud warning that if the current political corruption is not checked we are moving into a dangerous zone."
- Escalating civil society criticism from combination of restrictions on the two main sectors of governance.
- They not only succeeded in stopping any criticism from the legislative branch, but the executive branch has been chipping away at the judiciary. Without a legislature and a cornered judiciary, the ruling party was able to stifle the efforts of people calling for accountability. Things got even worse when the president started using presidential decrees without any discussion or debate for his own purposes and to keep certain people in position for a long time." *HMM SOUND FAMILIAR?*

16

Click to add notes

The Picture in Gaza – very hard to piece together

- Civil society reports also cover Gaza, where there is plenty of Hamas corruption (though opinion polls included in the text suggest that corruption is perceived to be lower by residents of Gaza than by those in the West Bank).
- Accountability on human rights is an area where we can see corruption of governance and political mandates.
- According to the US State Department Significant human rights issues included:
- With respect to Hamas: reports of unlawful or arbitrary killings, systematic torture, and arbitrary detention by Hamas officials; political prisoners; arbitrary or unlawful interference with privacy; serious restrictions on free expression, the press, and the internet, including violence, threats of violence, unjustified arrests and prosecutions against journalists, censorship, site blocking, and the existence of criminal libel and slander laws; substantial interference with the rights of peaceful assembly and freedom of association; restrictions on political participation, as there has been no national election since 2006; acts of corruption; reports of a lack of investigation of and accountability for violence against women; violence and threats of violence motivated by anti-Semitism; anti-Semitism in school textbooks; unlawful recruitment and use of child soldiers; violence and threats of violence targeting lesbian, gay, bisexual, transgender, or intersex persons; and forced or compulsory child labor.

17

Click to add notes

The **Times of Israel** published in January 2023 a rare opportunity for ordinary, courageous Gazans to tell the world what life is like under the rule of Hamas. All interviews were conducted over the course of 2022. The speakers, those who remain alive, all currently reside in Gaza.

Gazan men and women described their professional disenfranchisement by Hamas and the repression of their personal freedoms. They told of arbitrary arrests, shakedowns of small-time merchants, and the silencing of journalists. Voicing staunch support for Palestinian self-determination, they also denounced Hamas as harming that cause by starting wars with Israel it cannot win while hiding in bunkers and leaving civilians to suffer casualties. They conveyed an understanding of Hamas warfare, moreover, as a play for aid money that the movement goes on to plunder.

How fully valid is this picture? It's hard to say. Some rings true, some does not. There are misleading and often totally false narratives common to the Israeli press, Israeli courts and right wing political narratives.

But the animated videos they shared are compelling also. I'll include the links here for access from the ebook:

- https://youtu.be/p7fFYHN5CEI

- https://youtu.be/Ctu4W6Vj8eI

- https://youtu.be/LBT2Rab-MjA

- https://youtu.be/9B_sojyYzHI

The cumulative burden of all this is of course huge. It's interesting how some elements – corruption at political levels – find echoes back and forth between Palestine and Israel.

Extremism, violence, corruption and impunity to accountability feed on each other and are contagious. All this also adds up to an important national and regional security burden.

CHAPTER V

AN OPEN BLEEDING WOUND AND NATIONAL SECURITY

We've known for decades that the unaddressed and unresolved Palestinian situation was and would remain essentially an open wound. If it did not heal, it would fester. This has been the larger problem of the Palestinian people for decades, within the region. Consider this: the Palestinian people and their aspirations are a problem not just left to fester but deliberately so. From the start, with the *Nakba* and the displacement and dispossession of over 700,000 Palestinians from the State of Israel, over half moved into refugee camps in the surrounding countries.

There is a lot of mythology built up around this displacement, including a lot of half-truths and outright prevarication. Peter Beinart has done some scholarly writing about this, including recently an article for **The Jewish Forward**. The work coming out of that is challenging and painful since it confronts what Zionism was and came to be, and the early choices and actions of the Jewish settlers who arrived from Eastern and Central Europe during the first half of the twentieth century.

Teshuvah: A Jewish Case for Palestinian Refugee Return (jewishcurrents.org)

Beinart describes with ample detail the inconsistency in Jews supporting the right of return for Jews and every other population group, but not for Palestinians. But he goes much further; he documents the degree to which the Jewish settlers in Palestine encouraged and terrorized Palestinians to leave and challenges the long-held view that it was the Arab Palestinian leadership calling on the Palestinians to flee. He argues that this may have contributed to no more than a fraction of the cases. And he shows how Jewish leadership insisted on the need for the expulsion to bring the percentage of Arabs in the proposed Jewish state in 1947, even though the Jewish population at the time was at best one third of that across the Palestinian Mandate. It's beyond the scope of this book to delve too extensively in all that – I recommend Beinart's article above – but I would like to share a meaningful quote towards the end of his article that speaks to the core of the conflict:

"By refusing to acknowledge the Nakba, the Israeli government prepared the ground for its perpetuation. And by refusing to forget the Nakba, Palestinians—and some dissident Israeli Jews— prepared the ground for the resistance that is now convulsing Jerusalem, and Israel-Palestine as a whole.

"In our bones, Jews know that when you tell a people to forget its past you are not proposing peace. You are proposing extinction.

""We are what we remember," wrote the late Rabbi Jonathan Sacks. "As with an individual suffering from dementia, so with a culture as a whole: the loss of memory is experienced as a loss of identity." For a stateless people, collective memory is key to national survival. That's why for centuries diaspora Jews asked to be buried with soil from the land of Israel. And it's why Palestinians gather soil from the villages from which their parents or grandparents were expelled. For Jews to tell Palestinians that peace requires them to forget the Nakba is grotesque. In our bones, Jews know that when you tell a people to forget its past you are not proposing peace. You are proposing extinction."

I believe many mainstream and progressive American Jewish communities have members who profess to care deeply about Palestinian rights but have not yet come to terms with the idea that Palestinian return does not require or even necessarily imply Jewish displacement from Israel. Obviously for the extremists and hardliners, it easily becomes an all or nothing question. But nothing in life really works that way. I think reading Beinart's essay, even if you don't agree with all or most of it, forces a thought-provoking exercise to step out of the usual paradigms and assumptions and attempt to look more for solutions.

As someone from a Jewish background, and doubly so as a member of the Baha'i community who has lived and worked in Muslim and other countries and cultures, I still believe in the importance of the state of Israel and as a Jewish homeland. And I believe that what should be the lessons of the Holocaust, as expressed in memorials like Yad Vashem, really go beyond a narrowcasting view of "Never Again." When Yad Vashem in the Jerusalem Hills and the U.S. Holocaust Memorial Museum in Washington DC talk about and praise the "Righteous Among the Nations" this is no mere simplistic recognition that there were "good Gentiles" who stood up against genocidal behavior and the destruction of the Jewish people in Europe. It's not just a Hollywood feature film. It must surely go beyond that. The late Elie Wiesel understood this, and the legacy of his Foundation surely attempts to shine a sharp and painful light on the many instances where humanity falls short. There is a need for open questioning about some aspects of the mythological narrative that has built up over many decades about the displacement and the dispossession of the Palestinian people, but we also need to challenge the mirror image of mythologies that are sustained by many Jewish people.

I understand the fear and the willful blindness that exists in the hearts of many Jews and many Israelis about what they see as a zero-sum game, a contradiction between the two realities. In fact, if there is a contradiction, it is not just because Israel's history includes shameful episodes about the driving out of innocent Arab villagers, Christian, Muslim and even Druze. It is because Israel has refused to acknowledge this sin and has refused to accept the need for "*teshuvah*" and making amends.

In my mind, making amends does not require undoing some basic facts of history. It doesn't mean that all Palestinians must be fully returned to their homes in what is now Israel. I don't believe most Palestinians when supported from emotional reactions to the Occupation believe that either. But it does mean serious efforts at making amends, at negotiating compromises, reparations and compensation. Despite the mythology, Israel has rarely made any serious efforts to do so.

I understand that there is also culpability on the Palestinian side. Certainly, this is not a case of black and white but many nuances of gray. There is a history of corrupt and authoritarian leadership among Arab neighbors. There is a history where many Palestinians, unlike virtually every group of displaced peoples in the past century, have been kept artificially long in refugee camp arrangements, and often not permitted to integrate into the societies hosting them. They have been isolated under poor conditions, rights less and stateless, without any power of agency. There has been cynicism from many Arab Palestinian and Guf Muslim leaders as well in this regard.

But all of this is then a collective culpability that must be acknowledged. Had this been done so decades ago, we could have long seen and accommodated a Palestinian State and a Jewish one. But once again, the shiftlessness in Palestinian leadership simply does not free Israelis from a moral obligation that has been ignored for three-quarters of a century, if not longer.

In April 2023, this is how I conveyed my understanding for my ENCORE class online, which I led simultaneously from Gaza City and Sheikh Jarrah East Jerusalem:

Setting the stage in terms of country level security

- Israel just celebrated its 75th anniversary.
- In the eyes of many, it is going through perhaps the most internally divisive and polemic filled time of all its history.
- Political agendas of the incumbent government are testing the loyalty of many Israelis like never before. Senior and midlevel military officers have abandoned or threatened to abandon duties.
- Israeli President Herzog has called out in last 60 days to govt: **"Come to Your Senses!"** **"Halt the Madness"**
- The whole world is looking at you", Herzog said in a statement. "For the sake of the unity of the People of Israel, for the sake of the necessary responsibility, I call on you to halt the legislative process immediately." He urged all the leaders in power to place country's citizens above all else.

2

Setting the stage in terms of country level security (2)

- A brief pause of 2-3 weeks with Passover and Ramadan came to an end with no resolution.
- Protests have continued weekly: opposition says they will worsen unless IL govt drops plan for judicial reform and other extremist measures.
- Meanwhile, Diaspora World Jewry is facing its own crisis: continue to support Israel above all or convert statements of concern to harder choices to punish Israel.
- Meanwhile...

3

150

Setting the stage in terms of country level security (3)

- Israeli President Isaac Herzog and Palestinian President Mahmoud Abbas spoke on the phone before Ramadan in March to express their hopes for peace and stability in the Palestinian territories and the wider Middle East.
- But against a backdrop of unrelenting resurgent violence, not only since January but covering all of 2022.
- Hundreds of Palestinian prisoners in Israeli jails, under 'administrative detention'; no trial, no human rights, no sentence. No accountability.
- PIJ leader Adnan Khader just died this week after 86 days hunger strike, sparking more protests, over 100 rockets to Israel Tuesday and Wednesday. Multiple missile strikes in Gaza.
- Parents told me their children were terrified. The booms and explosions went on all Tuesday night too dawn.

4

Setting the stage in terms of country level security

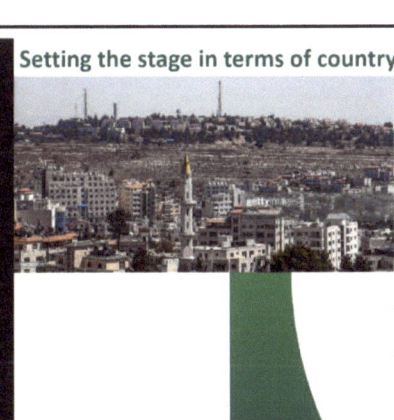

- So far, a Wednesday morning ceasefire but for how long? Increasing frequency of violent exchanges in 2023, 2022 and 2021.
- Deaths, home demolitions and detentions: But what's the Endgame here?
- Multiple Israeli governments, not just the current one, have acted with impunity over the oPt for at least 15 years.
- Creeping settlements, and some boundaries between legal and illegal ones, have changed now since January.
- Senior govt members frequently calling for outright annexation and possible attempts at expulsion.
- Apartheid realities? How does that work in a so-called democratic state? Isn't that Israel's primary perch of moral superiority?

5

151

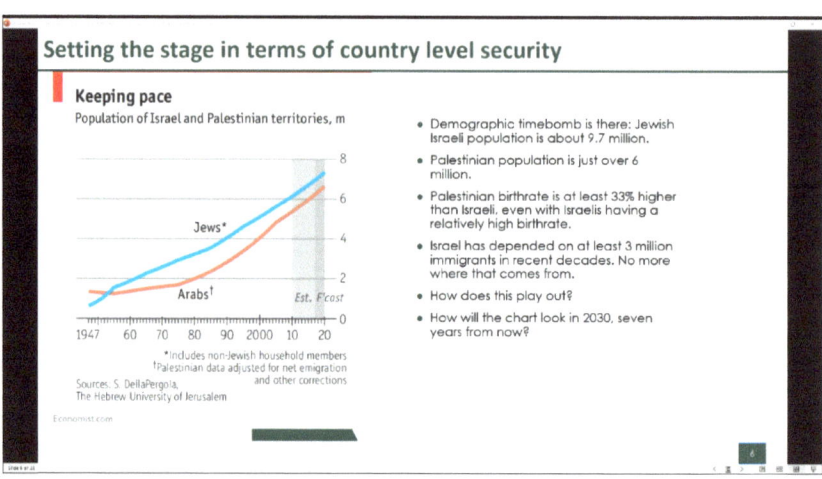

Setting the stage in terms of country level security

Keeping pace

Population of Israel and Palestinian territories, m

Jews*

Arabs†

Est. F'cast

1947 60 70 80 90 2000 10 20

*Includes non-Jewish household members
†Palestinian data adjusted for net emigration and other corrections

Sources: S. DellaPergola,
The Hebrew University of Jerusalem

Economist.com

- Demographic timebomb is there: Jewish Israeli population is about 9.7 million.
- Palestinian population is just over 6 million.
- Palestinian birthrate is at least 33% higher than Israeli, even with Israelis having a relatively high birthrate.
- Israel has depended on at least 3 million immigrants in recent decades. No more where that comes from.
- How does this play out?
- How will the chart look in 2030, seven years from now?

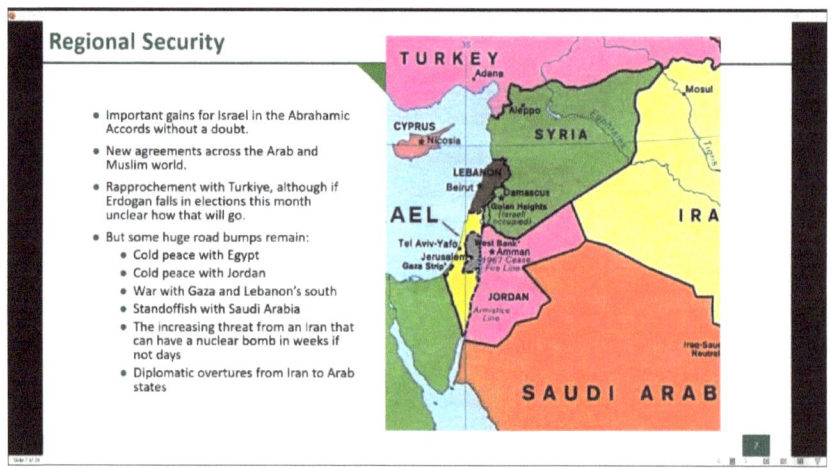

Regional Security

- Important gains for Israel in the Abrahamic Accords without a doubt.
- New agreements across the Arab and Muslim world.
- Rapprochement with Turkiye, although if Erdogan falls in elections this month unclear how that will go.
- But some huge road bumps remain:
  - Cold peace with Egypt
  - Cold peace with Jordan
  - War with Gaza and Lebanon's south
  - Standoffish with Saudi Arabia
  - The increasing threat from an Iran that can have a nuclear bomb in weeks if not days
  - Diplomatic overtures from Iran to Arab states

The Iran Dilemma

MIDDLE EAST CONFLICT MAP

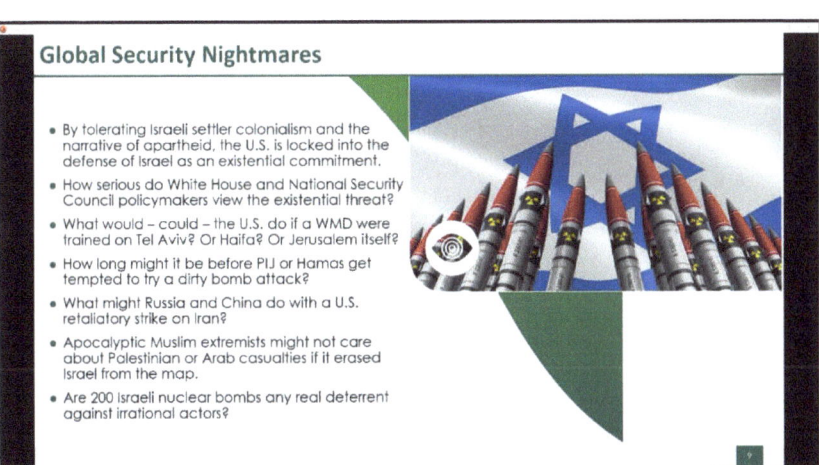

But according to the European Union, Israeli West Bank Settlements are the "Greatest Threat" to Peace!

- Israel keeps hinting at a pre-emptive strike on Iran
- But what hope is there that any pre-emptive strike can stop Iranian nuclear retaliation, or the nuclear program?
- The nuclear threat among others is largely fed by the marginalization, imprisonment and apartheid of Palestinians. How long would that last if the bleeding wound were healed?
- Doesn't the hook of the 'Little Satan' just encourage the impunity and continuance of the Islamic Republic Regime, in the face of economic collapse and other social forces?

Global Security Nightmares

- By tolerating Israeli settler colonialism and the narrative of apartheid, the U.S. is locked into the defense of Israel as an existential commitment.
- How serious do White House and National Security Council policymakers view the existential threat?
- What would – could – the U.S. do if a WMD were trained on Tel Aviv? Or Haifa? Or Jerusalem itself?
- How long might it be before PIJ or Hamas get tempted to try a dirty bomb attack?
- What might Russia and China do with a U.S. retaliatory strike on Iran?
- Apocalyptic Muslim extremists might not care about Palestinian or Arab casualties if it erased Israel from the map.
- Are 200 Israeli nuclear bombs any real deterrent against irrational actors?

The Start of Artificial Security of Settler Colonialism

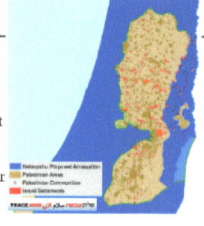

- The belief that the outcome of 1967 was a miracle reinforced to religious and messianic Zionists who believed that they had a right to the entirety of the Holy Land.

- The war unleashed the settler movement; a young generation of messianic Zionists decided to establish houses in the West Bank and Gaza, territory that is occupied and is not part of the state of Israel. At first regulated, legal and illegal settlements.

- The 1967 war gave fodder to the Zionist movement's 'colonial nature.' Instead of exchanging land for peace, as per UN Resolution 242at the end of the 1967 war, Israel encouraged citizens to move into the territories it occupied and supporting them as they did so.

- Shortly after ceasefire Israel began building illegal settlements for its citizens on land it does not own.

- Just one year after the 1967 war, there were six Israeli settlements built in the Syrian Golan Heights. By 1973, Israel had established 17 settlements in the West Bank and seven in the Gaza Strip. By 1977, some 11,000 Israelis had been living in the West Bank, Gaza Strip, the Golan Heights and the Sinai Peninsula.

10

The Start of Artificial Security of Settler Colonialism

- "Israel today maintains an entrenched system of institutionalised discrimination against Palestinians in the occupied territory – repression that extends far beyond any security rationale." Human Rights Watch

- All the while, Israel, since 1967, has proceeded with illegally building homes and transferring its Jewish citizens into the West Bank and East Jerusalem, or stolen Palestinian land. Today, at least 750,000 Israelis live in Jewish-only settlements scattered across the West Bank and East Jerusalem.

- Settlements, which are accompanied by roads and infrastructure built especially for the settlers, control at least 40 percent of the West Bank's surface area. As such, Israel has created an apartheid reality in the Palestinian territories whereby Israelis and Palestinians live under a system that privileges Jews over non-Jews.

- "By establishing two separate systems for Israelis and Palestinians, Israeli authorities also violate the international law prohibition on discrimination," a report by the London-based European Council on Foreign Relations think-tank.

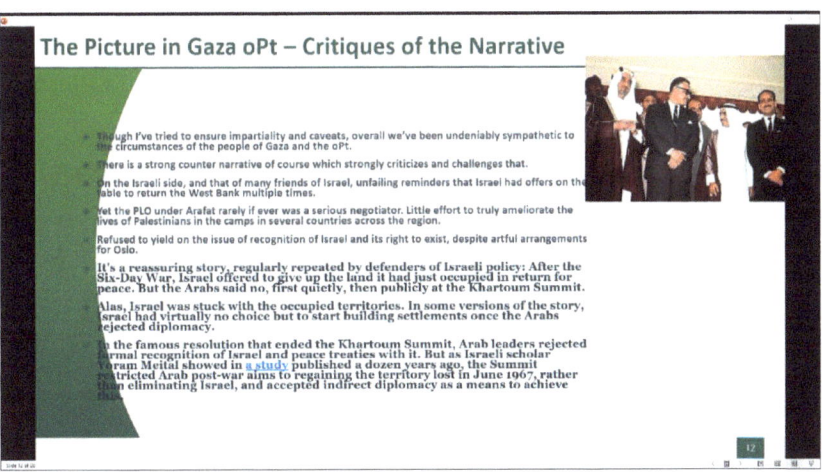

11

The Picture in Gaza oPt – Critiques of the Narrative

- Though I've tried to ensure impartiality and caveats, overall we've been undeniably sympathetic to the circumstances of the people of Gaza and the oPt.

- There is a strong counter narrative of course which strongly criticises and challenges that.

- On the Israeli side, and that of many friends of Israel, unfailing reminders that Israel had offers on the table to return the West Bank multiple times.

- Yet the PLO under Arafat rarely if ever was a serious negotiator. Little effort to truly ameliorate the lives of Palestinians in the camps in several countries across the region.

- Refused to yield on the issue of recognition of Israel and its right to exist, despite artful arrangements for Oslo.

- It's a reassuring story, regularly repeated by defenders of Israeli policy: After the Six-Day War, Israel offered to give up the land it had just occupied in return for peace. But the Arabs said no, first quietly, then publicly at the Khartoum Summit.

- Alas, Israel was stuck with the occupied territories. In some versions of the story, Israel had virtually no choice but to start building settlements once the Arabs rejected diplomacy.

- In the famous resolution that ended the Khartoum Summit, Arab leaders rejected formal recognition of Israel and peace treaties with it. But as Israeli scholar Yoram Meital showed in a study published a dozen years ago, the Summit restricted Arab post-war aims to regaining the territory lost in June 1967, rather than eliminating Israel, and accepted indirect diplomacy as a means to achieve that.

12

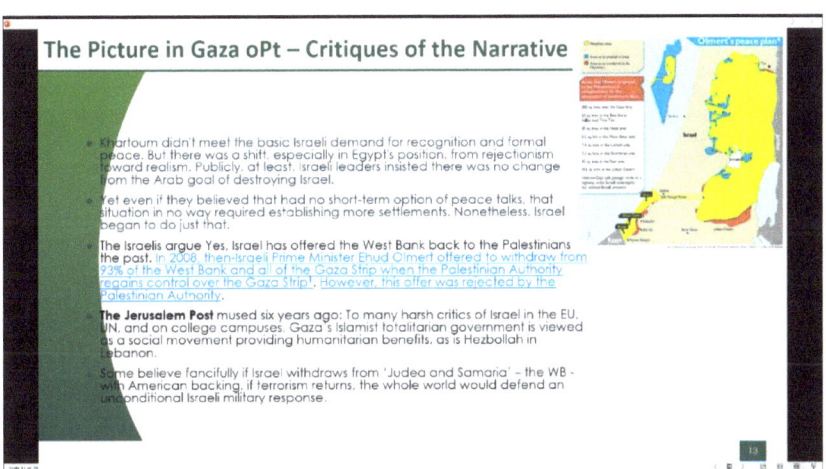

The Picture in Gaza oPt – Critiques of the Narrative

- Khartoum didn't meet the basic Israeli demand for recognition and formal peace. But there was a shift, especially in Egypt's position, from rejectionism toward realism. Publicly, at least, Israeli leaders insisted there was no change from the Arab goal of destroying Israel.

- Yet even if they believed that had no short-term option of peace talks, that situation in no way required establishing more settlements. Nonetheless, Israel began to do just that.

- The Israelis argue Yes, Israel has offered the West Bank back to the Palestinians the past. In 2008, then-Israeli Prime Minister Ehud Olmert offered to withdraw from 93% of the West Bank and all of the Gaza Strip when the Palestinian Authority regains control over the Gaza Strip'. However, this offer was rejected by the Palestinian Authority.

- **The Jerusalem Post** mused six years ago: To many harsh critics of Israel in the EU, UN, and on college campuses, Gaza's Islamist totalitarian government is viewed as a social movement providing humanitarian benefits, as is Hezbollah in Lebanon.

- Some believe fancifully if Israel withdraws from 'Judea and Samaria' – the WB - with American backing, if terrorism returns, the whole world would defend an unconditional Israeli military response.

13

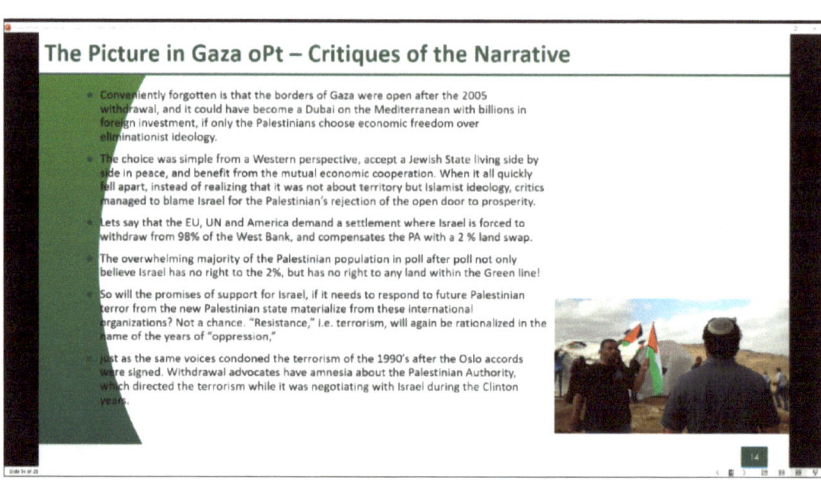

The Picture in Gaza oPt – Critiques of the Narrative

- Conveniently forgotten is that the borders of Gaza were open after the 2005 withdrawal, and it could have become a Dubai on the Mediterranean with billions in foreign investment, if only the Palestinians choose economic freedom over eliminationist ideology.

- The choice was simple from a Western perspective, accept a Jewish State living side by side in peace, and benefit from the mutual economic cooperation. When it all quickly fell apart, instead of realizing that it was not about territory but Islamist ideology, critics managed to blame Israel for the Palestinian's rejection of the open door to prosperity.

- Lets say that the EU, UN and America demand a settlement where Israel is forced to withdraw from 98% of the West Bank, and compensates the PA with a 2 % land swap.

- The overwhelming majority of the Palestinian population in poll after poll not only believe Israel has no right to the 2%, but has no right to any land within the Green line!

- So will the promises of support for Israel, if it needs to respond to future Palestinian terror from the new Palestinian state materialize from these international organizations? Not a chance. "Resistance," i.e. terrorism, will again be rationalized in the name of the years of "oppression,"

- Just as the same voices condoned the terrorism of the 1990's after the Oslo accords were signed. Withdrawal advocates have amnesia about the Palestinian Authority, which directed the terrorism while it was negotiating with Israel during the Clinton years.

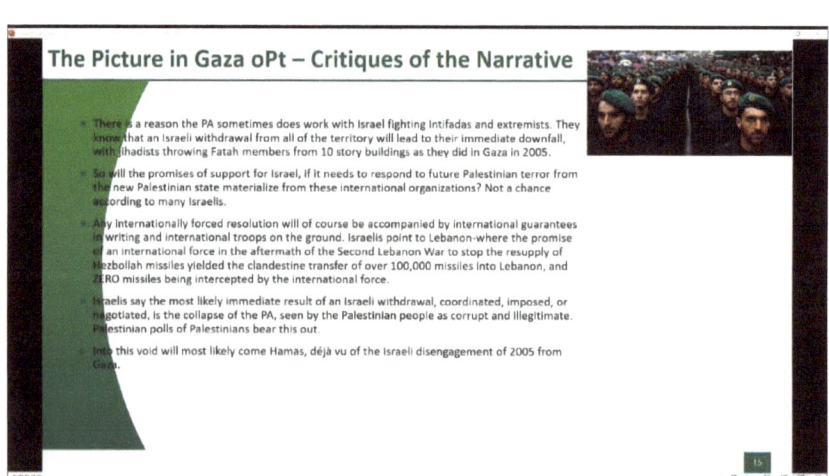

The Picture in Gaza oPt – Critiques of the Narrative

- There is a reason the PA sometimes does work with Israel fighting Intifadas and extremists. They know that an Israeli withdrawal from all of the territory will lead to their immediate downfall, with jihadists throwing Fatah members from 10 story buildings as they did in Gaza in 2005.

- So will the promises of support for Israel, if it needs to respond to future Palestinian terror from the new Palestinian state materialize from these international organizations? Not a chance according to many Israelis.

- Any internationally forced resolution will of course be accompanied by international guarantees in writing and international troops on the ground. Israelis point to Lebanon-where the promise of an international force in the aftermath of the Second Lebanon War to stop the resupply of Hezbollah missiles yielded the clandestine transfer of over 100,000 missiles into Lebanon, and ZERO missiles being intercepted by the international force.

- Israelis say the most likely immediate result of an Israeli withdrawal, coordinated, imposed, or negotiated, is the collapse of the PA, seen by the Palestinian people as corrupt and illegitimate. Palestinian polls of Palestinians bear this out.

- Into this void will most likely come Hamas, déjà vu of the Israeli disengagement of 2005 from Gaza.

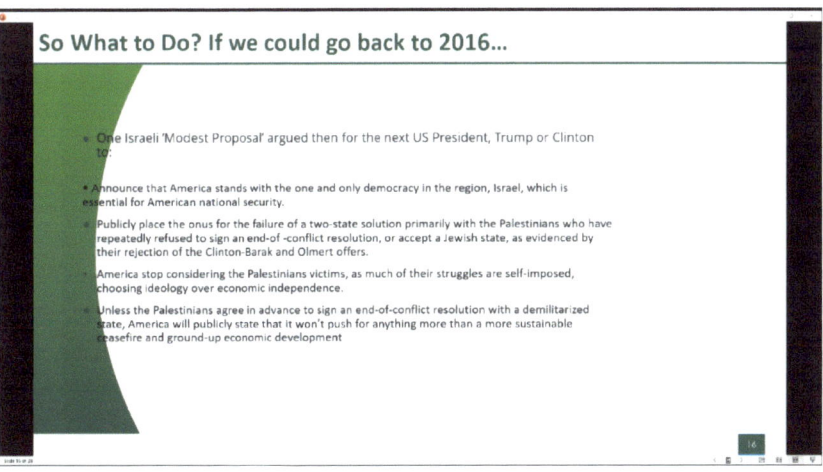

So What to Do? If we could go back to 2016...

- One Israeli 'Modest Proposal' argued then for the next US President, Trump or Clinton to:

- Announce that America stands with the one and only democracy in the region, Israel, which is essential for American national security.

- Publicly place the onus for the failure of a two-state solution primarily with the Palestinians who have repeatedly refused to sign an end-of -conflict resolution, or accept a Jewish state, as evidenced by their rejection of the Clinton-Barak and Olmert offers.

- America stop considering the Palestinians victims, as much of their struggles are self-imposed, choosing ideology over economic independence.

- Unless the Palestinians agree in advance to sign an end-of-conflict resolution with a demilitarized state, America will publicly state that it won't push for anything more than a more sustainable ceasefire and ground-up economic development

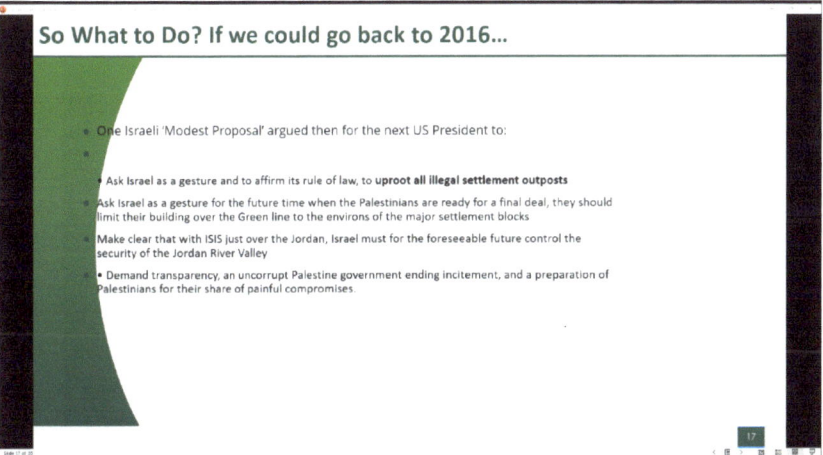

So What to Do? If we could go back to 2016...

- One Israeli 'Modest Proposal' argued then for the next US President to:

-

- Ask Israel as a gesture and to affirm its rule of law, to **uproot all illegal settlement outposts**

- Ask Israel as a gesture for the future time when the Palestinians are ready for a final deal, they should limit their building over the Green line to the environs of the major settlement blocks

- Make clear that with ISIS just over the Jordan, Israel must for the foreseeable future control the security of the Jordan River Valley

- Demand transparency, an uncorrupt Palestine government ending incitement, and a preparation of Palestinians for their share of painful compromises

So What to Do? If we could go back to 2016...

- One of the reasons the peace process has failed is that almost nothing is ever asked of the Palestinians, and worse, no consequences are imposed for their rejection of every deal that allows Israel to exist.

- They need to see sticks as well as carrots to prompt them to come to the table and do more than take what they can and then walk out, as they have every single time so far.

- Speaking frankly to the Palestinians, working with the Sunni Gulf states, Egypt, and Turkey to accept a reasonable security deal for Israel, and getting rid of UNWRA's definition of Palestinian refugees, a lethal poison pill for Israel, would be the beginning of the road to a two-state solution.

- Realistic?

So What to Do? 2022 Peace Proposal Yossi Beilin

- Israeli and Palestinian public figures have drawn up a new proposal for a two-state confederation that they hope will offer a way forward after a decade-long stalemate in Mideast peace efforts.

- The plan includes several controversial proposals, and it's unclear if it has any support among leaders on either side. But it could help shape the debate over the conflict and will be presented to a senior U.S. official and the U.N. secretary general this week.

- The plan calls for an independent state of Palestine in most of the West Bank, Gaza and east Jerusalem, territories Israel seized in the 1967 Mideast war. Israel and Palestine would have separate governments but coordinate at a very high level on security, infrastructure and other issues that affect both populations.

- The plan would allow the nearly 500,000 Jewish settlers in the occupied West Bank to remain there, with large settlements near the border annexed to Israel in a one-to-one land swap.

- Settlers living deep inside the West Bank would be given the option of relocating or becoming permanent residents in the state of Palestine. The same number of Palestinians – likely refugees from the 1948 war surrounding Israel's creation — would be allowed to relocate to Israel as citizens of Palestine with permanent residency in Israel.

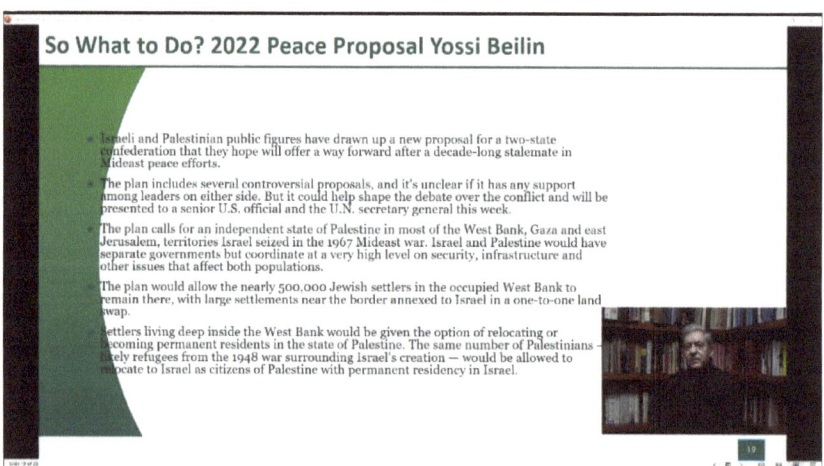

158

So What to Do? 2022 Peace Proposal

* Israeli and Palestinian public figures have drawn up a new proposal for a two-state confederation that they hope will offer a way forward after a decade-long stalemate in Mideast peace efforts.

* The plan includes several controversial proposals, and it's unclear if it has any support among leaders on either side. But it could help shape the debate over the conflict and will be presented to a senior U.S. official and the U.N. secretary general this week.

* The plan calls for an independent state of Palestine in most of the West Bank, Gaza and east Jerusalem, territories Israel seized in the 1967 Mideast war. Israel and Palestine would have separate governments but coordinate at a very high level on security, infrastructure and other issues that affect both populations.

* The plan would allow the nearly 500,000 Jewish settlers in the occupied West Bank to remain there, with large settlements near the border annexed to Israel in a one-to-one land swap.

* Settlers living deep inside the West Bank would be given the option of relocating or becoming permanent residents in the state of Palestine. The same number of Palestinians — likely refugees from the 1948 war surrounding Israel's creation — would be allowed to relocate to Israel as citizens of Palestine with permanent residency in Israel.

So What to Do? 2022-2023 Peace Proposals

Settlements are a major obstacle

* The initiative is largely based on the Geneva Accord, a detailed, comprehensive peace plan drawn up in 2003 by prominent Israelis and Palestinians, including former officials. The nearly 100-page confederation plan includes new, detailed recommendations for how to address core issues.

* Yossi Beilin, a former senior Israeli official and peace negotiator who co-founded the Geneva Initiative, said that by taking the mass evacuation of settlers off the table, the plan could be more amenable to them.

So What to Do? 2022-2023 Peace Proposals

- Israel's political system is dominated by the settlers and their supporters, who view the West Bank as the biblical and historical heartland of the Jewish people and an integral part of Israel.

- The Palestinians view the settlements as the main obstacle to peace, and most of the international community considers them illegal. The settlers living deep inside the West Bank — who would likely end up within the borders of a future Palestinian state — are among the most radical and tend to oppose any territorial partition.

- "We believe that if there is no threat of confrontations with the settlers it would be much easier for those who want to have a two-state solution," Beilin said. The idea has been discussed before, but he said a confederation would make it more "feasible."

So What to Do? 2022-2023 Peace Proposals

- **Thorny issues easier to address by two states in a confederation, architects of the plan say**

- The main Palestinian figure behind the initiative is Hiba Husseini, a former legal adviser to the Palestinian negotiating team going back to 1994 who hails from a prominent Jerusalem family.

- She acknowledged that the proposal regarding the settlers is "very controversial" but said the overall plan would fulfill the Palestinians' core aspiration for a state of their own.

- **There have been no serious Mideast talks for a decade**

- It's been nearly three decades since Israeli and Palestinian leaders gathered on the White House lawn to sign the Oslo accords, launching the peace process.

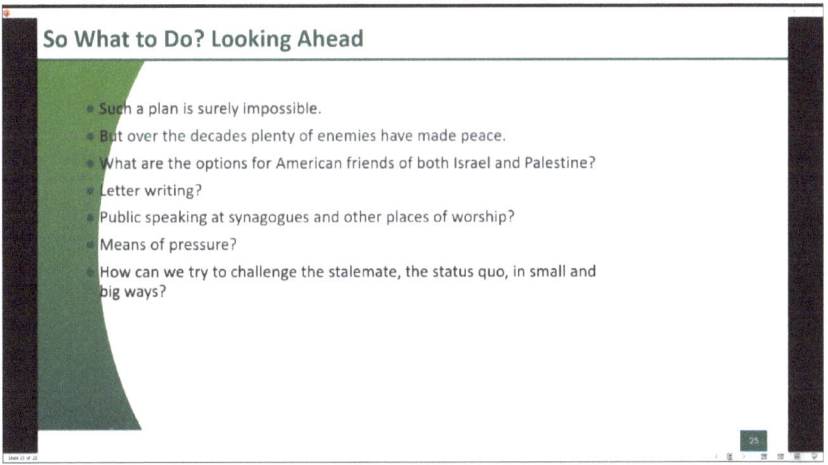

So What to Do? 2022-2023 Peace Proposals

- Several rounds of talks over the years, punctuated by outbursts of violence, failed to yield a final agreement, and there have been no serious or substantive negotiations in more than a decade. Former Prime Minister Yair Lapid supported the two state solution... but the current Israeli government vehemently opposes it.
- On the Palestinian side, President Mahmoud Abbas' authority is confined to parts of the occupied West Bank, with the Islamic militant group Hamas — which doesn't accept Israel's existence — ruling Gaza. Abbas' presidential term expired in 2009 and his popularity has plummeted in recent years, meaning he is unlikely to be able to make any historic compromises.
- The idea of the two-state solution was to give the Palestinians an independent state, while allowing Israel to exist as a democracy with a strong Jewish majority. Israel's continued expansion of settlements, the absence of any peace process and repeated rounds of violence, however, have greatly complicated hopes of partitioning the land.

24

So What to Do? Looking Ahead

- Such a plan is surely impossible.
- But over the decades plenty of enemies have made peace.
- What are the options for American friends of both Israel and Palestine?
- Letter writing?
- Public speaking at synagogues and other places of worship?
- Means of pressure?
- How can we try to challenge the stalemate, the status quo, in small and big ways?

25

Unfortunately, we can't go back in time. We can't wipe away all so easily the psychic and physical burdens and trauma from the *Nakba*. While all could have plausibly been resolved productively so many years ago, we can't just close our eyes and make it so. We can't return to 2016, 2022, or even 2023 conditions. The trauma for Israelis, Palestinians, and the world at large utterly changed on 10/7 and in the months since.

CHAPTER VI

SINCE 10/7 AND ONWARDS – HEARTBREAK, HUBRIS AND HORRORS

On October 5th, I found myself in Jerusalem unexpectedly. USAID had called a meeting of AIDA ExCom members with the Mission Director. This was a long-postponed quarterly meeting that had slid by from late August.

As I mentioned, we had a visiting technical advisor from Milan, Italy, for the GBV team, Laura Canali, working with Joy Mashedi, our Kenyan GBV Coordinator. I had planned to remain in Gaza over the weekend to spend time with Laura and Joy, visiting some historical sites outside Gaza City. With the change in plans, and since Friday and Saturday are the weekend in the Middle East, I spent Friday in Jerusalem taking care of shopping and other chores. I had initial plans early Saturday morning to drive down to the beach south of Tel Aviv near Holon to catch some sun. I preferred being outside of Jerusalem during *"Shabbat"* because of the virtual shutdown of most stores and services, either going to the beach or visiting one of the national parks around the country.

I awoke early Saturday morning to alarms and alerts from my phone. As a precaution, I installed at least one app to notify people of rockets. I would end up downloading others. It was clear immediately this would not be a beach day. But the news was sketchy; I first learned of the rockets and little else. I contacted our country security manager and some of our senior staff in Gaza to find out what they knew and to ask them to exercise extreme caution. I then contacted fellow members of the Executive Committee of the INGO network AIDA, the Association for International Development Agencies, to find out what others might know. Following protocol, I also briefed our global security specialists overseas from IMC HQ.

The news of the physical breaches in the fence with Gaza and the atrocities of Hamas on the ground would take hours. And it would seem to take even more hours for the Israeli Defense Forces to mount any resistance and counterattack to respond.

Following the usual precautions and practices in what we initially thought was a typical escalation, we instructed our staff to shelter in place and hibernate at the guest house. Joy and Laura were in Gaza that weekend, as another colleague had left with me for Jerusalem. Our soon-to-depart Medical Coordinator was the husband of the Mercy Corps International Country Director, who lived in Jerusalem. We compared notes; it was Shabbat, so the border was closed in any case, as it routinely was until at least Sunday morning.

To our surprise, it was clear that the rocket salvo from Gaza was far more significant than it had been in past escalations. There were alerts for the border regions of Israel with Gaza, but they also extended to alerts of incoming fire for Tel Aviv, central Israel, and even Jerusalem. Booms in the sky above Jerusalem and contrails pointed to the Israeli air defense system Iron Dome being activated by a massive number of rockets even there. There was little we could do but to hunker down and wait and see what would happen.

There had been minor rocket attacks in April, and in May, there was a significant escalation. During five days in May, nearly 1500 rockets had been launched from Gaza to Israel. At least ten percent were duds, falling back to earth in Gaza. Others fell into the Mediterranean. This attack in October, falling on the Jewish religious holiday of Simchat Torah and about two weeks after Yom Kippur, should not have been unexpected. The date was just after the symbolic 50th anniversary of the surprise attack of the Yom Kippur War; you'd have expected a certain level of readiness.

Moreover, things were polarizing and tense from the late summer. At meetings with the UN OCHA Humanitarian Country Team, different UN agencies expressed alarm at the drying up of available resources to support operations in Gaza. UNRWA, responsible for paying over 12,000 teacher and health clinic salaries, warned that they could not make payroll. The World Food Program representative warned that food and flour rations to Gaza would have to be cut, likely affecting bread prices on the streets in Gaza.

UN diplomatic security personnel previously noted other indicators that suggested a high likelihood of another escalation in September that might be deeper than the brief May 2023 spasm of violence. Some UN officials joked morbidly that September would be an excellent time to take a vacation and be away from the country. While this was all speculation, I had shared the same with our HQ visitors, but we concluded nothing actionable would force us to pull back or lower our profile in Gaza. Indeed, when October 1st came and went, it seemed things had eased.

The rockets continued to fly, and the initial delayed Israeli response came in the form of punishing airstrikes in Gaza from the Israeli Air Force to try to take out the mobile rocket launchers being used. But there was no let-up, and it seemed impossible to stop. I had a WhatsApp number to call and text for the Coordination Liaison Authority from COGAT, and I and other agency country directors sent messages confirming and attempting to de-conflict the locations of our expat staff in Gaza. Again, this was not unheard of and happened at least once a year. By the late afternoon on Saturday, news reports were coming in that dozens of Israelis had been taken hostage, something that had never happened before at this scale.

We told our local staff late Saturday that we would not open the office in Gaza on Sunday and that they should stay home and wait for further news. Panic buying started in Gaza in many shops, as the locals sensed this would not end soon or well. I called Israeli friends in Holon, Modiin, and the Galilee to check on them and express my deepest sympathies and shared horror at the unfolding disaster.

Over the next few days, the horror of the attack began to sink in. Reported casualties started coming in, and photos and videos from the border communities near Gaza. Over 1500 Israelis were initially reported dead; that number would be scaled back a bit eventually, but the magnitude of the loss of both civilians and security personnel was incalculable. This was as if over 40,000 Americans had been suddenly extinguished in terms of population proportion. The number of hostages was over 250, a mix of foreigners and Israelis, infants, children, and elderly among them.

The UN Humanitarian Country Team for the oPt in Sheikh Jarrah invited us to attend emergency meetings; I joined them with other AIDA colleagues to learn what they were finding out from UN personnel in Gaza and the West Bank. I stayed in constant contact with Joy, Laura, and our Gaza security manager to share what I knew and offer them solace and reassurance. I spoke frequently with our Palestinian country program lead at home in Bethlehem and with many of our Gazan staff. At the advice of our global security leads, our team activated a WhatsApp emergency channel to stay in contact with the 60 or so local staff in Gaza.

I don't want to offer a blow-by-blow description here of the savage and depraved attack by Hamas and Islamic Jihad militants. This is not journalism or an attempt to offer a comprehensive record.

Nothing I can say can make sense of or rationalize the violence, particularly the bloodthirsty horror committed by the Gazans who broke through the fence to Israel on 10/7. Israeli leaders called them *"animals, just human animals"*; that is an emotionally dehumanizing term that falls far short of reality. I don't know of any animals that suddenly attack the innocent unless they are predators for food, and no animal indulges in rape and desecration with another. No animal I know captures hostages for fun and bargaining chips. Unfortunately, as experts in conflict know, hostage-taking, gender-based violence, and rape are sadly not uncommon in conflict-fueled arenas. Nor is the giddy glee of violence associated with sudden explosive popular uprisings unknown elsewhere.

As the dust began to clear a bit in October from the inevitable fog of war, there were many sidebar reports that the 10/7 attack had "gotten away from Hamas," that they had had no idea of the success they would have in making several dozen breaks and penetrations into the fence separating Gaza from Israel. They had punctured the image of Israeli invulnerability. But when they managed to break through the wall with mobile arms, motorcycles, and even bulldozers, folks claimed that there was little apparent discipline to the many who surged across into southern Israel. There were reports that many criminals and other extremist groups surged across to commit murder and mayhem to take advantage of Hamas' unexpected success. In the ensuing week, it took many days, even weeks, for Israeli security forces to report with confidence that vast stretches of southern Israel were once again re-secured and cleared of terrorists and extremists.

One can't help but feel skeptical about this facile distinction, mainly if it is intentional or not to somehow exculpate what happened in the Nova Festival and the border communities. The Hamas extremists and terrorists were disciplined enough to be methodical in their attacks not only against the Israeli soldiers at the guard stations that dotted the fence but also the many hundreds of civilians hunted down. In this attack, Hamas and its associates were following the gamebook of terror; it's not the attack itself and the casualties it produces that is enough, but it is the terror induced in a civilian population because of the attack and the fear that they are no longer safe. The taking of hostages, particularly among civilians and even more so among children and older adults, also fuels terror, and it is at the heart of the utter rage that Israelis came to be swept by, of the sort found in so many Greek mythology tragedies.

Some would say that as an American, I have no right to comment or reflect on this rage and the terror. But I'm afraid I have to disagree. It's painful, but as an American Jew then living in the localities, I can be both empathetic to the horror of what happened and yet be able to distance myself sufficiently to be aware of the consequences.

I have been fully absorbed by the consequences in the almost eight months since the attack as of this writing. It was clear as day within days that the Israeli response to 10/7 would be ferocious, unforgiving, and uncompromising. It was also clear that this would be precisely what Hamas wanted through their hostage-taking and most depraved actions of desecration of the dead and violation of the living.

I stand in solidarity with my Israeli friends over the suffering and horror they've experienced. But that does not free me or absolve me of the heavy burden of empathy I also must feel over the dispossessed and innocents of Gaza and the West Bank.

During October, I remained in East Jerusalem, 100% focused on the well-being and safety of our staff in Gaza. During the first week of the month, things were initially stable in terms of lockdown, but we all began to worry as Israel announced it was poised for a massive invasion of Gaza. I called Joy, Laura, and our global security team daily. They were making connections with their counterparts at other organizations for crisis management.

In addition, AIDA was in emergency mode. The war had come at a challenging time for the NGO network. The previous

Executive Director, Joseph Kelly, had given notice in the spring as he and his family were moving to Kampala. For a number of reasons, we had followed a particularly lengthy recruitment effort to try to find a suitable replacement. I was on the panel that summer with the candidate reviews and interviews, and we had settled in the end on a choice that at any other time would have been seen as admirable and noteworthy.

After looking at the best candidates, we selected by consensus a young Palestinian development professional from Ramallah rather than the usual expat. He was dynamic and both wrote and spoke persuasively throughout the process, with relevant experience with the European Union and other project donors. We felt that he could help us move forward with a refreshed advocacy and strategic vision approach as a Palestinian. He had asked in September for about a month to start the new job, and with the start of the war, he was still not yet onboarded.

He started in mid-October, over a week after the 10/7 attack. But by that point, the West Bank was on a new level of lockdown, and he couldn't travel out of Ramallah and come to Jerusalem for meetings. The Israeli authorities were not issuing travel permits for Palestinians, and any prior ones had been automatically revoked. This did create a bit of a handicap for us from the start, which we had hoped we would eventually be able to manage.

The AIDA Gaza Coordinator, Dr. Moner Murtaja, who I had come to know for almost 18 months, was in hunker-down hibernation mode with his family but ably tried to open and sustain communications from the field with the AIDA Executive Committee, with AIDA members operating in Gaza and with UN officials in Gaza. He followed up with different NGOs with staff in Gaza, asking periodically for details of staff location to help collate master lists to provide to his counterparts in the UN Access Coordination Unit that negotiate regularly with Israeli COGAT officials who would presumably work with the Israeli Defense

Forces on deconfliction. This frequently did not fully work and would only get more problematic over time.

Meanwhile, UNRWA officials were raising the possibility that expat staff trapped in Gaza City might want or need to evacuate to a presumed safer location at the UNRWA compound, which was across the street from IMC's offices. They had initially resisted this support, wanting to limit access only to UN staff. Still, some INGOs without safer locations had been lobbying for this support from the UN inside Gaza.

The so-called safer space was actually just the interior lower-level ramps of a parking garage, where any NGO staff could bring their sleeping bags. It would be strictly BYOB, with no UN commitment to access to food or supplies.

It seemed problematic to me, and in discussing it with Joy and Laura, I didn't encourage the move. I thought they might be safer staying in our furnished and reasonably stocked expat apartments in what we called the Save the Children building. We'd also picked up some additional guests since Dr. Moner had asked if we could house two young Italian nationals from other organizations with nowhere else to go with the sealing off of Gaza. He was in contact with several diplomatic missions and received an urgent request from the Italian consulate; he immediately called me first and said, "You are always my lifesaver; we have people stranded with nowhere to go. Could you help?"

Though our HQ security team was concerned about liability issues, I authorized Eyas, our country security officer, to open the other apartments we rented and provide support. Our country security officer had access to the IMC vehicle, but it was also getting increasingly dangerous to circulate on the streets with the impending Israeli ground assault.

Unfortunately, within a few days, they did have to move. While the Israeli COGAT officer I spoke with by WhatsApp assured me our building was deconflicted, there were significant strikes by

Israeli bombs and shelling just nearby, which destroyed adjacent buildings and damaged our own, blowing in the windows.

Dr. Moner offered to take them to his command post just a few blocks away. There were multiple ways to enter and exit, making it hopefully safer for our people. That lasted a few nights, and they could ferry over food and mattresses. He went out and found other expats stranded from different organizations, and this area included several INGO guest houses. He provided immediate shelter in several cases and hosted them for quite some time. Soon, however, that building became less secure, and among the INGOs, we discussed other options. A WhatsApp group of different NGO country directors in AIDA with staff trapped in Gaza and some of the leaders from MSF and other groups debated the safer choice. Our staff relocated to the UNDP compound in Gaza City, crowded with people desperately seeking a safe haven. Almost all expats, including IMC staff, moved immediately. Moner was there to support.

At that point, we began to receive the alarming demands from the Israelis – evacuate Gaza City now. The Israeli military was ordering all civilians to move south below the midpoint like of Gaza at Wadi Ghazza and leave behind northern Gaza and Gaza City. This was the first of what would be a first of what would be a cascade of nightmare scenarios. The UN and the international NGO community protested loudly; an evacuation from the north of so many people with so short notice would create panic and suffering for innocent civilians. The Israelis insisted that this must be done; otherwise, people would be in grave danger. Indeed, many parts of the Remal neighborhood where our offices and guest house lay were being methodically flattened. Yet it was near-impossible for many, such as the elderly, the disabled and their caregivers, to relocate so swiftly.

I also reached out to our local staff to share the regular updates I was receiving from the Israeli military in terms of the demands for evacuation. Most of our local Gazan staff were indignant. Many refused to move. They did not want to leave their homes. I understood this attitude and could not order them to do so. Still, I felt I had to responsibly convey each threat and warning we were receiving from Israeli authorities with increasing impatience and alerts to impending danger. Where would people go? Where could they go?

At first, the demands were to move at least south of Wadi Ghazza, but that was clearly a line drawn in the sand, and with no clear place to stop there. Among the INGOs, it was also contentious.

Dealing with MSF as a group was not the easiest. *Medecins sans Frontières* was remarkable globally for its elevated mission to provide emergency medical assistance where few others dared to tread. But they had something of a cowboy ethos and did not play well with other organizations. Their local leadership would multiple times convey a message of "Our way or the highway," they had resisted formally fully joining AIDA as a network of organizations, staying as 'observers.' However, that didn't stop them from turning to AIDA when they needed information or assistance that AIDA, at times, was best able to provide.

UNRWA's compound was severely damaged after strikes nearby, which also blew in the walls and windows across the street at our offices. Our security manager entered and sent me photos and videos. The office on the second and third floors was essentially trashed and uninhabitable. It was striking and sobering. We'd been there just a year since our move in September 2022. So much equipment was damaged; it brought home to us that we could not return. We speculated among the INGO leadership what the Israelis were planning to do. Many thought the Israelis were going to come in and pancake and flatten almost every building in Gaza City. It was inconceivable.

We negotiated where to go next. AIDA pushed UNRWA to give us access to our expat staff at UN compounds further south. We finally got word that UNDP and other UN agency staff were planning a convoy south to the UNRWA Khan Yunus Teaching College (KYTC) on the outskirts of Khan Yunus. Our people did not drive; our country security officer was becoming increasingly unavailable because he was focusing on his family in northern Gaza and did not want to risk leaving them.

A Mercy Corps staff member from Nigeria admitted he drove and could drive the IMC vehicle south with Joy Laura and other NGO staff we were becoming responsible for. The convoy would include a half dozen vehicles and two dozen staff from MSF who were a significant presence in Gaza. We all had misgivings about the move, but we did not seem to have any alternative. We hoped our expats would be safe there and perhaps closer to a possible exit corridor if opened in Rafah that would permit the escape of expat staff to Egypt.

Based on the MSF security assessment and the UN plans for departure, we agreed on a time for departure in the early morning hours from the UNDP compound in Gaza City, only to discover a major disturbance outside the UNDP gates. A group of Gazans were blocking the exit. They said they did not want the expats to leave if there was no way for them to go, too. It was unclear if any instigation to protest or engagement came from the DFA. The UN had some security and some means to call the police, to the degree they were still active. No one, however, wanted to risk things to get out of hand and lead to any incitement of violence.

There was a lot of negotiation from the UNDP staff on the ground and others. Our people were delayed for hours, finally the gate opened, and they were able to leave. The IDF had supposedly deconflicted the convoy of vehicles but that was never a guarantee.

We carried a half dozen in the IMC car, and 34 expat staff from all of the AIDA agencies were in several other cars, notably two vehicles from Catholic Relief Services driven by local volunteers. MSF had another twenty staff in their cars.

I was told by Dr. Moner, who was leading in the field, that the situation was a terrible mess. AIDA co-led the convoy, but also Moner, who was in touch with several missions, informed the embassies of nationals in the convoys about the route and tried to ensure an extra layer of safety during the relocation. Despite the UN and Diplomatic missions, the road was perilous, and attacks were very close to the route. The people of Gaza were scared and followed the convoy to Khan Younis and other locations. The convoy was finally sent to the KYTC UNRWA facility. Shortly after INGO and UN staff arrived, the place was jammed with thousands of people hoping to find a safer shelter next to expats.

The UN staff numbered far more, and it was clear that they seemed to barely tolerate the NGO staff that sought to tag along under their protection during emergencies. In truth, we'd all experienced a similar attitude from the UN agencies on several occasions. During a hairy escalation of Israeli retaliatory rocket fire earlier in May of that year, the UN agencies would not agree to INGOs joining an evacuation of international staff from Gaza towards Erez Terminal, and there had been similar incidents in 2022 and 2021. There wasn't universal diffidence from UN colleagues; the then-UNRWA director in Gaza, Tom White, was an Australian and known friend and associate of INGOs. Several people supporting humanitarian assistance from UN OCHA were also INGO friends and sought to facilitate our work, although frankly, not always.

Part of the problem was also with the very concept of "evacuation." Several organizations and the UN agencies did not want locals to believe that they were fleeing and evacuating and leaving them in danger of Israeli forces. While humanitarian solidarity was understandable, most of these NGO staff, except for perhaps MSF, had not intended to have to endure total conflict and fighting. Many agencies argued for the ability to "rotate" out their staff and have some guarantees that the Israelis and Egyptians would open the Rafah Gate to allow expats to leave and others to take their places in Gaza. There were no guarantees on that, though.

It was a perilous journey south for Joy, Laura, and the others. Our people had a vital satellite phone for contact in addition to their cell phones and WhatsApp channels. We were in constant contact, and so were our global security managers. The trip south to Khan Yunus had previously been only about a half-hour drive, but it was far more with the increasing destruction and the Gazans beginning to flee Gaza City. Joy and Laura brought what supplies they could manage. Some of the expats in the convoy were younger and had less experience and were getting understandably frightened of the high-risk situation. In that, Laura and particularly Joy projected a calm and serenity, which was admirable and hopefully eased the nervousness of others.

The teaching college compound was in a terrible state and would only get worse as a point of temporary evacuation. UN local staff were also beginning to flee to the area with their families, and other Gazans began to come into the compound despite the efforts of security staff to hold them off. The vehicles initially thought of parking outside the compound and bringing in foam mattresses and supplies, but that proved a little problematic from a security standpoint. They brought the cars and tried to cordon off a space for the INGO expat staff. Food was minimal, but our local NGO colleagues from CRS were able to find food and safe water for them.

Unfortunately, within a couple of days, there were unconfirmed reports that specific extremist terrorist forces were coming too close to the teaching college compound and using it as a cover for mobile rocket launchers. This could easily be disastrous because even though COGAT and the IDF were notified of the locale to deconflict it from Israeli targeting solutions if there were rockets fired, then they would surely draw retaliatory responses. In addition, every six hours more and more people were fleeing into the facility. Within a short time, they had occupied all the classrooms and the washrooms available there. The population of refugees surged to reportedly close to 20,000 or more, huddled and looking for a safe space, many coming in from Gaza City or the Middle Area of Gaza. The refugees completely surrounded our expats and those of the UN and there was virtually no security at the UNRWA location.

Some of the IMC local staff, including our Program Team Lead in Bethlehem and the Technical Coordinator in Rafah, found several rooms for shelter in Rafah itself, further south. It had some electricity and solar panel cells, which was vital as Israel had cut off the fuel supply to Gaza, as well as electricity and water. While part of the space would be used for our Technical Coordinator and his family, I proposed that we make this space available for the expats on behalf of IMC. In discussions with our HQ security personnel, the fact that it would be closer to the Rafah Gate if and when that would re-open was also a positive.

However, this proved a bit controversial for some. Some, including MSF, were very opposed to separating from the rest of the UN convoy. Though we were not wanted by much of the UN, the argument went that if and when Rafah were to be re-opened, at least for the exit of international personnel, we should be ready to roll with the UN staff. Within another day or so, the UN team itself seemed to fracture. We learned that some staff from UNDP had moved away in the dark of night to rented apartments in Khan Yunus. IMC had been promised some of that space by the landlord in separate negotiations as well, but the landlord decided to cut and run to the higher bidder, and we could not afford to pay the price that UNDP would pay.

We brought up the plight of our NGO expat colleagues before the UN OCHA and the Humanitarian Country Team. There, we found some folks very bemused and still of mixed minds regarding any justification for the evacuation of the NGO staff. We were receiving all through this time daily situation reports from UN OCHA, with detailed information regarding losses and casualties on both the Israeli side and the Palestinian side. The situation on the ground was unraveling fast. We also received increasingly strident warning messages from the IDF regarding the need for Gazans as well as humanitarians to evacuate further south, despite repeated protestations from the UN that trying to force the mass movement of over one million Gazans could, in fact in itself, constitute a war crime.

Tom White from UNRWA suggested a compromise and told AIDA and the INGO community that he would support the move of the NGO staff to the UNRWA Logistics Base on the edge of Rafah. This would at least sustain a tie with some UN staff if they were at some point in a position to make a break for the border.

The cognizant AIDA country directors consulted and discussed the situation with the help of the Save the Children Country Director, who was serving as an interface and liaison with UN authorities. We consulted with Joy, Laura, and the other NGO staff – what did they feel would be best on the ground? Though consulting with them, it ultimately would be the call of the country directors, together with the help of our respective security staff from HQ.

We decided to drive the short distance to Rafah and the Logs Base, hoping it would be safer and more secure.

Up north, terrible atrocities had taken place. In a globally controversial attack, we learned on October 17th of a horrendous attack on our partner Ahli Arab Hospital in Gaza City. News reports from BBC and Al Jazeera conveyed reports from Palestinian officials of hundreds killed in an Israeli strike on the hospital, which was one of a few NGO facilities able to continue to offer services in the emergency room. But in a

reminder that a lie will fly around the world when the truth is tying its shoes, this was debunked, but the damage was done. There had been falling debris and explosions in the front parking lot area of AAH, where, unfortunately, perhaps 100 or more people were gathered. There were many casualties. But it proved to be from a falling Palestinian Islamic Jihad rocket that misfired and exploded midair and came down from an adjacent launch trajectory near the hospital. By that time, there were riots all over the West Bank and protests in many capitals worldwide. I repeatedly reached out to Sohaila Tarazi, the hospital director, and finally got word from her that she and her staff were OK and that the hospital was still functional.

This was a dreadful and complicated story. It was not the Israelis' fault – that time. But there had already been multiple incidents of Gazan health facilities and ambulances hit by Israeli mortar shells, drones, and missiles. It was, in hindsight, a dark and infamous turning point in world opinion for many. Before that, Israel had earned the sympathy of much of the world for the horrendous 10/7 attack and the fate of the hostages. Sadly, for many it seemed that Palestinians and some of their sympathizers seemed incapable of recognizing the barbarity of 10/7 regardless of the history of the suppression and oppression of Palestinians in the occupied Palestinian territories. But generally speaking, this was not the case. Many Palestinian activists and analysts explicitly condemned Hamas' attack and mistreatment of Israeli civilians on 10/7, even while political leaders stayed quiet. But the nature of the Israeli retaliation after 10/7 quieted many if not most of those.

The tide began to turn when Israel hardened a bombing campaign across Gaza within days and began its ground operation into Gaza a week later, on October 14. The attack on AAH three days later was catastrophic in terms of public relations and crisis management by Israel. And it seemed to those of us on the ground that rather than use this incident to reflect and re-assess what they were doing, the Israelis doubled down on the level of violence, which all too often appeared to be indiscriminate. The violence would come close again and again near AAH and the nearby Christian church facilities protecting hundreds of refugees in improvised shelters.

The UNRWA logs base was reasonably well organized and outfitted. The expats moved the NGO vehicles into a sheltered area of the compound inside an inner gate near the garage area housing UNRWA vehicle assets. However, UNRWA staff on the ground said that the NGO staff would be allowed to stay there only temporarily, perhaps only 24 hours, and under no circumstances would be allowed to get shelter inside the compound buildings and offices. That would be reserved only for UN staff. The NGO staff could stay outside with the cars in an area partially protected from the crowds of refugees making their way to Rafah.

Our NGO staff were courageous, resilient, and resourceful. Though there was no real protection against the sun or elements, they managed to improvise some lean-tos. They began to set up regimens of yoga, meditation, and language training to take their minds off the risks, danger, and tremendous uncertainty. They politely ignored the local UNRWA demands about staying only 24 hours. We protested this back to other UN officials in Jerusalem and contacted Tom White from UNRWA, who had been caught outside the country. We kept making constant calls with them through WhatsApp, sat phone, or any other means, and we tried to keep their spirits up. Some of our staff slept in the IMC car occasionally. Still, they were also sharing space with the Gazan family of a local CRS driver who had come to help drive the vehicle in return for safer accommodations with the expat team. The few local staff helped to scout for provisions and supplies. It would also help make contact between our expat team and the local IMC staff in the region, many of whom had regrouped, fleeing with their families to Khan Yunus and Rafah ahead of the Israeli invasion force.

It was not the most comfortable arrangement. I asked myself how I would have handled things if I had, too, been stuck in Gaza and forced to flee and camp out without much protection from base to base. Would I have measured up as well as some of our NGO staff there?

As we debated with our security team and other NGO colleagues, the situation on the ground continued to deteriorate. After a week or so there, with temperatures beginning to drop outside in the evening, the Logs Base was also becoming untenable. Security was compromised in several ways.

Reportedly, some UNRWA and other UN agency staff were planning on fleeing the location soon and moving to villas located in what the Israelis had taken to call the Al Mawasi Humanitarian Zone to the west, near the shoreline.

The group of INGO country directors debated again on WhatsApp. I pushed again for the IMC rented space to be considered a realistic option. MSF was still worried about staying close to the UN and insisted on following them. One French NGO, PUI, dropped a bomblet on us to say they had found a small house near the Humanitarian Zone, but there would only be room for them and MSF. So much for the universal push for unity and sticking together. We absorbed this news and shared it with our expat staff in the field. Some colleagues worried when others expressed concerns that the IMC space might be too congested an area in part of Rafah. PUI was joined brashly in the end by an Italian-Palestinian couple from a small Italian NGO. But in the end, most of our people from the five NGOs stuck together and decided to move out to the IMC space after considering other alternatives that might have implied doubling back to Khan Yunus, even further from the Rafah Gate portal, which remained sealed.

There was a frankly hare-brained idea from some USAID Mission staff for a way out of Gaza, which I won't entirely go into. Still, it would have subjected the humanitarian staff and agencies to considerable risk and danger. It was impractical and it would have represented a violation of our humanitarian code. It was clear that though they claimed to be in constant negotiations with the Israeli government and military leadership, there was no special powers or influence that American officials had or were willing to exercise in the effort to rescue our expat colleagues, who included some elderly Americans from one organization. And of course, given the continuing adherence to the no-contact policy, they had zero influence over the de facto authorities in Gaza without any intercessions from third party countries like Egypt or Qatar.

The IMC space was not a cake walk but it proved safer than other options. Our local space Emergency Technical Coordinator, an acerbic and sometimes cranky and idiosyncratic older Palestinian physician, who I had designated earlier as the senior IMC Gaza staff member on the ground in Gaza, received the 34 expats with a mix of welcome and resignation. He tried to help with water and electrical connections for the team, so that they could re-charge cell phones and the sat phone. He too had an IMC sat phone as well, although a different and more problematic model. Our expat staff, however, were initially startled and fearful when they saw the amount of destruction in some nearby buildings and worried about the choices we'd made.

In the end though it proved providential and safe. There was less stress than at the UNRWA base; Joy and Laura told me the next day that they and other expats had slept better than they had for many days, and it certainly must have helped to be indoors and away from the weather and prying eyes.

We continued to push U.S. Embassy and USAID Mission staff for help in getting the Israelis and Egyptians to open Rafah Gate. Our lobbying was incessant, at the field level but also at the HQ levels. Not limited by any means to just the rescue of our expats, some of whom were in precarious conditions of health. Most of our agencies pushed constantly for a humanitarian ceasefire, and for free passage of the huge amount of humanitarian assistance goods that were beginning to pile up on the Egyptian side of the border, and at the El Arish airbase in northern Sinai. We also pushed constantly for the safe passage across Gaza of humanitarian assistance. But the Israelis were hearing almost none of it.

Some of the more junior humanitarian USAID staff were at least on the face of it empathetic and seemingly concerned and asked daily for updates on our expat and local staff presence and movements in Gaza. They wanted to know how many remained in the north and why, and what the status was on injuries. They seemed to understand that virtually all our local staff were not able to actually work productively but were in survival mode. Like many others, our organization had advanced pay within a couple weeks of the onset of the broader war and had looked for ways to make resources available electronically for them. At that point, as we approached the end of October 2023, food was still available in many places but getting more expensive, and it was risky to go out and forage for supplies.

I was contacted several times by Italian Consulate officials regarding some of the Italian nationals that were in our party in Gaza. I also spoke several times with officials from the UK Foreign, Commonwealth and Development Office, including their newly arrived Humanitarian Officer, and we shared the driblets of news that each had been secured from different parts. We sent word to the Egyptian Foreign Ministry about our expat staff and shared the relevant passport information. I worried primarily about Joy as I and my HQ colleagues could only guess whether she as a Kenyan would get the same treatment as Americans and Europeans.

There were some false alarms that Rafah Gate would open imminently. The Israelis sent word, as did the Americans. But several times it was supposed to happen, nothing changed. There was an Israeli airstrike close to the Rafah Gate, which, according to the Egyptians, damaged some of their infrastructure, and so they halted the opening. A series of short humanitarian pauses were put into effect by the Israeli Defense Forces to reportedly encourage more traffic south on two critical routes from northern Gaza to the south, and Khan Yunus and Rafah were beginning to swell even more with populations of internally displaced people. We worried about how this would affect an exit from Gaza.

CRS had sent some of their Egyptian vehicles and staff to the other side a few days before, waiting for the possible exit of the INGO staff. Finally, on November 1st, Rafah Gate opened, and we instructed our vehicles to head to it. The queues were agonizingly long, and the Egyptians had announced that only foreigners could leave at that point. Still, it had turned out that there were many thousands of dual national, and in some cases tri-national, Gazans who were able to claim and demonstrate citizenship outside of Gaza and the occupied Palestinian territories. We worried whether our people would make it through.

It took many hours for them to negotiate multiple gates and checkpoints set up by the Egyptians. Finally, after over eight hours of queueing and as the sun was setting, we got word – they were through without a hitch or mishap. As it turned out the Italian Consulate in Cairo had also sent a vehicle for some of its nationals, and Laura was able to connect with them. However, thanks to our friends from CRS, there was room for all the expats to be transferred from the Egyptian side of Rafah to Cairo, though it would be another five hours on a relatively insecure road with lots of Egyptian checkpoints until they finally were able to make it hotels there.

Our expat staff would rest a couple of days in Cairo but then catch flights home; Joy would go back to Nairobi to join her family with some well-deserved extended leave to help recuperate from the arduous experience of the three and ½ weeks of internal displacement and danger; Laura flew back ever quicker to Milan to be with her parents.

Though we briefly paused, we remained focused on what we could do for our local staff remaining in Gaza and elsewhere. As it turned out, we had a few who had been caught outside of Gaza. Our local senior finance manager had been in Croatia for training when the fighting had started;. At the same time, his Croatian colleagues encouraged him to stay and be safe, he was worried about his Gazan family in north Gaza and two weeks later travelled to Amman first and then to Cairo to be able to return to Gaza when IMC would be able to rotate humanitarian staff into Gaza. Two other program staff were in support of activities on the West Bank and within a few weeks were able to surrender to Israeli military authorities and faced a painful but relatively safe process of repatriation to Gaza, as Israel did with hundreds of Gazans who were similarly caught by surprise outside of Gaza.

During November, IMC's HQ was approached by USAID's Bureau of Humanitarian Affairs with the idea of staging a field hospital in southern Gaza. Could it be done, and if so how and at what cost? IMC had undertaken a comparable effort in war-torn Ukraine. The logistics demands were far more complex and dangerous in Gaza.

Deploying limited temporary field hospitals was a controversial question for the World Health Organization (WHO) Mission in Jerusalem and other UN agency partners as well as some INGOs. Emergency medical care facilities and practitioners were needed precisely because of the increasing scale of destruction of Gazan hospitals and health clinics. By that point only a dozen hospitals were working on a minimally functional basis and within another few weeks almost all would be taken offline.

So many health clinics managed by UNRWA were hit in strikes and so many doctors and nurses were killed. Even by mid-November it was clear that medical personnel and humanitarian assistance workers were not only victims of happenstance in attacks, but there was an increasing body of evidence suggesting that they were in fact being targeted in Gaza by the IDF. So, installing a small field hospital with 50-100 beds, in the face of thousands of Gazan casualties, would be a drop in the bucket. In any case, the management of this question was quickly set aside from the country mission and put in the hands of the HQ Emergency Response Unit.

In the local Israeli media the focus was understandably on the hostages, both Israeli and foreign. Huge protests had begun again against the Israeli Prime Minister and the Cabinet for not prioritizing the steps needed to save the hostages. There had been some brief humanitarian pauses achieved for a few days at a time, in which small groups of hostages were released in exchange for the release of many Palestinian prisoners in Israel, many of whom had been held for years without trial or convictions.

I felt great empathy for the Israelis in this situation. This had been arguably the first time in Israeli history that no obvious or major efforts were being made to secure the release of the hostages, many of whom were elderly or children. Israelis I met were stunned by this aberration, which they saw as a breaking of faith by the Israeli government. After a month of the Israeli military retaliatory operations against Gaza, I could not see how the remainder of the hostages would survive long enough to be rescued or released given the intensity and seeming abandonment of care to avoid civilian casualties.

Almost every day of the week I fielded messages from our local staff. While the initial "shock and awe" of Israeli ground forces, the drones and other naval and aerial attacks left all scrambling for cover, slowly a few staff began to let us know they wanted to do more than just survive; they wanted to help in any way they could. About a dozen sent messages along those lines, and a half dozen were able to share photos of care being to neighbors, family members and anyone they could reach showing wound dressing, psychosocial counseling sessions and directed play activities to help traumatized children.

In mid-November, our Senior Health Advisor Dr. Jill John-Kall had managed to find some funds to set up a Primary Trauma Care training of trainers for medical and nursing practitioners who might be willing to consider deploying into Gaza when that proved possible, most likely through the Rafah Gate on the Egyptian border. This was a great initiative. Dr. Jill had actually visited us in Gaza in late June for a ten-day field visit, working with our health team staff and she had previously been to Gaza a couple years before I had arrived.

Dr Jill looked at options for locations, and ultimately planned to go with the Egyptian Pediatric Association in Cairo, adjacent to the Cairo Pediatric Cancer Hospital. I offered to travel to Cairo to observe and see how we might be able to apply this more broadly.

I flew to Cairo, which was suddenly not easy. Since the start of the war, many different international airlines had stopped flying into Ben Gurion Airport outside Tel Aviv. Egypt had also interrupted direct flights to Cairo. The IMC travel office had difficulty finding connections. At last, we managed to find seats flying to Cairo via Athens and a return four days later via Larnaca, Cyprus.

When I arrived at the airport on the morning of November 27, I was taken aback by a virtually empty terminal. There seemed to be only 10% of the usual number of people for a Monday. The only flights operating appeared to be those of Israel's flag airline, ELAL.

Dr. Jill had arranged for the course to be deployed by three experienced British trauma doctor volunteers under the umbrella of the Primary Trauma Care Foundation. I met them at the Cleopatra Hotel, just off the famous and traffic-clogged Tahrir Square, near the huge looming Egyptian Museum.

After a little bit of a slow start, there proved to be a good number of Palestinian doctors as well as Egyptians who claimed to be interested in serving in Gaza. Dr. Jill reached out to the Palestinian Red Crescent Society branch hospital in Cairo. All this was done at a modest cost and would be followed by a later replica in Amman, Jordan.

The trauma training was a low-budget but hands-on affair. Though Dr. Jill had secured some training tools and partial mannequins to work on, the British doctors wanted more life-like tools. A short walk one evening from the Cancer Hospital, it turned out there was a livestock market with sheep, goats, and cow heads and a camel market.

It was hilarious walking through this with the trauma docs while they picked out the vivisection pieces from the market that would most do, while we dodged the speeding minibikes, scooters, and taxis

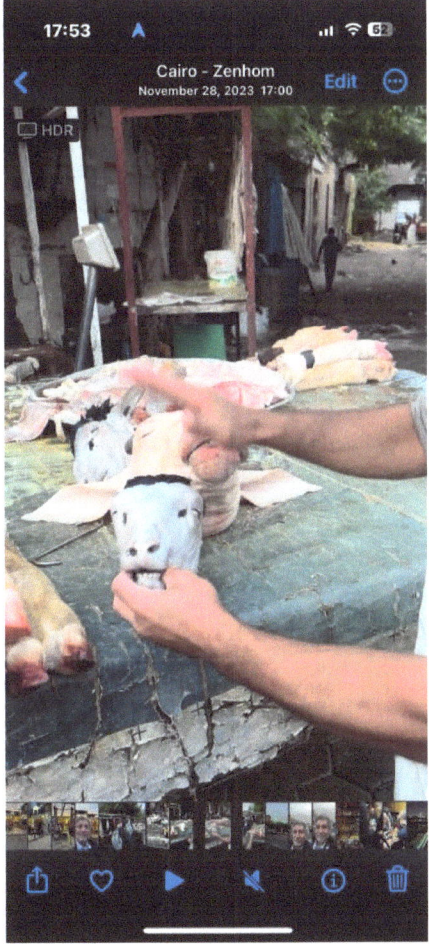

going through brazenly the market streets.

I took advantage of being in Cairo to head to the south of the city where the HQ Emergency Response Unit and the Regional Logistics Team had set up a provisional base of operations to support the entry of the field hospital on pallets – 'the hospital in a box' -and other logistics. I met with some of the staff members and discussed the challenges with logistics on the Egyptian side. They described many of the problems as being very high risk; there were many stories from many organizations about the constant problem of pilfering of foreign humanitarian assistance.

Moreover, Egyptian security did not allow continuous tracking and monitoring of the supplies when they landed by plane at the El Arish airbase in northern Sinai. In theory, there were UN officials keeping tabs on things. Still, clearly, there was a lack of strong enough security and no guarantees that materials coming in would make it to the border with Rafah. On the Egyptian side, sole control of distribution was in the hands of the Egyptian Red Crescent, which was not an organization known for its competence and management capabilities. Also, on the Gaza side, the Palestinian Red Crescent Society controlled distribution in Rafah, and it was hard to ensure that the full integrity of specific shipments would remain intact in the face of the tremendous need on the Gazan side. The UN had introduced a QR code system with shipments, which was still inadequate.

It was unclear, of course, how the entry of foreign emergency assistance would play out. All during the previous five weeks, when the Israelis had grudgingly indicated they would allow the flow of humanitarian assistance into Gaza and even had contacted me to see how they might help in some way with the deployment of outside field hospitals into Gaza, it remained a hotly disputed question. When INGOs like IMC or Save the Children attempted to get clearance for humanitarian assistance, there would inevitably be delays and obstructions, and even when approvals were forthcoming, they would often be held up at the border of Rafah with a demanding inspection routine.

Medical supplies would be routinely blocked due to claims by the Israelis that items in shipments were 'dual-use' and could be captured and manipulated by Hamas for military purposes. Oxygen tanks for field hospital purposes were blocked like that. So were straightforward birthing and OB/GYN kits desperately needed in Gaza because they held small sterile scissors to help cut the umbilical cords of newborns.

It was an almost impossible situation, and I wondered how IMC would get the field hospital in. The planned equipment, installation, and supplies would add up to three shipping containers

of goods carefully packed for deployment; they would require entry with three trucks and with care and oversight that no items from the trucks would be disturbed or removed, otherwise putting at risk the entire enterprise.

On my third morning in Cairo, the day before I departed, I took a taxi very early to the pyramids and visited briefly before the scheduled training. Traffic was light, and the Uber I found got me there in less than a half hour. After some technology

problems at the cashier point of sale – it was hard to pay with a card when the internet was wobbly, and no cash was accepted – I walked inside the pyramid complex and marveled first at the Great Sphinx of Giza.

I studied it in the early morning light. The Egyptians claimed it was 4,500 years old. Yet some recent studies showed evidence that it was mainly carved out in one entire piece much earlier, perhaps 12,000 years ago, during catastrophic melts from the last Ice Age. I found the arguments and controversies fascinating.

My family and I visited Egypt on a vacation in 2008 from Nigeria; my last visit was on a work visit in 2014 while assigned as Deputy Mission Director for USAID in Iraq. In the intervening nine years, it had been entirely built up further. But I went loping up the trail to reach the first of the three pyramids a mile from the gate. It was early morning, before 8 am, and I was almost the only "tourist" there.

I snapped plenty of photos from my phone while fending off at least a half dozen camel drivers and horse carriages, trying to secure my business for touristy rides. I didn't want to start all that since I had planned to visit for less than an hour and then head back to the Egyptian Pediatric Association. I tried to walk and contemplate the scenery without many tourists and interruptions.

However, this old, scrawny Egyptian carriage driver followed me and pleaded with me. "Please bless my day, be my first customer, and bring me luck. You look like you have a kind face.

I sighed and asked how much.

"Only 400 Egyptian pounds. For you, 300." That was only about $6.30.

"Ok, Ok," I said. "But only for about 30 minutes, and we don't need to stop at tourist traps. Just let's head up and around them."

The old horse pulling the carriage was unconvinced and didn't seem to want to go anywhere. I should have taken it as a sign, though we got underway and hoofed along the stone way. We went up between and around the pyramids, and I took plenty of photos and some videos. The horse carriage driver spoke in broken English and joked and laughed, and I laughed along with him. After a bit, I asked him to head back and bring me down to the complex's front gate, where I would try to catch a taxi to the outside.

We were trotting along, and suddenly, I saw the horse lurch to the left, and the left carriage wheel went up a cement barrier in the middle of the path. We hit hard, and as time slowed, I saw us all flipping into the air. The carriage flipped to the right and upside down in the air; the horse flew upside down, and the two of us went airborne. I remember thinking I had to protect my head, neck, and hips when we came down, and I tried to roll out of the way. The carriage driver on my left was flying across to my right, and the carriage came down on top of his legs and the side of my knee. It must have been less than a second, but it all seemed in slow motion.

I found myself in severe pain, but the carriage driver was even worse. Suddenly, vendors and others appeared where few people had been noticeable before. Tourist police came running. Someone brought me a chair out of nowhere, but I couldn't easily sit.

"Help him, help him!" I shouted.

They pulled the old man out from under the carriage. Others seemed to take the horse away. It seemed like the horse was shaken but able to walk. The old man, though, looked like he had two broken legs, and he was howling constantly in agony.

Everyone was asking in English and Arabic if I was OK.

"Please call an ambulance," I asked.

No one moved.

"Ambulance. Doctor for him. *Al Assaf! Tabib!*" Several went running, and soon an ambulance came.

My back and side were hurting fiercely, as was my knee. I wondered if I'd hurt my right kidney or something. I called Dr. Jill back in Cairo. She was alarmed and told me to go to the ER. She mentioned a few places but I thought they looked far away on my phone.

Finally, the ambulance arrived, and after they carried the old man into it, I tried to climb in and join him.

"*La la la la.*" No, no, not for you. They were very reluctant to let me ride in the same ambulance as the carriage driver. The tourist police took me to a small sub-office and questioned me briefly about what had happened.

The cop looked at me meaningfully and asked, "Do you want to file a complaint against the carriage driver?" This seemed to be what he most wanted to talk about.

I shook my head. It was a freak accident. How could I file charges against this poor man? I imagined he must have somehow gone into a daze of distraction and didn't realize where he was steering the cart.

"*La la. Min fadlik*, please I need a taxi to take me away. If you can't do that I will search for myself."

Soon, I was crossing town, and I decided against going to the ER for now. I wanted first to go to the Egyptian Pediatric Association, where the course was being held, and we had several highly qualified trauma doctors there.

Sitting in the car was agony, but I made it, even though morning traffic was already building up. I called Dr. Jill to let her know I was coming in. She said she would arrange a hired car at the location to go to an ER, and she would take me herself.

Meanwhile, our trauma doc volunteers, Dr. Swati, got on the phone and teased me a bit with Dr Jill. "We come a few thousand miles to teach trauma to these Palestinian doctors, and who knew the first trauma case we would have been our Mission Director here!"

I was rueful. It had been such a freak accident. I wished I had followed my gut feeling and not accepted the carriage offer. After arriving at the training site, Dr. Jill promptly took me to the Dar el Fouad Hospital Emergency Room with a driver. I soon realized that to get to it meant close to another hour in the car with the midday traffic, as the hospital was on the Giza right bank side of the Nile, across the river from our training center. I probably should have just gone on my own to it and met up with Dr Jill there.

Nonetheless, Dr. Jill was enormously helpful in insisting they give me prompt care at the ER. Compared to what would have been the wait in an American Emergency Room, I got kingly service in less than an hour. The chief resident quickly scheduled X-rays, CAT scans, and Ultrasound checks. What he didn't do, to my slight amusement, was do a physical eyeball check of the injured sites, which I suggested after he might want to also do. He did this quickly and with aplomb, and after a short wait for the price of about $100, I got all the results.

I got the sense that he was embarrassed at what he thought was charging me too much, care that in the States would have been probably in the thousands. He decided, however, that there were no broken bones, just contusions and internal bruising.

I was given anti-inflammatories and simple painkillers and told to be patient since the pain would probably get worse for a couple of days before getting better over time. Dr. Jill and I returned to Cairo, where she dropped me at the hotel after we picked up the

prescriptions from a local pharmacy. I decided to rest a bit for the remainder of the afternoon, although, in truth, it hurt far less when I stood up and walked rather than sitting down. We met again with the team for dinner at a nearby local restaurant within walking distance from the hotel and Tahrir Square.

That night, I texted Dr. Zahra, a trauma doc friend in London, who warned me that if I felt some congestion in my chest, to cough up and bring up whatever was building up there. Zahra had formerly worked with IMC in Syria, was also a talented poetess and calligrapher and had been a candidate for the Medical Coordinator job in IMC Palestine after the war started, until she opted to return to Syria with another organization. She explained that one of the secondary consequences of an injury like this, even if I had not punctured a lung, was that due to the pain of coughing from the ribcage and diaphragm, a patient might typically suppress the cough. Doing so and not coughing up any accumulated fluid could inadvertently allow that fluid to build up in the lungs, potentially risking pneumonia.

I followed Dr. Zahra's advice and was glad that I did. Though the Egyptian emergency room attending physician had assured me nothing was broken, as I felt myself along the side, I had a strong sense that at least one rib was indeed broken, and maybe more. Indeed, as I would come to confirm with my doctor in Tel Aviv the following week, two ribs had been broken, and I had been fortunate they had not shifted and punctured the lung or pleural cavity.

I left Cairo on Friday, December 1. I had decided to spend a long weekend relaxing and taking it easy in Cyprus rather than directly continuing to Tel Aviv. I had never been and took advantage of seeing a bit of the western and eastern reaches of the island, and even spent one day crossing the border into 'occupied Cyprus,' the northern 40% of the island which had been illegally invaded by Türkiye which had created the separatist Turkish Republic of Northern Cyprus. I wasn't in the mood for any tourism, of course, but I did psychologically need to decompress and manage my healing.

The border, with UN observation lines still traversing the city of Nicosia, was not too complicated to cross and then return. Still, I couldn't help the reminders in some way of the border wall divisions between Israel and Palestine, particularly with the West Bank. The whole world, except for Türkiye (and perhaps Russia), refuses to recognize the TRNC, just as the entire world, except Israel, refuses to acknowledge the occupation and annexation of Palestinian lands.

However, though some neighborhoods in Nicosia still looked damaged and pockmarked from the Cypriot civil war, there had been a cold peace and coexistence for years. The amount of Russian and other foreign housing, hotel, and tourist investment in the rump piece of Cyprus and the northern coast was remarkable. There was a fantastic ancient castle in Girne (Kyrenia), northern Turkish Cyprus. I found it quite healing to spend a few hours walking along the sea wall, breathing in the Mediterranean, and pondering the next steps.

I got back to Tel Aviv and Jerusalem a few days later. To my dismay, I learned that HQ had made decisions that I was deeply troubled by. The attacks on the Gazans in both the north and the south had increased, and many INGOs had increased their calls for a humanitarian ceasefire.

Ours was not one of them, and I was warned not to sign any statements on behalf of IMC that would suggest otherwise.

Though official U.S. government policy had tiptoed in the direction of some partial calls for a humanitarian pause to provide a space for the release of Israeli hostages, it seemed that the State Department was following uncritically the position of the Israeli government that no cessation of combat would take place until the destruction of Hamas.

Several resolutions would come up in the UN Security Council for Gaza ceasefire votes, and I was ashamed to see that the U.S. would veto them. I found it impossible to defend or explain these actions to our desperate local staff and other INGO colleagues.

Within days, I had an even more acute emotional blow from a loss I could not come to terms with or accept. Up to December 7, by some miracle, none of the local staff of IMC nor other INGOs in Gaza had died in the two months of the war. Some, of course, had tragically lost family members or had been hurt in building bombings and airstrikes. But there had been no deaths yet of staff themselves.

This changed with the tragic and senseless news of the death of Hassan al Ramlawi, the young logistics assistant whose wedding I had attended in Gaza a little over four months before. Our entire staff was crushed and demoralized by the hateful news. When I called my wife in the States to tell her, she could not stop crying. I felt paralyzed and dead inside, hit by waves of horror, rage, and impotence at being unable to protect the wellbeing of my staff.

In the days just before, I had heard that his older sister had been arrested at an Israeli checkpoint, and no one knew her whereabouts. She had been working with UNRWA. This was a widespread fear of Gazans as they moved about from the north to the south. They feared arbitrary and unjustified detention, with no explanations or clue of the reasons. Their mother, Sahar, who was the manager of our child protection team in Gaza, called me in tears to ask my help and to try to find out where she was and when she would be released. I had been checking all my UN contacts to ask for help and had confirmed that UNRWA itself was also asking questions about the safety and whereabouts of their staff.

And now – to learn of the reported death by a sniper of Hassan – we all felt a blow like a punch to the stomach. Hassan had remained behind in Gaza City as many had fled south if they could. His mother had refused to leave, and he wanted to help his mother. I heard from colleagues in Gaza that Hassan had gone out one day with his brother in the dusk, looking for pure water, and he had been shot dead and his brother wounded.

I shared the news with the USAID Mission staff, who offered words of bereavement and condolences. I shared it with fellow members of the Executive Committee of AIDA, and all came together in solidarity with me. Some of our local staff prepared a death notice and wanted to post it on the IMC Gaza Facebook page and other social media.

International Medical Corps
الهيئة الطبية الدولية

We were deeply saddened to learn of the passing of our colleague and friend,

HASSAN N. RAMLAWI
May 7, 1990 - Dec 7, 2023

Who was tragically killed while searching for water to provide for his family in Gaza. Our thoughts and prayers are with his family during this difficult time. May he rest in peace.

To my great consternation, IMC HQ's Global Comms lead forbade us from doing so. We were instructed not to post it because it was supposedly against IMC policy. I had examined the wording, which was moderate to me and not excessively polarizing, simply stating the facts as we knew them. I could not understand that posture, nor could my AIDA colleagues.

Hassan's death was horribly just the beginning. But it would not be the last; within days, humanitarian staff at CARITAS Jerusalem, Save the Children, Humanity & Inclusion, Mercy Corps, and others were wantonly killed, sometimes even in Christian churches. Indeed, there are so many victims in a war like no other this century, with so many humanitarians, aid workers, doctors, nurses, and journalists targeted and killed. Just like our colleagues at World Central Kitchen.

This was a December of horror, despair, and disillusionment. The Christian episcopal leaders in Jerusalem announced that there would be no holiday celebrations for Christmas in the Old City, as

Christians were equally under siege and under attack and not only in Gaza. Even in East Jerusalem and the West Bank, a series of attacks against Christian properties and organizations had been unleashed. These attacks on Christians and Christian institutions were not coming from Muslims; they were coming from extremist orthodox Jewish groups and, in some cases, by institutions of the State of Israel.

I felt like damaged goods. I thought that I was powerless to do more constructive and assertive things to help my staff and the people of Gaza. And I wasn't the only one to feel that way. Many of my AIDA colleagues felt the same. My friend Jason Lee, a young Australian who was the Country Director of Save the Children in Palestine, bravely volunteered to re-enter Gaza under UN auspices and to spend two weeks at an improvised UN logistics base in the Al Mawasi corridor. But he came away with a bad taste in his mouth from the lack of faith and fidelity from donor governments and UN Member States and the ability of the UN to push the needle at all in terms of demanding the protection for unobstructed delivery of humanitarian assistance. Jason, however, had been able to speak out forcefully on social media and in new interviews with Al Jazeera and other international news outlets. Save the Children and other organizations were fearless in their expressions of outrage and demands for accountability. I had no such ability to advocate publicly and no means to deliver a comparable message.

I felt obliged to resign as Mission Director, effective at the end of December. I would remain in Jerusalem and do what I could but depart the country just before Christmas. As a free agent, I hoped that I could do more in speaking out. When I shared the news with my AIDA country director colleagues, all were sympathetic and understanding, and I saw that at least three of them were also planning to leave within a month or two more.

In the ensuing weeks, I began to make my goodbyes. I notified our points of contact with the Israeli Defense Forces and COGAT, an acronym for the Israeli military branch, which served as the Coordinator of Government Activities in the [occupied] Territories. I was correct and even-tempered in my messaging because I did not want to burn any bridges at operational levels. To my great surprise, I received multiple calls from them, expressing deep sadness and regret that I had resigned and would be leaving. They said they hoped I could return to Israel, perhaps under other circumstances and arrangements. Though I had been critical repeatedly with them, including their messages demanding the evacuation of local staff in Gaza from one part of Gaza to another, they said they had always respected and appreciated my candor and apparent impartiality.

I met with Anton Asfar, the genial and deeply experienced General Secretary and Executive Director, and his staff of CARITAS Jerusalem in an emotional goodbye in their offices at the Notre Dame Catholic Archdiocese compound, across from the Old City New Gate. We shared and prayed in solidarity for the suffering of the Gazan and Palestinian people we served and the safety of our humanitarian staff on the ground.

I visited Israeli friends in Holon, Poria Illit, and elsewhere to say goodbye and to pray for a resolution of the horrors afflicting all peoples in the Holy Land. The daughter of dear friends lost her fiancé at the Nova Festival massacre; their son went off to quickly re-mobilize. Everyone knew someone directly or indirectly killed or with upended lives from the war.

Some Israeli friends had difficulty talking with me initially after 10/7. I understood that they couldn't avoid the association of me in their minds with the catastrophic attack. Most, however, respected and admired my efforts despite all in the occupied Palestinian territories. The younger brother of a high school classmate from New York, from a Syrian Jewish family, had made "Aliyah" to Israel a decade before. He was very empathetic and supportive of my work and efforts, and philosophical about the way the future of Israel was being held hostage not only from the tragedy but from the revanchist extremism. I appreciated Steve's balance; he had been very sympathetic to the situation of Palestinians, but I sensed he was often swimming against the tide between family, in-laws, and others. Support for Netanyahu and the war divided some families and marriages.

This was also true of some Jewish friends and family back in the States. I understood that they had a profound emotional reaction to the horror of Gaza and disgust to the hubris that I must surely have in having helped for so many months the Palestinians. For some, but not all, it was hard for them to disentangle support for the protection of the innocents and the delivery of humanitarian assistance with some perceived collaboration with Hamas. That was patently ridiculous, but I largely tried to avoid getting into unproductive disputes with them about that.

All of this, of course, would presage what I would find in the United States on my return. Jewish friends and contacts were all over the map. Most valued my commitment to amplifying social media posts to attempt to inform, educate, and counterbalance an appreciable amount of false and misleading information on the air in the news.

I had to spend some time physically healing from the broken ribs from Cairo, but also take stock psychologically of all that had happened. I mourned what I saw as the ever-worsening toll of what I viewed and witnessed as indiscriminate retaliatory violence with no respect for proportionality for human life. I remained part of several WhatsApp chat groups in the oPt for months after returning, hearing the cries for help and appeals for assistance from many.

I even continued to receive a constant flurry of warning messages of COGAT, which would alert me to brief interruptions in the battlespace of different neighborhoods and areas across Gaza, ostensibly to allow the flow of humanitarian assistance on the ground. It was difficult to find these carefully crafted messages from the Israeli military believable. They published these newsletter updates of their humanitarian work online as a counter-narrative to the UN OCHA offices. They had been filled with inaccuracies and misstatements. From experience in Jerusalem and continued contact with former colleagues and agencies, I knew that many, if not most, of these messages were effectively not credible. I knew that humanitarian convoys were still generally being blocked or canceled at the last minute or interfered with by onsite Israeli military commanders and forces. I knew that despite denials otherwise, there were repeated incidents of unwarranted military strikes against people racing to secure assistance from water and food delivery trucks, admittedly often in their desperation rioting and sacking trucks that might make it through the lines.

There were always the post-humous justifications of intent to go after Hamas militants and leaders. They were always the repetition of the claims, many likely true, that Hamas forces used the civilian population as 'human shields.' I have no doubt this took place, although I also know there were repeated incidents of artificial manipulation of photos and reports claiming far more Hamas presence in tunnels adjoining hospitals, often not accurate if not wholly and intentionally deceptive.

None of this is acceptable according to the international standards of the Geneva Conventions, the rules of war, and international humanitarian law. Collective punishment of noncombatants is not justifiable because they 'all dress the same.' It is not allowable to write off vast numbers of civilian deaths and injuries because they were collateral damage to military operations that were otherwise be difficult. I don't want to relitigate so much of what is in the media regarding this, as that is not the book's purpose and is far beyond its scope. However, our toxic public debate in the U.S. and Europe, and certainly at major fora such as the UN Security Council, has still only lightly treaded over this hard, brutish reality.

On the other side, I confess to having serious problems with the accusations of genocide against Israel, particularly about how so much of the hatred from those who reject the continued military occupation of Gaza has painted as collateral unindicted co-conspirators the Jewish community in many institutions across the States. This was the mirror image of the collective punishment of innocents and the suffocation of any attempt to find balance from the extreme polarization reasonably. Genocide is a horribly charged word that simply doesn't apply without caveats, but it is also understandable from some who decry the apparent efforts at cultural eradication and erasure all too common in Israel. Similarly, apartheid is a charged and provocative word I usually avoid. Yet across Israel, second-class citizenship and marginalization is common, and the situation in the West Bank certainly easily finds echoes in the word of apartheid.

For this reason, within a couple of months of my return and recovery from Israel and Palestine, by late February, I had come to meet and get acquainted through mutual friends Sasha Ghosh Siminoff, the CEO and Founder of People Demand Change (PDC Inc.), and through him the group of the Friends of Standing Together (FOST) in the Washington DC (DMV) area. I willingly joined to see how I could help with some specific committees, including advocacy, vigils, and education within the Jewish community, and find ways to complement my experience with that of Sasha.

Sasha invited me to a timely IPSOS roundtable discussion on the Palestinian Cause and its impact on regional stability. It was largely co-led by Sasha and his Palestinian colleague, a survivor of Palestinian refugee camps in Syria and Lebanon. It included online contributions and thoughts from Nasser Judeh, a Jordanian former Deputy Prime Minister and former Minister of Foreign Affairs. The roundtable followed "Chatham House" rules, but it was a valuable half-day spent discussing the key drivers of instability in Gaza and Palestine and the dangers and risks from the militias that support Hamas as well as Iran's provocative actions.

As part of the Standing Together movement, which is a collaborative effort of Jews and Palestinians in Israel and around the world, I've come to admire and appreciate the grit of those who try to work to bridge the chasm between many Jews and Palestinians in the U.S. and back in Israel. Here in the Washington DC area, there have been initiatives of all sorts: public advocacy events and protests about the conduct of the war, the need for a humanitarian ceasefire and the return of the hostages, protests to the continued U.S. complicity in sending weaponry without any faithful compliance with restrictions such as the Leahy Amendment, efforts to associate with and support with solidarity Palestinians in the DC area including the Museum of the Palestinian People near Adams Morgan, and most significant for me, opportunities to educate and encourage open and respectful discussion in the Jewish community about the protection of civilians and humanitarian assistance.

One former colleague from USAID resigned loudly due to perceived hypocrisies from USAID and State Department leadership and has since gone on to loudly characterize President Biden and U.S. State Department leadership in inflammatory and controversial ways. While I shared her opposition to repeated U.S. policy calls on weapons, even finding much of the same policies reprehensible, I felt that this was going too far. The resignations have continued in both agencies, with some speaking out more than others.

In recent months, I've met online and in person with the CEO Heather Moran and Senior Rabbi Aaron Potek at the Historic Sixth & I synagogue in Washington, DC to share my story and experiences and encourage a possible education outreach event there. Though that has yet to materialize, I joined a thoughtful small group discussion organized by Resetting the Table, an advocacy and facilitation group specializing in helping people sort through and discuss thorny and difficult topics. At Sixth & I, about 60, mostly young people in their 20s and 30s, gathered and formed eight small groups. After an initial conversation, trained facilitators motivated and guided frank and helpful discussions about loss, insecurity, and overcoming the pain of antisemitism in a world upside down. It was a good event, and I was happy to add to the group from my unique experience.

Heather Moran facilitated an invitation for my wife and me to join a larger group in the Sanctuary with several guest speakers. They included noted and somewhat controversial Jewish journalist Peter Beinart, who typically advocates for a 'one-state' rather than a 'two-state solution' as the most realistic and pragmatic solution for what amounts to a state of apartheid in Israel. He was joined by Rabbi Jill Jacobs, the CEO of *Tru'ah: the Rabbinical Call for Human Rights*. We were there as listeners, but it was a large crowd addressing a topic for which Heather had suggested there was a great deal of social justice fatigue from many of the usual congregants there, in part because of the drains of the brief campus occupation movement, the Palestinian protests across many U.S. cities and the seeming disregard for concerns about antisemitism in the minds of many.

Another key representative from Sixth & I, musician and social justice advocate Aaron Shneyer, arranged with his father, the Senior Rabbi at Temple Am Kolel, an online Zoom event about a month ago for the Education Subcommittee of FOST. In that event, Tara, the subcommittee chair, ably managed and there were speaking roles for me and Sasha Siminoff to talk about Gaza and the flow of humanitarian aid. About 30 people participated, and we included time for small group discussions. There was an animated discussion from the largely progressive Jewish participants, with a great deal of sympathy for the Palestinian cause combined with a sense of hopelessness for overcoming the antisemitic attacks and threats against the State of Israel's existence around the world. We all learned from it; we saw that in these kinds of discussions, we have to use the time wisely to end on a hopeful note and a call to action for concrete and favorable things people could do.

We have other events in mind and under discussion with some synagogues. Many of us went down to the campus protests in Washington to listen to the students (and professional protestors). The Washington protest on the campus of George Washington University was, to all appearances, peaceful, unlike UCLA and Columbia University in the news. It also involved students from American University and Georgetown University. I visited one day and spoke to the nearby mobilized police about it. I was assured that students have the right to protest as long as they are peaceful and don't interfere with the responsibilities of others.

One MPD officer told me, "As long as they are peaceful, they can protest as long as they want." Yes, intolerance was in the air, and within a couple of days, allegedly, the Mayor of Washington ordered the students removed from the yard, the day before planned Congressional testimony, which ultimately was canceled in any case. It had been a little surreal; there were sometimes more reporters and citizen journalists than actual protestors. They had teach-in classes on the summer grass, and one group of young people were somehow writing letters of solidarity to "the children of Gaza." I doubted any children would see these. There were plenty of signs with some slogans and epithets more objectionable than others, but even a corner of Jewish student groups protested on behalf of the Palestinian people.

My wife and I also participated in a fundraiser with ANERA at the Martin Luther King Jr. Library in Washington DC, held as part of an Iftar dinner during the final week of Ramadan. The event raised about $5000 and was well attended. ANERA has always done serious and substantive work in the region; their CEO, Sean C. Carroll, has spoken out bravely and forcefully regarding the delivery of humanitarian assistance in Gaza. We also signed up for the fundraiser held by **HEAL Palestine**, which is affiliated with the notable medical and surgical assistance organization **PCRF**. Their work and leadership in providing critical care for Palestinians across the oPt has been known for years.

We were introduced to **Abrahamic House** by Aaron Shneyer, who had helped host a concert for peace and justice fundraiser for humanitarian assistance on March 4th at ***Busboys & Poets***, which included noted Israeli performer and thinker Gabriel Meyer-HaLevy. At the fundraiser, we met Mohammed al Samawi, the Abrahamic House founder, and we were charmed and moved by his story and that of the multifaith incubator for social change. During Ramadan, we were honored to join him in Washington DC for their own interfaith Iftar dinner and learn of this worthy bridge-building effort to support a co-living, co-learning, and co-creating space between the fellowship members who included a Muslim, a Christian, a Jew, and a Baha'i.

I became very impressed in April and May by Instagram and other social media posts from Standing Together in Israel itself. They had recognized that one of the most obnoxious and violent aspects of the Israeli reactions came from those who you can only call the settler colonials, the right-wing infatuated and obsessed settlers who had over two decades moved to increasingly large outposts of stolen West Bank land, using guns indiscriminately without any real IDF control or oversight, killing and hurting Palestinian villages adjacent to the lands they had taken. Increasingly groups of these armed brigands would sweep down into Israel proper and attack convoys of humanitarian assistance intended for the ravaged poor of Gaza. They would attempt to destroy it, or at least waylay it and delay it.

Standing Together organized a self-styled Humanitarian Guard of Israeli volunteers, not just for counter-protests but to protect the aid shipments largely coming from either UN agencies or INGOs. This is how they described it in one IG post:

"@standing.together.english This year, Israel's Independence Day and Nakba Day fall one day apart, as Israeli Independence Day falls on the 14th of May and Nakba (catastrophe) Day is commemorated as usual on the 15th.

"In the 76 years since Israel was declared a state, there has been little acknowledgment of the Palestinian Nakba: violent displacement, destruction, and land expropriation in 1948 (and ongoing). Since Israel's creation, many have believed that the strength of the society rests on its ability to cling tightly to and reinforce the Israeli narrative and ignore or hide the Palestinian narrative. The reality is that this is not what true strength of a society is - if anything, it is one of its biggest weaknesses. A strong society is a society that is able to confront the most brutal, painful parts of its history, and learns from the horrors of the past.

"76 years since 1948, we are witnessing the biggest loss of life and destruction for Palestinians since 1948, and October 7th marked the biggest loss of life and destruction for Israelis since 1948. Palestinians have always paid the biggest price, facing ongoing displacement, dispossession and ethnic cleansing, and Israelis have never managed to find true safety in the state that promised to be a haven.

"In order to move forward, to reach a place where all of us are able to live with freedom, dignity and equality, we must acknowledge the existence of these two fundamentally opposing narratives and grapple with the complexity that they contain. It is on us, as Jewish and Palestinian citizens of Israel, to continue to push our society to confront its dark history and pave the way toward a just future.

"Settlers are attacking aid trucks on a daily basis and law enforcement is doing barely anything to stop it. In the coming weeks, Standing Together is setting up a humanitarian guard - activists who will go to the aid trucks themselves to protect the aid from violent attacks.

"To do this we need to fund legal assistance, security, rental cars and trucks, and plenty of other equipment necessary to protect the aid. We need your help! "

Share this call on:

- Instagram: https://omdi.me/3ymZqX3

- Facebook: https://omdi.me/3V0OaZi

- Donate to the campaign: https://omdi.me/3WMfD2g

Thanks to Heather Moran from the Historic Sixth & I synagogue, she introduced me to her Senior Rabbi at Washington's Temple Micah and brokered a conversation. That led to Senior Rabbi Daniel Zemel's invitation for coffee and his welcoming me to join his congregation on June 23 to talk about my view from Gaza and how I came to see the delivery of humanitarian assistance and the protection of civilians.

This synagogue talk was surprisingly well-attended, with about 50 people in person and another 50 online by Zoom. I talked about breaking through the stalemate of Gaza and the reality I had observed on the ground during two years in both Israel and Palestine. I also talked about Standing Together and shared a sign-up list for those who wanted to learn more and look for practical things they might do as individuals or as Friends of Standing Together. Sixteen more people volunteered on the spot. Kudos to Rabbi Danny and Rabbi Stephanie at Temple Micah and to some local Jewish activists opposed to the conduct of the war for taking meaningful steps to speak out and counter the pro-conflict narrative. I and other members of Friends of Standing Together hope to join other public talks about humanitarian assistance, Gaza, Palestinian human rights and the vulnerabilities Israel faces in the coming weeks.

My long-time friend and collaborator Rachel Zelon recently shared with me a New York Times column from Nick Kristof, who I generally admire as a thoughtful and out-of-the-box thinker. He offered some valuable overarching points about approaching and understanding the toxic debate about the Gaza war and the key protagonists and antagonists. As Nick noted, there are inflamed passions on both sides, and neither he nor I are trying to draw a moral equivalence between the actions of one or the other. Much of the anger and hostility arise from this question and the idea that the vicious brutality of 10/7 represented a legitimate and justifiable act of Palestinian armed resistance and self-defense. It was not.

Whatever the evils associated with the decades-long Israeli occupation of the oPt, whatever truths there are in the continued denial of statehood and national determination, these do not wash away a heinous historical stain from Hamas' depravity. But there are very legitimate ethical and moral questions that are exceedingly complex and contradictory. These paraphrased points by Kristof are:

1. This is not merely right vs. wrong. It is "a collision of right versus right. Israelis have built a remarkable economy and society. They should have the right to raise their children without fear of terror attacks, while Palestinians should enjoy the same freedoms and be able to raise their children safely in their own state."

2. All lives have equal value, and all children must be presumed innocent. "So while there is no moral equivalence between Hamas and Israel, there is a moral equivalence between Israeli civilians and Palestinian civilians." If you champion only one side and ignore the other, you don't actually care about human rights.

3. It's a positive albeit long-delayed step for President Biden to finally advocate recently for a proposal for a temporary cease-fire that could lead to a permanent end to the war and a release of hostages; as he said, "It's time for this war to end." However, it's also true that "Biden's failure to apply enough leverage over the last seven months has made the United States complicit in human rights abuses in Gaza, because it has provided weapons used in the mass killing of civilians, and because it has gone too far in protecting Israel at the United Nations."

4. "You can say you are pro-Israeli or pro-Palestinian, but we must agree on being anti-massacre, anti-starvation, and anti-rape. Hamas is an oppressive, misogynistic, and homophobic organization whose misrule has hurt Palestinians and Israelis alike. However, not all Palestinians are members of Hamas, and civilians should not be subject to collective punishment. In the words of a 16-year-old Gaza girl: "It's like we are overpaying the price for a sin we didn't commit."

5. "There was no excuse for Hamas attacking Israel on Oct. 7 and murdering, torturing and raping Israeli civilians. And there is no excuse for Israel's reckless use of 2,000-pound bombs and other munitions, such as the globally proscribed white phosphorus, that have destroyed entire city blocks and neighborhoods and killed

vast numbers of innocent people, including more than 200 aid workers.

6.   When Israel began military operations after Oct. 7, it was a just war and justifiable retaliation and self-defense. But what starts as a just war can be waged unjustly.

7.   "Israel was entitled to strike Gaza after the Oct. 7 attack but not to do whatever it wanted. In particular, there should be no argument about Israel's practice of throttling food aid. Using starvation as a weapon of war against civilians, as the prosecutor of the International Criminal Court alleges Israel has done, is a violation of the laws of war.

8.   "Each side justifies its own brutality by pointing to earlier cruelty by the other side. Israelis see Oct. 7. Palestinians see the "open-air prison" imposed on Gaza before that. This goes all the way back to the displacement of Palestinians at Israel's founding in 1948, the 1929 massacre of Jews at Hebron, and so on.

9.   Hamas' brutality toward Israeli hostages, such as credible reports of sexual assault and starvation, is unconscionable. So is Israeli brutality toward Palestinian prisoners, such as CNN accounts that some Palestinians have had limbs amputated because of constant handcuffing.

10. War nurtures dehumanization that produces more war. We've all heard too many Palestinians dehumanize Jews and too many Jews dehumanize Palestinians. When we dehumanize others, we lose our own humanity.

11. Zionism is not a form of racism. And criticism of Israel is not antisemitism. Both sides are too quick to fire such epithets. Each side sees itself as a victim, which is true — but each side is also a perpetrator. Pro-Palestinian demonstrations have too often tolerated strains of antisemitism, which in recent months has shown itself to be stronger than many imagined. How can a

movement that claims the moral high ground make excuses for any bigotry?

12. "Apartheid" isn't the right word for Israel proper today, where Palestinians are treated like second-class citizens but can still vote, serve in the Knesset, and enjoy more political freedoms than in most of the Arab world. But "apartheid" is a rough approximation of Israeli rule in the West Bank, where Arabs have long been oppressed under a system that is separate and unequal.

13. "From the river to the sea" refers to the dream of a single state from the Jordan River to the Mediterranean Sea, encompassing what is now Israel and the Palestinian territories. The slogan, as used by protesters, can mean many different things, some peaceful and some the militaristic vision of the Hamas charter, while a parallel vision is in the original platform of Prime Minister Benjamin Netanyahu's Likud party. Hamas imagines a Palestinian state with no room for Israel, and Netanyahu wants perpetual Israeli sovereignty from the river to the sea to deny a place for a Palestinian state. I think a two-state solution is infinitely preferable instead of either version of a one-state solution.

14. We probably know what an eventual Israeli-Palestinian peace deal would look like. The plan was outlined in the Clinton Parameters of 2000 and the Geneva Accord of 2003. The only question is how many innocent people on both sides will die before we get there.

15. To establish peace, both Israel and the Palestinian Authority will need new leaders with vision and courage. This won't be achieved tomorrow. But there are peacemakers on each side."

AIDA released a humanitarian assistance brief several months ago; conditions have only worsened since. It hasn't been updated but some key points from then are still worth sharing here.

Since 26 January, only one-third of INGOs operating in the Gaza Strip have been able to import humanitarian aid trucks into the enclave. Not all organizations are registered in Egypt and have the capacity to overcome the complexity of the logistical process of entering supplies into the Gaza Strip. On the other hand, organizations that can send aid convoys through Egypt are facing great challenges in ensuring the transport of humanitarian aid trucks, including in obtaining Egyptian and Israeli approvals.

Trucks held up for unknown amounts of time at the border

INGOs are raising concerns about the lack of transparency surrounding the process of entry of trucks into the enclave. Organizations indicate a lack of clarity regarding the timing for their trucks to be granted passage through Israeli crossing points. **As of 15 February 2024, for the total INGOs surveyed, 78 trucks loaded with food, medicine, water, and survival equipment are still waiting on the Egyptian side of the border**, just a few hundred meters away from a population in desperate need of this aid. Some INGOs' trucks have been waiting for months for authorization to go through Israeli crossing points at Rafah or Karam Abu Salem / Kerem Shalom.

Delays and denials at Israeli crossing and inspection points

INGOs report long delays and denials of entry due to Israeli inspection mechanisms. One organization indicated that all 35 of their trucks had at one point been delayed by Israeli inspection mechanisms at the crossing points. Among the 7 INGOs who sent trucks from Egypt to the Gaza Strip, 2 reported that some of the items were denied entry by Israeli authorities on grounds of potential "dual use" materials. According to these INGOs, these shipments contained much needed assistance, such as water pipes, water quality control testing kits, hygiene materials, survivor blankets or candles. Israel's classification of certain items as "dual-use" may not align with international standards because it potentially includes a broader range of goods than those internationally recognized as dual-use.

No safety assurances during the crossing process

Figure 2 UN OCHA

In addition, some organizations report challenges due to the lack of security for their trucks and traffic jams in the "no man's land" area in-between the crossing points.

The barriers to INGO aid trucks entry into the Gaza Strip create substantial challenges for aid operations on the ground.

Many lifesaving services and supplies are delayed as INGOs could not receive the expected humanitarian trucks. 3 health organizations have been postponing the launching of mobile clinics as their medical emergency kits are still impeded from accessing the strip, effectively obstructing the provision of medical treatment to thousands of people in dire need of health services.

Many organizations have also reported a critical fuel shortage inside the enclave, directly impeding their ability to deliver humanitarian aid effectively. This fuel scarcity exacerbates a broader crisis, including the severe lack of medical supplies, food, and clean water due to a compromised supply chain. Consequently, INGOs face substantial challenges in fulfilling the basic necessities of Gaza's population, underscoring the urgent need for a streamlined aid delivery system to mitigate the humanitarian crisis.

ALMOST NO AID DISTRIBUTED BEYOND RAFAH

The intensity of hostilities and Israeli-imposed movement restrictions means that almost no aid is distributed beyond Rafah. INGOs who completed the survey reported the following:

• Only 50% of INGOs said they were able to deliver any aid at all beyond Rafah.

• Most of the organizations are able to reach the Khan Younis and Middle Area governorates qualify their access as "merely partial" or "minimal."

• 80% of INGOs reported aiming to reach other governorates than the ones where they currently operate but are hindered by Israeli military operations, including constant bombardment and checkpoint closures. Some used to operate in all five governorates but now work exclusively in Rafah due to access and security challenges.

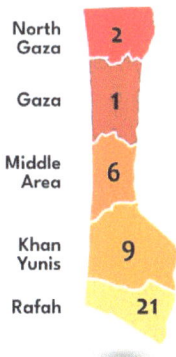

North Gaza: 2
Gaza: 1
Middle Area: 6
Khan Yunis: 9
Rafah: 21

Number of INGOs able to reach each governorate across the Gaza Strip

Despite residents in areas north of Wadi Ghazza facing some of the most severe food shortages, the people of northern Gaza are receiving almost no assistance, with aid convoys repeatedly denied the ability to enter the area by Israeli forces.

• **Only 3 INGOs are able to deliver aid in Gaza and North Gaza governorates.** Among these three, one INGO said they exclusively facilitate the delivery of supplies sourced from local vendors in the area as they cannot dispatch aid convoys from Rafah to northern areas.

What stops humanitarian aid from moving inside the Gaza Strip?

Extreme levels of danger for the lives of humanitarian personnel

Lack of protection for humanitarian personnel is the main reason impeding INGOs from expanding operations beyond Rafah. International non- governmental actors report on extreme levels of risk for field operation teams during their work in areas across the Strip. **Since the beginning of the hostilities, INGOs reported that a total of nine humanitarian workers were killed in strikes or sniper fire.** INGOs reported that the presence of Israeli ground forces has posed critical levels of risk for the lives of their personnel, local partners and their operations. The consistent unpredictability of the bombardment poses an additional security threat to humanitarian workers, rendering more places unreachable for aid in the Strip.

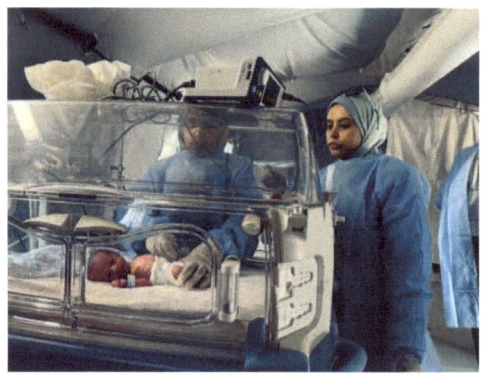

The lack of progress in the above grips me daily with emotions ranging from frustration, disbelief, anger, and determination. That the IMC field hospitals (now only one functional in the Middle Area after multiple forced relocations and closures) exist and care for patients, along with other field hospitals mounted by ICRC, PCRF, and other organizations, are all positive efforts, and I know many of my former Gazan staff can remain engaged and support of these efforts

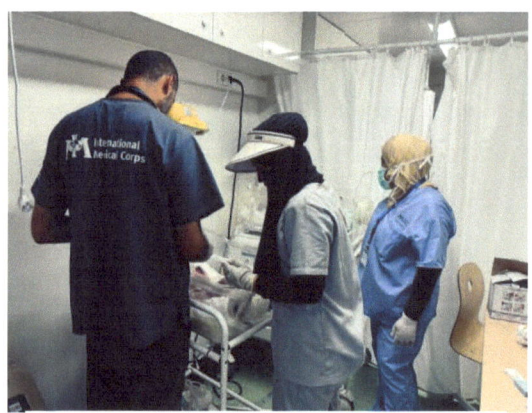

Figure 3 IMC field hospital from Khetam LinkedIn

and related community outreach.

Many or most facilities were interrupted for several weeks in May and June but seem to have resumed some level of functioning and rotation of expat staff together with local Palestinians. But that shouldn't lull us into thinking that humanitarian assistance is resolved since this type of acute and emergency assistance is a mere drop in the bucket of the real needs of children and families in Gaza. Governments continue to grasp at straws, considering poorly considered ideas such as the airdrops in earlier months or the floating pier, almost immediately disabled, all at tremendous cost compared to ground access of trucks with humanitarian aid into Gaza.

I continue to receive regular situation updates from UN OCHA. Having joined OCHA Humanitarian Country Team meetings many times in recent years, I can challenge from personal experience the frequent disparagement and easy mocking of UN authorities by the Israeli government authorities at both the senior and petty levels. It's not universal, but it is very broad, self-serving, and a disrespectful unwillingness to listen to hard truths.

Now I confess, from time to time, I have sometimes heard comments about Israel and Israelis, particularly from a few younger European colleagues, which would make me cringe occasionally. There is a different language and perspectives perhaps some of them bring which from my social and cultural paradigms I find excessive. But that doesn't mean I completely disagreed with them either. It was more a nuance and a tone that I might take issue with.

This was never reflected in the attitudes of more senior UN OCHA staff, such as the Humanitarian Coordinator, the Resident Coordinator, the Chiefs of Office etc. They were fair, neutral, and impartial humanitarians who nevertheless chose to speak truth to power when they could and were sometimes punished for it. The former Resident Coordinator found that the Israelis refused to renew her diplomatic visa, and government officials and Members of the Knesset, the Israeli Parliament, threatened periodically to expel all UN staff.

Let me cite points from the most recent **UN OCHA Situation Update, #179**:

Key Highlights

- Only two stabilization centres for severely malnourished children remain functional across the Gaza Strip as catastrophic hunger grips a significant portion of Gaza's population, warn UN agencies.
- Displaced families face significant challenges in accessing basic services, with critically low access to water, according to recent humanitarian assessments.
- Jordan, Egypt and the UN co-organize a "Call for Action" conference to urgently strengthen the humanitarian response in Gaza, as fuel shortages and access constraints continue to severely disrupt the delivery of life-saving aid.

Humanitarian Developments

- Israeli bombardment from the air, land, and sea continues to be reported across much of the Gaza Strip, resulting in further civilian casualties, displacement, and destruction of houses and other civilian infrastructure. Ground incursions and heavy fighting also continue to be reported across Gaza, including in Beit Hanoun, south of Gaza city, eastern Deir al Balah, northeastern Khan Younis, as well as in eastern, central and western Rafah.
- Between the afternoons of 10 and 14 June, according to the Ministry of Health (MoH) in Gaza, 142 Palestinians were killed and 396 were injured. Between 7 October 2023 and 14 June 2024, at least 37,266 Palestinians were killed and 85,102 were injured in Gaza, according to MoH in Gaza.
- The following are among the deadly incidents reported between 10 and 12 June:

- On 10 June, at about 12:20, at least five Palestinians were reportedly killed and 30 injured when several residential buildings were hit in Al Qarara, north of Khan Younis city.
- On 10 June, at about 13:20, five Palestinians, including four women and one man, were reportedly killed and others injured when a house was hit in Al Fukhari area, southeast of Khan Younis city.
- On 11 June, in the morning hours, eight Palestinians were reportedly killed and others injured when a house was hit in Ad Daraj neighbourhood, in Gaza's Old City.
- On 12 June, at about 1:30, seven Palestinians were reportedly killed and others injured when a house was hit in Ash Shuja'iyya neighbourhood, east of Gaza city.
- On 12 June, at about 2:30, eight Palestinians, including an unidentified number of children, were reportedly killed and others injured when a house was hit in Ad Daraj neighbourhood, in Gaza's Old City.
- On 12 June, during the morning hours, at least four Palestinians were reportedly killed and others injured when a residential building was hit in Az Zaytoun neighbourhood, in southern Gaza city.
- On 12 June, at about 23:55, four Palestinians, including a man, a woman and their two children, were reportedly killed and at least six others were injured when a house was hit in Al Hassayna area in western An Nuseirat Refugee Camp, in Deir al Balah.

- Between the afternoons of 10 and 14 June, four Israeli soldiers were reported killed in Gaza. As of 14 June, 299 soldiers have been killed and 1,940 soldiers have been injured in Gaza or along the border in Israel since the beginning of the ground operation, according to the Israeli military. In addition, according to the Israeli media citing official Israeli sources, over 1,200 Israelis and foreign nationals, including 33 children, have been killed in Israel, the vast majority on 7 October. As of 14 June, it is estimated that 120 Israelis and foreign nationals remain captive in Gaza, including fatalities whose bodies are withheld.

- Israeli evacuation orders and military operations since early May have so far forced the displacement of about one million people from Rafah and more than 100,000 people in northern Gaza. Assessments by humanitarian organizations over the past month have highlighted the dire conditions facing displaced families, with significant challenges to their ability to access basic services.
    - Between 14 and 16 May, a light-touch rapid assessment by the Site Management Working Group (SMWG) found that more than half (51 per cent) of 47 assessed locations across all five Gaza governorates reported that people were displaced in new sites, 31 per cent were displaced in existing sites, and 16 per cent returned to destroyed houses. The majority of displaced people from Rafah sought refuge in the already overcrowded and resource-depleted governorates of Khan Younis and Deir al Balah. Interviewed key informants highlighted that new arrivals were facing a range of challenges in accessing basic services and identified food as their first priority, followed by water and sanitation, and health. The main reported barriers to accessing water and health services included the lack of a sufficient number of water points, the long distance to available water points and health facilities, overcrowded health facilities, and the lack of water tanks, storage containers, medicines and transportation.
    - On 7 June, two inter-cluster assessments led by OCHA were carried out at two informal displacement sites in Deir al Balah. At both Abo Dalal and Ard Al Ghusain displacement sites, which house 3,000 and 7,000 displaced people respectively, families reported

irregular food distributions, overcrowded and dilapidated shelters with an average of eight to 10 persons per shelter, lack of sanitation infrastructure, and a range of health issues such as skin diseases, hepatitis A, gastroenteritis, and respiratory illnesses. Moreover, domestic violence and mental health issues were highlighted as prevalent, with children having no access to child-friendly spaces or educational activities. A critically low access to water was also reported as a critical concern; average water availability per person per day was less than two litres at Abo Dalal displacement site and only 0.7 litres at Ard Al Ghusain displacement site. This is less than the internationally recognized minimum requirement for the survival of three liters per day and significantly lower than the minimum amount of 15 liters per day needed in an emergency for drinking, washing, and cooking.

- The water and sanitation infrastructure in Gaza continues to sustain significant damage. According to the Water, Sanitation, and Hygiene (WASH) Cluster, the recent intensification of military operations has resulted in additional losses of critical water and sanitation assets, including five water production wells in Jabalya, and two water wells, the supply line from the Egypt-based desalination plant and two desalination plants, all in Rafah. Over the past eight months, WASH Cluster partners estimate that approximately 67 per cent of water and sanitation facilities and infrastructure have been destroyed or damaged due to conflict-related activities, with damage to mobile assets yet to be assessed. Damaged facilities include 194 water production wells, 40 high volume water reservoirs, 55 sewage pumping stations, 76 municipal desalination plants, four waste water treatment plants and nine warehouses. Many other facilities have also been rendered non-operational due to a range of challenges, including insecurity, constrained access, lack of power supply and fuel to operate generators, and limited to no availability of spare parts, consumables, basic building materials and equipment. As a result, while water production through the Coastal Municipalities Water Utility/Palestinian Water Authority (CMWU/PWA) and municipal service providers has increased to 95,000-108,000 cubic metres per day across the Gaza Strip, this figure represents only 28 per cent of water production prior to October 2023 and is unevenly distributed across the various production points. The Cluster further notes that there is a 50 per cent water loss in the distribution network due to large scale damage, limiting actual water availability. Families in informal displacement sites face additional challenges given the lack of infrastructure that needs to be newly installed to ensure service delivery. People's coping mechanisms are heavily stretched, the Cluster emphasizes; the most vulnerable people are collecting water from unreliable sources in inadequate containers and lack hygiene items such as soap or facilities for handwashing and other basic hygiene practices. Combined, these factors have contributed to elevated levels of acute watery diarrhea, skin diseases and an outbreak of Hepatitis A.

- No international Emergency Medical Teams (EMTs) are currently deployed in Rafah or in northern Gaza due to rising insecurity, reported the World Health Organization (WHO). Medical evacuations of critical patients outside of Gaza also remain suspended, and persistent fuel shortages continue to threaten the functioning of vital medical infrastructure and equipment. Moreover, while 17 of Gaza's 36 hospitals are partially functional, 14 are partially accessible due to insecurity and physical barriers, such as damage to patient and ambulance entrances and surrounding roads. In Rafah, where no hospitals are currently functional, the ICRC field hospital represents a lifeline for the population, while the UAE field hospital remains only partially functional amid severe access challenges. In a positive development, in Khan Younis, Al Khair Hospital resumed partial functionality, and 15 dialysis machines to serve 250 patients were provided to Nasser Medical Complex with support from the World Bank. However, the CT scanner at Nasser remains out of service and diagnostic capacity has severely shrunk. In North Gaza, following the Israeli forces' withdrawal on 31 May, access to the Al-Awda, Kamal Adwan and Indonesian hospitals has been partially restored; the Indonesian Hospital now offers only basic emergency services while inpatient services have resumed at both Kamal Adwan (144 beds) and Al Awda (40 beds) hospitals, with Al-Awda also providing critical maternal care. On 9 June, WHO and its partners reached both facilities, delivering 24,000 liters of fuel and medical supplies to support an estimated 2,000 patients. Two tents were also provided to Al-Awda to expand the facility's premises.

- The inability to provide health services safely, coupled with the lack of clean water and sanitation, are exacerbating malnutrition risks in Gaza. On 12 June, the WHO Director-General, Tedros Adhanom Ghebreyesus, stressed that a "significant proportion of Gaza's population is now facing catastrophic hunger and famine-like conditions." While over 8,000 children under the age of five have been already diagnosed with acute malnutrition, ongoing insecurity, access constraints, and large-scale displacement continue to hamper the critical scale-up of identification of cases of malnourished children at the community level, explains the Nutrition Cluster. On 11 June, UNICEF further warned that almost 3,000 children who were receiving treatment for acute malnutrition in the south prior to the military escalation in Rafah, have now been cut off from life-saving services due to displacement and shrinking treatment capacity; only two stabilization centres for severely malnourished children are now functional in Gaza, one in North Gaza and one in Deir al Balah. "Our warnings of mounting child deaths from a preventable combination of malnutrition, dehydration, and disease should have mobilized immediate action to save children's lives, and yet, this devastation continues," stated the UNICEF Regional Director for the Middle East and North Africa, Adele Khodr. On 14 June, the Director of Kamal Adwan Hospital in North Gaza reported to the media that they have recently documented more than 200 cases of children with multiple signs of malnutrition.

- A new assessment by the Education Cluster, based on satellite imagery collected on 3 and 7 May, reveals a further increase in the scale of damage and destruction of schools in the Gaza Strip compared with the 1 April analysis. Over 76 per cent of schools in Gaza are now assessed as requiring full reconstruction or major rehabilitation to be functional again, up from 73 per cent. The assessment also highlights a "continuous spike in the direct targeting of schools," with 23 facilities that had already been classified as "damaged" in the previous analysis being affected by additional direct hits in April. Among school buildings used as IDP shelters, 69 per cent have been directly hit or damaged, up from 65 per cent in March. Overall, some 54 per cent of school buildings (307 out of 563) have been "directly hit," 22 per cent (123) of school buildings have been "damaged," while 15 per cent (86) are classified as "likely or possibly damaged." Of note, more than 96 per cent (296) of all directly hit schools are in areas subject to evacuation orders issued by Israeli authorities. Furthermore, out of all damaged schools, 61 have been totally destroyed and 39 have lost at least half of their structures. North Gaza and Gaza governorates have been the most impacted, with about 90 per cent and 89 per cent of their school buildings directly hit or damaged, respectively.
- In May, humanitarian access in Gaza was severely hindered by intense military activities, the closure of crossings, volatile security conditions, unexploded ordnance, complex and inconsistent movement notification and coordination procedures, damaged and overcrowded roads, and inconsistent checkpoint procedures. These challenges have persisted in June; between 1 and 13 June, out of 44 planned coordinated humanitarian assistance missions to northern Gaza, 23 (52 per cent) were facilitated by Israeli authorities, four (nine per cent) were denied access, 10 (23 per cent) were impeded, and seven (16 per cent) were cancelled due to logistical, operational or security reasons. In addition, out of 151 coordinated humanitarian

assistance missions to areas in southern Gaza, 108 (71 per cent) were facilitated by Israeli authorities, seven (five per cent) were denied access, 24 (16 per cent) were impeded, and 12 (eight per cent) were cancelled. Many missions classified as "impeded" experienced extended delays imposed by the Israeli army. During the same period, a humanitarian convoy was delayed for over nine hours at an insecure checkpoint leading to northern Gaza, preventing the organization from delivering critical medicines and nutrition supplies for more than 10,000 children. Another humanitarian mission to northern Gaza, which involved the delivery of critical medical supplies to hospitals and transfer of one patient, faced a delay of over five hours at a checkpoint, undermining these critical medical activities.

- On 11 June, the World Food Programme (WFP) stressed that while it has been able to reach over one million people in the Gaza Strip last month, aid operations have been severely affected by the escalation in fighting and urgently need "regular access, the ability to transport aid safely, and fighting to stop." On the same day, WFP took the precaution of temporarily halting operations at the floating dock, pending a thorough security assessment needed to ensure the safety and security of staff and partners. On 12 June, Humanity and Inclusion (HI) reported that the Israeli army bulldozed the NGO's warehouse in Rafah, "where nearly 200 pallets of humanitarian equipment were stored," noting its location and function had been reported to the Israeli authorities.

- A high-level conference, titled "Call for Action: Urgent Humanitarian Response for Gaza," was held in Jordan on 11 June. Co-organized by Jordan, Egypt and the UN, the conference aimed to identify means of strengthening the humanitarian response in Gaza, including the operational, logistical, protection, and other conditions necessary for establishing sustainable pipelines to immediately deliver sufficient aid. The conference also discussed preparations for early recovery and garnered commitments for a coordinated collective response. It was attended by Heads of State and representatives of governments and international organizations, including UN Secretary-General Antonio Guterres, Under-Secretary-General for Humanitarian Affairs and Emergency Relief Coordinator Martin Griffiths, and Humanitarian Coordinator for the Occupied Palestinian Territory Muhammad Hadi. In his remarks at the conference, Guterres saluted "the brave humanitarians in Gaza working in nightmare conditions to stem the suffering," called for full accountability for the deaths of 193 UNRWA staff members, and reaffirmed that UNRWA is the backbone of the humanitarian response. The UN Chief further stated: "Deliveries require safe routes and effective deconfliction mechanisms to ensure their security. They require unimpeded access for security and communications equipment, commensurate with the risks of working in a war zone. They require immediate efforts to clear routes inside Gaza, which are littered with mines and unexploded ordnance. Civilians must be allowed to seek safety. And civilians and the infrastructure they rely on must never be militarized or targeted." As of 12 June, at least 273 aid workers have been killed in Gaza, including 197 UN staff members, 33 PRCS staff and volunteers, and 43 other aid workers. According to MoH and Palestinian Civil Defense, 498 health workers and 70 Civil Defense staff have also been killed.

Funding

- As of 13 June, Member States have disbursed about US$1.06 billion out of $3.4 billion (31 per cent) requested to meet the most critical needs of 2.3 million people in Gaza and 800,000 people in the West Bank, including East Jerusalem, between January and December 2024. For funding analysis, please see the Flash Appeal Financial Tracking dashboard.
- The oPt HF has 109 ongoing projects, for a total of $78.9 million, addressing urgent needs in the Gaza Strip (86 per cent) and West Bank (14 per cent). Of these projects, 69 projects are being implemented by

international non-governmental organizations (INGOs), 26 by national NGOs and 14 by UN agencies. Notably, 43 out of the 83 projects implemented by INGOs or the UN are being implemented in collaboration with national NGOs. Since 7 October, the oPt HF has mobilized over $100 million from Member States and private donors, designated for programmes throughout Gaza. A summary of the oPt HF activities and challenges in May 2024 is available through this link and the 2023 Annual Report of the oPt HF can be accessed here. Private donations are collected directly through the Humanitarian Fund.

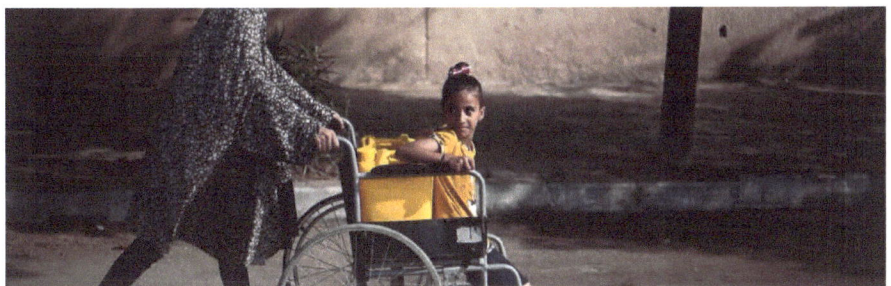

Reports like these have gone out almost daily since the start of the war, over 250 days ago.

So, where does that leave us today, in late June 2024, as I share this? What can we all do?

It's so hard to take stock in crises like this, which take on existential dimensions for both sides.

I am profoundly sympathetic and empathetic to the realities faced by Israelis, American and other Diaspora Jews, the people of Gaza, Palestinians on the West Bank, and in the dispersal of their own diaspora. I don't lump all Israelis into the same bundle, nor do I do that with all Palestinians. I'm not naïve. But I also know this is no longer the Israel of the 1980s, 1990s, or even fifteen years ago. There's been a categorical change since among many Israelis, as there has been among many Palestinians.

I realize that with this book, I might be misinterpreted for trying to be mindlessly evenhanded, and even some might rush to judge that I am insufficiently focused on the suffering of the people in the West Bank and Gaza or fueling anti-Israel propaganda. Nothing, of course, could be further from the truth.

There's a resonant danger with proximity to the fuse in many situations. It's easy to get yourself blown up. But also, when you are too close to the situation, inevitably, your frame of reference and scale shrink precipitously, and you can often only focus on what is in front of your face.

Existential fears and trauma have overwhelmed both Israelis and Palestinians. This is not the first time that has happened; it has occurred many times before and, sadly, at this point, will easily happen again without outside intervention. The Israeli people, including many of the most sympathetic to the overarching cause of social justice and fair play for Palestinians, were first to be infused with that trauma. Many, if not most, Israelis reacted with extreme rage and trauma after 10/7. Some have been able to take a step back and question that rage by now, although not enough.

The Palestinians and particularly the Gazans have, of course, been delivered into an ongoing horror show in the retaliation since 10/7, a retaliation far beyond any proportionality, reason, or likely military success for the other side. The deaths of 40,000 or more from a population of 2.2 million are only made more tortured by how many children, elderly, and noncombatants have paid the ultimate price. Trauma with compounded interest has been delivered unto the next generations even when the fighting eventually stops or pauses; so many crippled and reduced of their humanity will never forget the last 10-11 months.

Having lived in Gaza, I recognized that even in relatively peaceable times, there was always the lurking shadow of Hamas' presence. There were also the incompetent and corrupt authorities of the West Bank, unmoved and seemingly disinterested in the wellbeing of the Palestinian people. Hamas is a deadly danger we are often not allowed to address fully; on the one side, we have Mission Order 21 and the USG No Contact Policy blocking engagement, and on the other side, apologists for Palestinian actions and those who protest Israeli disproportionate aggression, calling it "genocide" often ignore what genocide really means, that Hamas and Islamic extremists directly threaten genocide in some of their founding documents, and even that Hamas is not even the greatest potential danger in the region. A strong case can be made that Palestinian Islamic Jihad (PIJ), as the most fervent proxy for Iran in the oPt, represents a truer threat.

Gaza itself is often vastly oversimplified. The fact that Hamas leadership is rooted in the Khan Yunus refugee camps is ignored. Attention is barely given to the psychopathy of Yahya Sinwar, the Hamas leader since 2017, a multi-decade-obsessed student of Israel and Israeli psychology from Israeli prisons, and the fact that he is far beyond rationality, reason, or any interest in negotiations.

I loathe the term "genocide" when applied to Israel and its immediate post-10/7 retaliation against Hamas and Gaza. I know Israelis are furious with it. But I must reluctantly admit there is a basis for it now, to my shame and disgust. Aryeh Neier, the Jewish co-founder of **Human Rights Watch**, offered compelling arguments on the ICJ case against Israel in the **NY Review of Books.** This was preceded by a recent patient and well-reasoned discussion on **Fareed Zakaria's Global Public Square.**

(https://www.nybooks.com/articles/2024/06/06/is-israel-committing-genocide-aryeh-neier/)

(https://www.cnn.com/videos/world/2024/05/26/gps-0526-icc-charges-against-israel.cnn)

I confess to being hugely disappointed and ashamed of the Biden Administration to date. The few tentative positive steps our State Department and National Security Council took have been far too little, far too late. They have been far too enabling of a terrible existential threat to Israel, and that threat is, in fact, fundamentally the Israeli government in power.

Many responsible and respected INGOs have struggled to serve the need for humanitarian assistance in Gaza, but are hobbled with many interruptions and blocked access over and over.

Meanwhile, other critical disasters worldwide go untended and ignored, to our peril. So much money has been wasted on foolhardy efforts to deliver vital lifesaving humanitarian assistance. Vast sums were wasted on what some have called "humanitarian theatre" because that's all they amounted to. Airdrops of aid were costly and meaningless exercises that did more damage than any real good.

The much-ballyhooed naval pier south of Gaza City, designed to deliver humanitarian assistance by ship, has been another costly, wasteful disaster without any capacity to function. It has been mechanically and operationally disabled, in part because of the inability to set things up directly and efficiently.

The only way cost effective to deliver humanitarian assistance is by land, by combining it with commerce and private sector shipments, and by opening new and previous checkpoints from Israel proper, not by Egypt. The humanitarian INGOs demanded this from the start. They demanded that the U.S. Embassy in Jerusalem and President Biden's special envoy insist on this with the Israeli government. But the Americans demurred and promises of reopening Erez and other checkpoints to the north evaporated. Groups like ANERA, Mercy Corps, World Central Kitchen, PCRF, and others have struggled boldly but without the means to help at scale.

What can you do? Whatever your tribe, whatever your political affiliation, we must raise our collective voices and push Congress and the White House to lean heavily on Israel to stop now. Not a month longer. It's time to "declare victory" and leave.

We must stop the insanity now, rescue Israel and the Israelis from their blindspots, and push for an armistice, peace, and reconciliation. The government of Israel is staggering like a drunk reaching for the car keys. We must stop enabling the suicidal behavior of a corrupt and discredited government incapable of ending this. Extremists don't want to end this due to a messianic vision of a Greater Israel. We must stop them in their tracks.

Israeli (and American) military leaders well know that "Victory" won't be defined by the IDF annihilating a grassroots idea of national resistance. We need to listen carefully to people like Yoav Gallant and Rear Admiral Daniel Haggari: even with their many faults they know the catastrophic danger for Israel of continued fighting, efforts to re-occupy Gaza, and the cost in Israeli lives – not to mention Palestinian ones – in a reckless push forward to greater urban warfare in Rafah. Anything less is playing into Hamas and Islamic Jihad's hands and only strengthening the long game of Yahya Sinwar.

I believe we must insist on a suspension/revocation of all arms deliveries now for Israel beyond those strictly for national defense. We should put some teeth into our message by suspending all visas and visa-free travel from Israel for five years until a new Israeli government is elected and takes office. The United States and EU should jointly consider suspension of Israeli import privileges into their markets until an armistice and military withdrawal are in place, along with a rollback in West Bank settlements.

The U.S. Government has other readily available tools that should be immediately put into effect. These should include severely limited Israeli access to U.S. intelligence sharing and the abrogation of any further support or political cover in the United Nations Security Council and General Assembly.

Both American political parties and tribes must understand that supporting bad behavior by Israel, with political gestures such as the attacks on the ICJ and ICC, and the coddling of Netanyahu, has paradoxically increased the dangers for Israel and Israeli survival.

We must- seriously re-evaluate the consequences and impact of U.S. laws and policy measures such as Mission Order 21, the No-Contact Policy with FTOs, the Taylor Force Law, and similar political actions that thoroughly undermine and weaken U.S. diplomacy. They should be repealed. In our tribal politics, it may be impossible to reconcile disagreements, but this only weakens U.S. power and influence. There are far better and more effective ways to avoid the diversion and deviation of U.S. resources and assistance.

Even though many in the global community seem determined by default to drag this out as long as possible, the only solution to what we currently face is an impregnable, stainless international force to put everybody into a "time-out." Since people are not angels and often have all sorts of corrupt motivations, there must be strict and vigilant controls and expectations over that international force.

The Great Powers need to be willing to assign the resources and manpower and willing to sacrifice to work with Arab neighbors to completely overhaul security, governance, and administration in the entire oPt. Both Israel and the PNA must be set aside, willing or not, and we must exercise tough love in doing so.

We can no longer afford to indulge the virulent extremists on both sides. We must be willing to deliver stern ultimatums to all actors that severe consequences will be faced and be prepared to stop playing footsie with them in not ensuring accountability.

Unfortunately, we don't have a great track record in this. Look at Haiti and Venezuela in the Western Hemisphere and far too many kleptocratic regimes across Africa and Asia. Yet this is our great generational challenge. If we can "fix" Palestine after nearly 80 years of fumbling and foolishness, surely any other global problem will seem easy by comparison.

I believe we are talking about a 10-20-year trusteeship over the entire oPt, including Gaza, West Bank, and some portion of East Jerusalem, costing upwards of $100 billion per year. Perhaps it will be less. But if it costs $2 trillion, that is far less than the utterly useless adventurism of the United States and NATO allies in Afghanistan and Iraq, which further broke this world.

I know that some Israeli friends dream that they can do a reprise of the invasion of Beirut in the early 1980s, where the IDF was able to secure the departure of thousands of Palestinian militants from Lebanon to Tunisia. But this is not the 1980s, and Lebanon today hardly shows any gains from that time. Israel is in fact less secure. Very conservative political Islam is also far more a fact of life now than then. So, the space to maneuver is not what it was.

There were many chances in the past for peace. The Palestinians and Israelis made multiple fatal strategic and tactical errors. It's time for something entirely new. Surely, there are ways to incentivize Egypt, Jordan, and the Gulf Arab States so they will drop their diffidence and reluctance to find a permanent resolution to the Palestinian cause and the inevitable recognition and engagement with both states, Israel and Palestine, which is in their highest national interests and security concerns.

I am coming around reluctantly to the sense that a Two-State Solution is no longer possible. It remains the war our diplomats continue to fruitlessly fight, but like generals always fighting the last war, I sense this has passed its shelf date expiration. Perhaps it was possible up until 2007, but it has been undermined for so long and so effectively by Israelis and Palestinians that I think it is now as dead as can be.

I see the only viable alternative for now is to take it out of the antagonists' hands and create an ***Operation Overlord trusteeship*** with an enforced confederacy or federation for Israel and Palestine. Individual legislatures but a supra-national council that will oversee and veto the actions of the individual states. I wouldn't tinker with certain inevitable demands for functional autonomy in key areas, but I don't think we can allow individual states to continue unfettered and free to act without consequences. Perhaps there could be national referendums in 10-20 years about a peaceable divorce and reallocation of resources and population, with all the essential safeguards, but I think a two-state solution now is not viable.

There will be spoilers, of course. Iran remains irredentist. Hezbollah, as an Iranian proxy in Lebanon, also needs to be severely degraded in its ability to do mischief, including major consequences for missile and rocket fire on northern and central Israel. The Russian autocracy is a failed rogue state. China is uncertain of what best furthers its own national security concerns. However, some of these might also be coopted into a grand Great Power deal that could have ultimate payoffs far beyond Palestine and Israel regarding a remaking of global security mechanisms and the United Nations. There will be Israeli and Palestinian spoilers as well, of course. These must be also firmly and unconditionally dealt with.

I'm far from the only one making these calls for action. Yet inertia, fear, political tribalism, and shortsightedness have always kept us from dealing with this. There were times in the past when American Administrations made serious efforts to hold Israel accountable.

The Nixon, Ford, Reagan, GHW Bush, Clinton, Bush II, and Obama administrations all had moments trying to draw lines in the sand over decades, but they never went far enough. Clinton had perhaps the best possible tee-up for this after the end of the Cold War but failed to follow through in his triangulation of trials and distractibility. Obama also had huge opportunities, but that Administration also showed a lack of resolve and courage in overcoming and confronting political enemies who were gratuitously blocking his actions.

We can do this; we must do this. It's hard to imagine either candidate for the American Presidency being prepared enough to go the distance. Blind acquiescence to Israeli extremism is not acceptable as a means to defend the rights of the Jewish people or the existence of a safe and secure Israel. However, this is as much a life-or-death threat to the world as that confronted by the WWII Operation Overlord and the D-Day alliance 80 years ago.

DEAR READER

Thank you for taking the time to read *A JEW IN GAZA*. If you value and appreciate this book and its messages, please consider telling your friends about it and posting a short review on Amazon or where you obtained the book.

Word of mouth and reviews are an author's best friends, and we deeply appreciate every review and referral you give.

I hope to share more of my search for meaning, purpose, and discovery in subsequent books. There are still many adventures to share, with your help. Feel free also to join my mailing list and visit my website: https://enableennoble.net/subscribe/

Thank you again.

AUTHOR'S BIO

Allan J. "Alonzo" Wind served from February 2022 to December 2023 as the International Medical Corps Mission Director in Gaza and the occupied Palestinian territories (oPt), supervising a staff of seven expats of different nationalities and over 75 local Palestinian staff in Gaza and Bethlehem. He was elected in 2022 to the Executive Committee of the Association for International Development Agencies (AIDA) and asked to serve on the UN OCHA Humanitarian Fund Advisory Board.

Mr. Wind was resident in both Gaza and East Jerusalem for nearly two years and was in a unique position in Gaza as a senior Jewish American INGO leader, also connected with the Baha'i Community. Mr. Wind is a retired Senior Foreign Service Officer from the U.S. Agency for International Development (USAID), having worked for 22 years on diplomatic assignments with USAID primarily overseas in Peru, Nicaragua, Angola, Nigeria,

Iraq, Afghanistan and South Africa. He is a Senior Advisor and Scholar for the Foundation for Law and International Affairs (FLIA).

Mr. Wind previously worked for fifteen years for different nonprofit private voluntary organizations in Ecuador, Bolivia, the Dominican Republic, and the UK, among others, also serving as the Global Programme Coordinator of the International Save the Children Alliance Secretariat.

He began his career as a Public Health Peace Corps Volunteer in Ecuador, and his experiences described here led to his lifelong vocation for global service and international development, living in over a dozen countries and familiar with at least fifty more in Latin America and the Caribbean, Africa, Europe and Asia.

He and his wife reside in Fairfax County Virginia, and their daughter lives and works in Berlin. Mr. Wind also serves on the Boards of Directors of different NGOs, including Hunger Relief International, supporting their efforts with the neediest in Guatemala and Haiti.

www.ingramcontent.com/pod-product-compliance
Lightning Source LLC
Chambersburg PA
CBHW040843120626
46547CB00001B/10